Designing Modern Germany

Designing Modern Germany

Jeremy Aynsley

REAKTION BOOKS

For Sarah

Published by Reaktion Books Ltd
33 Great Sutton Street
London EC1V ODX, UK

www.reaktionbooks.co.uk

First published 2009

Printed and bound in China by C&C Offset Printing Co., Ltd

British Library Cataloguing in Publication Data
Aynsley, Jeremy
    Designing modern Germany
    1. Design – Germany – History – 20th century
    I. Title
    745.4'0943'0904

ISBN: 978 1 86189 401 4

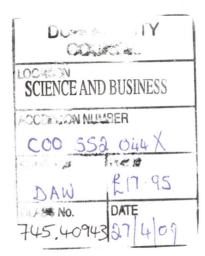

Contents

DIE KÜNSTLERISCHE FORMGEBUNG DES REICHS

VON

REICHSKUNSTWART DR·EDWIN REDSLOB

BØHM

Introduction: The Culture of Design in Germany

Ernst Böhm, cover design for *Die Künstlerische Formgebung des Reichs* (The Artistic Design of the Reich), published by Dr Erwin Redslob, the State Art Minister (Reichskunstwart) in 1926. The book considered the design of flags, currency, postage stamps and all manner of official works.

Reference to design in Germany can evoke strong, contrasting and even contradictory images. Design is understandably one of the leading cultural contributions for which the country has a deserved reputation. When we use the term 'German design', however, we must do so with caution. Immediately we need to qualify what we mean: when, where, who or what? To construct a history of the culture of design by nation is a naturally complex and to some extent artificial process for any country and all the more so for one with so many conflicting ideas of national identity. In particular, Germany had a turbulent political history during the twentieth century, encompassing two world wars and the ideological division into the Federal Republic of Germany and the German Democratic Republic in the second half of the century.

National identities can depend on stereotype, and on one level at least, Germany and its design traditions have been associated with a tendency towards organization, system and planning – 'rectangular and reliable' as one recent commentator suggested.[1] This is only reinforced if we contrast our immediate reactions to the term 'German design' to those to 'Italian design', with its hallmarks of flair, culture and style, or 'Scandinavian design', with its associations with the democratic, ergonomic and natural. At a popular level, such German dependence on the reliability of technology was parodied for a British audience in the television advertising campaign to promote Audi cars during the 1980s and '90s under the strap-line 'Vorsprung durch Technik' – advancement through technology. In this much remarked upon series, emphasis was placed on the highly developed 'German' technical strengths of the company's reputation, leaving other aspects of design, among them styling, unmentioned.[2]

But perhaps this stress on technology and modern design should be qualified. For if, on the one hand, Germany certainly has indeed been a site of a continuing and serious engagement with the implications of Modernism for design and its rationalist concepts of providing a well-considered environment for the benefit of a large proportion of the population, on the other hand, at significant moments in the country's history, anti-modern sentiments and forces have come to the fore, challenging the idea that continued progress towards a modern ideal could be achieved or should indeed be the ultimate goal. Most notably, on the coming to power of the Third Reich in the early 1930s, at the level of rhetoric at least, the 'rectangular and reliable', as we shall see, were perceived to be insufficient, if not at times antithetical to the National Socialists' extreme promotion of the 'German' soul. And in a rather different way, in the 1980s, another reaction against the rational, problem-solving version of design came under duress in the attempt to sustain the German Democratic Republic. The relatively sudden collapse of the GDR suggested that ordinary people's resistance to a political regime could be expressed by, among other things, consumer forces, driven in part by desire and ordinary pleasure in material goods. In so doing, they overthrew the planned, rational and ordered society that its leaders professed to have achieved. As this book explores, throughout the century, even within Modernist circles, there were those who argued against this too-easy dichotomy – stressing that the rational should be balanced by the spiritual, the machine-made by the handmade, and the artificial by the natural.

Designing Modern Germany

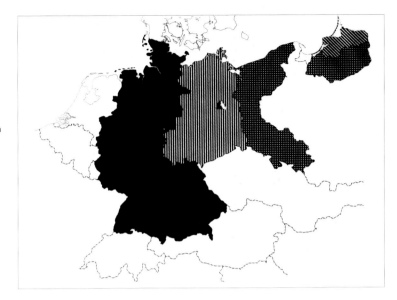

... and after the Second World War. The black zone shows the Federal Republic of Germany, the vertical striped zone indicates the German Democratic Republic with Berlin as an island within it. Other zones show parts of Poland and East Prussia that ceased to be German territory at the end of the war.

The particular character of German design, its tendencies and discourses, is the extended subject of this book. By way of premise, we can suggest that, for many, Germany is a country associated with leading the way in terms of promoting a modern understanding of the word 'design'. For although the English word 'design' only entered the German language in the post-war period, when it became adopted as part of a recognized international terminology for many branches of the field (as in *Grafikdesign* or *Industriedesign*), design had been recognized as an important cultural, industrial and commercial factor much earlier on. The historical terminology was varied in the German language, but within the period covered by this book, it evolved from *Kunstgewerbe* (Arts and Crafts), as informed by William Morris and the generation of the 1880s, as considered in chapter One, to *Gestaltung* (shaping) and *Formgebung* (form-giving) of the 1920s, discussed in chapter Three, and eventually to 'Design'.[3]

As has been commented, the concept of design acknowledges a level of self-consciousness in the relationship between people and things. At its most basic, design involves the arrangement of everyday life – and in this sense, anyone can be said to be a designer, and it is also possible to write about design before 'design', or at least without professional design.[4] The emphasis of this study, however, is on the history of a specialist activity called design, very often taught in art and design schools, and practised by specialists known as 'designers' who develop ideas and products, helping to shape and form them, often in relation to the manufacturer and potential retailer, and sometimes also the consumer. As used to describe a self-conscious discipline, this understanding of the word has a relatively recent history: many of the structures that shape design – the dedicated schools, museums, specialist publications and organizations – were in fact formed in the late nineteenth and early twentieth centuries and were symptomatic of the particular organization of culture under a democracy, which is still dominant today.

Although histories of design need not only be about designers, German design history is peppered with a number of 'stars' – what Nikolaus Pevsner, one of the first to write a design history of early modern design, called 'pioneers' in his extremely influential study of 1936, *Pioneers of the Modern Movement from William Morris to Walter Gropius* (later published as *Pioneers of Modern Design*. In this account, Pevsner identified figures from the first generation of Arts and Crafts reformers who were influential in defining how design might be conceived in the 1880s and '90s. Pevsner suggested that many of the ideas developed in Belgium, Britain and France, and reached their culmination immediately after the First World War in Germany, since the country's particular circumstances of relatively late industrialization and state formation after 1870 allowed it to become an important seedbed for design innovation. Of the famous architect and director of the Bauhaus, Pevsner wrote:

> Gropius regards himself as a follower of Ruskin and Morris, of van de Velde and of the Werkbund. So the circle is complete. The history of artistic theory between 1890 and the First World War proves the assertion on which the present work is based, namely, that the phase between Morris and Gropius is an historical unit. Morris laid the foundation of the modern style; with Gropius its character was ultimately determined.[5]

Along with the individual German designers who have claimed the world stage over the past century – among others Peter Behrens, Marianne Brandt, Bruno Paul, Wilhelm Wagenfeld, Dieter Rams, Jil Sander and Ingo Maurer – a sense of German design culture needs to be built up by looking at cultural institutions and the methods by which design was defined, taught, promoted and exhibited. In the late twentieth century discussion within the design press, for example, stressed how Germany seemed consciously to choose not to be a 'land of stars'.[6] Unlike the United States and other mature industrial cultures, the country seemed to resist promotion of its designers as celebrity individuals; its strength lay rather

Designing Modern Germany

in a long-standing tradition of considering design professionalism, education and philosophy seriously and with continuity.

This serious promotion of design spans the entire twentieth century at least. It was in Germany in 1907, for instance, that the Deutsche Werkbund (literally the German League of Work) was formed, becoming the first association to encourage relations between the designer, the industrialist and the retailer through exhibitions, publications and a form of lobbying and political promotion. This model of an agency for the furtherance of design was formative for many other countries, being adopted in Switzerland and Austria before 1914, and followed in other European countries subsequently, especially in the form of post-war design councils.[7] Along with this important organization, Germany's twentieth-century design history involves some of the most highly regarded educational establishments, notably the Bauhaus in its various stages of existence between 1919 and 1933, and the Ulm Hochschule für Gestaltung (HfG) between 1953 and 1968. Interestingly, these institutions immediately raise the complexity of writing about a 'national' design culture. In each case, the schools were attended by students and teachers who came from a variety of countries and whose aims were avowedly international in perspective. Exactly how 'German' was each establishment becomes an interesting point of discussion. They suggest that a conception of a national culture of design needs to be flexible, at least in the German case, if not in all other 'national' histories.[8]

For a country with such a complex political history throughout the twentieth century, encompassing internal conflicts, uprisings, attempted revolutions, radical political division and polarization, this study requires a consideration of how ideology and culture interact. Put more succinctly, we need to understand how political beliefs can inform some of the most visible expressions of design thinking: this book will examine how design can work ideologically and, in turn, how ideology can work on design.

With this question in mind, it is important to stress that this book respects the accepted political chronologies and major events of war and regime change as used in other forms of historical enquiry and takes these as its structuring principle, even if the purpose is to establish both continuity and rupture in relation to such political demarcations. It begins around 1870, although this year was by no means a straightforward starting point for modern design.[9] Chapter One covers the final stages of imperial Wilhelmine Germany, when the new nation established itself as a world power, and considers the development of design up to the country's defeat in the First World War and the abdication of the Kaiser Wilhelm II in 1918. In the last decades of the nineteenth century, following the military success

of victory over France in the Franco-Prussian war (1870–71), Germany, a newly unified country, turned its attention towards becoming a strong, impermeable nation state as a guise through which to enter the world arena – primarily by economic prowess, military strength and industrial growth. This was matched by a strong impulse towards cultural expression in the arts, as well as philosophical exhortations of a new destiny, often couched in nationalist terms. A considerable commitment was shown to the place of education in building up a strong workforce, and hence nation. In many respects, the first years of the twentieth century marked a culmination in this nationalistic growth. Germany held a distinct advantage in undergoing such processes at a later stage than its immediate neighbours and competitors, Belgium, Britain and France and their empires, and to an extent learned from their example, as well as that of the USA, an alternative model of ascendant world power. Such self-consciousness of living in modernity brought with it an accelerated acceptance of industrial and commercial culture, and the role of goods in forming modern social identity for which Germany became famous.

This photograph of Alexanderplatz in Berlin by Lucien Levy shows how by 1896 the city had all the signs of a modern metropolis.

Designing Modern Germany

A strongly contrasting image of Germany is conjured up by the Weimar years, defined as such by the move of the seat of government in 1918 from volatile Berlin to Weimar, following Germany's defeat in war, until the Republic's demise in 1933.[10] For its first years until 1923, this new republic floundered in economic chaos, which was matched nonetheless by great social, artistic and political experiment, encompassing a rejection of the past as well as enthusiasm for all that was modern. For the design historian, the period is most evocatively epitomized by the Bauhaus school of design and architecture (whose years in Germany neatly coincide with those of the Republic) and more generally by the formation of Modernism, for which Germany became extremely important. Weimar, the city where the Bauhaus was first established before its subsequent moves to Dessau, Berlin and eventually Chicago, was a city associated with the historical legacy of Goethe and the German Enlightenment.[11] This tradition was evoked by the modernizers of the Weimar period, who saw themselves as combining scientific knowledge with cultural novelty, but the historically conservative National Socialists, an increasing political force in the late 1920s, also laid claim to it. This highlights the central ambiguity of the Weimar period and the impossibility of maintaining the idea of a straightforwardly progressivist history toward the modern. Nonetheless, both at the Bauhaus and beyond, it was during this period that design in Germany more than ever became linked with a utopian wish to build a better life, and when many elements in Modernism were realized and for the first time acquired international significance. Fulfilment came at first on an experimental level, for instance, in avant-garde, abstract interiors and design prototypes. It was subsequently more publicly realized in social-housing estates and the proliferation of new forms of graphic design, magazines and film, as well as in early examples of modern industrial design.

The rise of the National Socialist party and the election of Adolf Hitler to the position of Chancellor of Germany in January 1933, from then on to be known as the Third Reich, marked an end to many of the forward-thinking ideas about design associated with Weimar, or at least the ease with which they could be publicly expressed and supported. As chapter Three examines, the National Socialist political regime attempted to establish a programme of autarky, through which indigenous raw materials for domestic manufacture became a crucial priority for the national economy.[12] As under other extreme political regimes eager to establish clear and dogmatic political messages, design was given heightened symbolic meaning at the level of propaganda within National Socialism. Accordingly, the material culture of everyday life was imbued with a national spirit through rhetoric

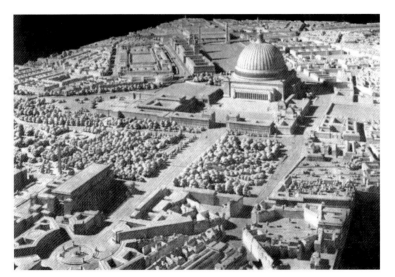

Albert Speer, model of the north–south axis of Berlin, part of the plan to develop it as 'world city Germania' between 1937 and 1942.

and display. Design played an overt role in establishing an identity for the Party, most obviously in the emblem of the swastika, with its characteristic blend of modernity and archaism.[13] Commentators have shown, however, that if on a political level the regime attempted to be consistent and non-contradictory, at the level of implementation it raised many complex issues of style and ideology, modernity and tradition. These reveal how far from straightforward it is to move between a political belief and its manifestation in design and material culture. Clear signs remain that a selective anti-Modernism existed during the Third Reich.

In many respects, the political history of Germany consists of a series of ruptures rather than continuities. The question, then, for the design historian, is the extent to which design itself can be considered to reflect these. In this sense, are the boundaries of 'German' design flexible and pervious? And what place do we give to the personal circumstances of individuals caught up in the events that surround them? In the twentieth century, in order to accommodate an expanded idea of a national design culture and its influences, we need to take into account the processes of emigration and exile, for instance, of German nationals such as Lucian Bernhard to the United States, Jan Tschichold to Switzerland, Hannes Meyer to the Soviet Union, Walter Gropius to Britain and the United States, Erich Mendelsohn to Britain, Palestine and the USA, and, much later, the decision of the designer Richard Sapper to be based in Milan.[14]

In a similar respect, account needs to be given of how modern design can occur under contrasting political circumstances. As will be discussed in

Designing Modern Germany

chapters Three and Four, the history of German industrial design and manufacture between 1930 and 1960 suggests that there were signs of significant continuity across ostensibly opposing political systems, just as there were breaks, divisions and changes, making our understanding of design and history complex. We will ask what it means to look for similarities as well as differences between the Third Reich and the Federal Republic of Germany or German Democratic Republic.

Rather than overlook the post-war history of one or other of the two Germanys, as has often been the case in earlier studies, treating them by default, as unrelated or independent developments, chapter Four seeks to analyse the two together.[15] Again, for the historian of German design, the period following the end of the Second World War provides a far from simple or straightforward narrative. After defeat, the two Germanys were divided according to the military occupations of the joint Allied forces in 1948 – the US, British and French zones in the south, north and west, the Soviet zone in the east. Berlin, revived capital of Germany from 1933, was in an extremely sensitive situation – the four occupying forces each took a sector, mirroring in their geography the greater division of Germany. Through this, the French, American and British zones formed an island and the seat

Columbus Haus in Potsdamer Platz, Berlin, 1951. The photographic postcard shows the facade with messages against the re-militarization of Berlin, 'Youth of the world – united in Berlin – help us to maintain peace'.

of the Federal Republic government was moved to Bonn. Between 1948 and 1961, during the height of the Cold War, and after 1961 and the building of the Berlin Wall, design, like all areas of public cultural life, became susceptible to various pressures, and a heightened awareness of its material, ideological and psychological potential grew. This situation presented the designer with a complex set of circumstances to negotiate. For those in the West, the tendency was to consider the Federal Republic as the natural inheritor of a liberal tradition of modern design applied to the benefits of an increasingly dominant consumer society, the latter in many respects based on the American model. The earlier commitment to the socialist or Communist political beliefs of Weimar was not necessarily carried over. As in many Western countries, arguments were put forward by designers to distinguish their achievements as *Gute Form* (good design), endorsed by the official tastemakers of the Rat für Formgebung (Council for Design), which was established in 1951. Whereas the emphasis of the 1920s (even if not fully realized) had been on developing qualities in design to provide for the largest proportion of the population through standards for minimum dwellings, much Western design of the 1950s moved in the direction that came to be identified as 'lifestyle' (*Lebensart*). Under renewed prosperity and shored up by the US subsidies of the Marshall Plan, the West German Economic Miracle, or *Wirtschaftswunder* as it became known, allowed for a large proportion of the population to benefit from this growth, levelling out the earlier severe class division. Designers were encouraged to believe that their work would contribute to a consensual form of social democracy, based on welfare state capitalism.

By contrast, the status of design in the German Democratic Republic (1949–89) reflected the complexities of the regime's own changing political situation. Initially, designers sought many parallels with the Federal Republic and often aspired to similar design principles and philosophies as their Western counterparts. For instance, in the first years of the regime, many argued for the new republic to become the inheritor of Modernist design, in education, professional practice and state policy, even if not through the consumer market. The situation was made more complex, however, with the increasing control from the Soviet Union in the early 1950s, when what was known as the 'Formalism debate' led to the repression of experimental cultural ideas in favour of policies oriented towards Stalinism. A period of relative freedom, often termed the cultural thaw, followed the death of Stalin and in response to the more moderate policies of Nikita Khrushchev.[16] Parallel developments in design included the award to well-designed industrial products from 1957 and the promotion of 'good design' by the Zentral Institut für Formgestaltung (Central Institute for Design) in the late 1950s to 1970s.[17]

As is discussed in chapter Four, the designers most directly influenced by state policies were those involved in the technologically oriented areas of industrial design for East German manufacture. By contrast, it was possible to sustain alternative forms of expression and a relative autonomy in some areas of the applied arts. These can be regarded as 'softer' design fields, less dependant on systems of formal provision and open to more individuality, such as, for example, the flourishing book, illustration and poster design industries and small-scale craft production, which seemed to thrive. For consumers in the GDR, the home-made, do-it-yourself and informal economy also provided an alternative means of access to everyday design.

Chapter Five considers the final stage of coexistence of the German Democratic Republic and the Federal Republic and sets the developments in design culture against these years, leading to the dramatic collapse of the Berlin Wall in 1989, the reunification of Germany in 1991 and the return of the seat of the united Federal government to Berlin.

On one level, in the 1980s profound dissatisfaction had been shown with defence policies, rearmament, nuclear power and the threat of environmental disaster. Prominent among the countries of Europe, the two Germanys experienced a deep ecological critique in which design was implicated. Some designers engaged with these issues through examining possibilities of sustainability and design for social need, although in many respects this counter-cultural stance could be regarded as undermining much of what the dominant design culture represented. At the same time in the 1980s, the Western-style design profession was also going through its own self-examination, asking how it compared with Italian design in the period of high Postmodernism, for instance. The debate revealed contrasting opinions on the place of the designer as part of contemporary cultural life, defined by a post-industrial economy in the context of increasing globalization of the spheres of manufacture. Other countries seemed to fare better in the face of this challenge. This brought to a head an increasing dissatisfaction from younger generations with the tradition of problem-solving and stress on formal values that had characterized much post-war German design, which by then was viewed as reductive. At a polemical level, mounting critique came from the next generation of designers, who argued for a more communicative, critical, expressive and cultural approach to design, which was in keeping with the radical Postmodernism of other cultural forms. In the early 1980s Berlin in particular became the location for an experimental design scene that matched a renewed energy in many other forms of visual culture.

This generation preferred a model of design as discourse, embracing semiology and celebrating signification through popular references to everyday life (*Alltagskultur*). They were also interested in more overtly politicized possibilities for design, which, in the West German situation, had been seen as taboo ever since Nazism.

Despite this radical critique, as the century came to a close, economic, social, legislative and cultural change introduced in the eastern sector after reunification confirmed that the winning model of political economy was free-market capitalism along with EEC membership. Germany held the difficult task of continuing to behave as the role-model European state, in a period of increasing inflation, growing unemployment and worldwide destabilization caused by an aggressive US foreign policy.[18] The country faced the costs of reorganization of many of its cultural institutions. Already in the 1980s a series of ambitious developments in the museum sector had led to great interest in the curation of design as part of modern leisure and culture industries. The question became whether the reunified country could afford to maintain these institutions at the level accustomed in the Federal Republic, while investing in rebuilding the infrastructure of the eastern parts of the country to bring them to similar levels as the western, through reforms in transport, communications and massive industrial reorganization, as well as investment in the renovation of their cities. After the jubilations of a newly reunited country, a period of intense self-questioning followed that importantly included the place of design as the new millennium dawned.

Germany and a Sense of Place

A word needs to be given about the geography of this book. To speak of 'German design', or even design in Germany, immediately prompts questions of the more exact location of design within the country's own national borders. If Berlin was one central force of gravity throughout the twentieth century, in a federal constitution regional cities also have great influence and offer alternative venues for the formation of culture. Historians of Germany always face the difficult decision about where to concentrate their attention – places are omitted, not because they are necessarily less important, but through force of circumstance – there would be simply too much to take on. Unlike Italy, for example, where a history of twentieth-century design could quite legitimately be focused on Milan, with occasional detours to Rome or Turin and a few other cities, or Britain, where again the official cultures of design could be said to have been centralized around a few crucial centres, there is no such clear map to the design of Germany.

Designing Modern Germany

Traditionally, design is associated with cities and metropolitan culture, where the mixture of ideas ferments. Design also requires links with industry. On one level, 'Germany' can be identified as a group of its 'big cities', the *Groszstädte* of Berlin, Cologne, Dresden, Frankfurt am Main, Hamburg, Leipzig, Munich, Nuremburg and Stuttgart. As the cultural history of Germany reveals, cities were developed with individual identities, Munich as an art city, Berlin for new technical industries, Nuremburg and the Ruhr district for heavy industrial culture based on extractive resources, and so on. Then there were centres identified for their art and design schools: Munich, Darmstadt, Essen, Magdeburg, Ulm, Breslau, Weimar, Karlsruhe and Düsseldorf. Other cities that claim attention include Frankfurt am Main, for its experimental municipal patronage of the new architecture and design of the 1920s. Then come regional cities with strong identities for a particular material or genre of design, as was the case for Leipzig in the East and Offenbach am Main in the West, each a centre for publishing, the book arts and graphic trades, and Burg Giebichenstein for ceramics, Jena for glass and Krefeld and Barmen for textiles. With the second industrial revolution of technical and electrical industries, cities were based around new engineering industries and the landscape again changed: MAN heavy vehicles in Nuremberg or single-industry towns, such as Wolfsburg in the case of Volkswagen and Zwickau in the German Democratic Republic where the Trabant was produced. With the advent of computer-aided design and the digital revolution, the map altered again.

To take a case in point, the already mentioned German Werkbund, while regarded as a 'national' formation, was in fact more active in certain regions than others. For example, in the 1920s Stuttgart in Baden-Württemberg became a leading city in the promotion of design, thanks to a number of active individuals who organized important design exhibitions, among them *Form Ohne Ornament* (Form without Ornament) of 1924, the modern housing exhibition *Die Wohnung* (The Dwelling) of 1927, better known as the *Weissenhofsiedlung*, and *Film und Foto* of 1929, which celebrated the radical photographic culture of the Weimar years.[19]

Other smaller cities or towns attracted international attention at the beginning of the twentieth century through association with design. Among these was Darmstadt, where a flowering of *Jugendstil* took off between 1898 and 1914 in all directions of the visual and performing arts, architecture, design and crafts in its artists' colony, formed under the royal patronage of the archduke of Hesse.[20] On the strength of the inheritance of the artists' colony, the museum, theatre and design institutions in Darmstadt became important settings later in the century. It was here, for example, that the Rat für Formgebung was established in 1951. It supported an important school of design, the Werkkunstschule Darmstadt, which in 1971 became a faculty of the Fachhochschule Darmstadt (FHD).

By contrast, Hagen in north-west Germany, a small, industrial town, was important only in the few years between 1902 and 1914, when the Museum für Kunst in Handel und Gewerbe (Museum for Art in Trade and Industry), founded by Karl Ernst Osthaus, proved that 'design for industry' could be a subject equal to the fine arts and worthy of museum display.[21] Both locations offer exceptional cases of the local promotion of design and material culture, which attracted international recognition and altered the geography of German design in the twentieth century.

German Design and Personal Reminiscence

Books are written for any number of reasons and they can reflect both the practice of research and priorities of the time of writing. Historians follow established conventions for gathering evidence and analysing it: in the case of the design historian, for example, these can range from sources in archives and libraries, interpreting designed objects held in museum collections, measuring the value of oral testimony, design journalism, and many other kinds of formal and informal evidence. History is also often informed by subjective experiences, and these should be acknowledged by way of conclusion to this introduction.

I started writing this book in 2005 in a converted factory that now serves as low-cost, rented accommodation in Kreuzberg, a central district of Berlin. When originally constructed in the 1880s, the building had served as a combined small-scale basic workshop and domestic space, a *Hinterhof* (backyard) of plain brickwork with little adornment. From the formal street facade of greater Wilhelmine grandeur, through successive courtyards, one accesses the most modest of blocks such as this. These places are emblematic of the multi-layered character of many cities in Western Europe in the early twenty-first century, whilst holding their own particularly distinctive character and composition. In the case of Kreuzberg, once a thriving inner-city district, industries were disrupted and discontinued following the Second World War. While much of the street plan of nineteenth-century buildings survived sufficiently to be restored eventually, the district became considered by many to be no longer desirable. Gradually the suburban development of modern housing estates removed many original residents from the former inner city, and the area became home to successive generations of poor migrant workers, initially largely from Turkey. The large

An improvized house, 'Baum Haus an der Mauer' (Tree House on the Wall) built into part of the remains of the Berlin Wall in the Kreuzberg district of the city, photographed in 2007.

empty buildings were also prime sites for occupation, and squatting proliferated in the 1970s. In this respect, the district became both a site of wilful disregard for the more modern social amenities afforded to other areas of the city, and a locus for forceful resistance from some of its inhabitants, hippies, punks and anarchists, whose anti-establishment values, alternative scene of squats and impromptu cultural activity formed as a culture of protest. With the fall of the Wall, these lively streets again became prime sites for speculative development in the reconfigured city centre of Berlin. At the time of writing, graffiti and flyers attest to the controversial encroachment of middle-class café culture and the risk of gentrification and vocal resistance to this, while aspects of the alternative scene migrate to other areas of the city.

At an imaginative level, it is a challenge for the design historian to reconcile this view of everyday life in the contemporary German city, however impressionistically built up through the eyes of a foreigner, with the well-ordered, clean-cut design that continues to appear on the pages of the official design press such as *Form, Design Report* and *Novum Gebrauchsgraphik.* These still privilege exemplary objects as worthy of attention, very often removed from social practice.

I conclude with another perspective, again impressionistic and experiential. My first encounter with the full impact of material culture and the strength of its ideological and emotional power was in 1971 – it came from a growing awareness that cultural difference can be acutely perceived through design. As a young student visiting Berlin for the first time, I experienced what all those who took the journey through the political border of Checkpoint Charlie, from West to East Berlin, might encounter. On the western side, a strong sense of decay in the streets around the Kochstrasse district of Kreuzberg pervaded, at a time before it became associated with artistic revival. It simply felt like the end of the line. It was a point of no return, blocked by the Wall, and an area that the West Berlin authorities were uncertain how to develop, in an atmosphere of neglect. The exception was Axel Springer Haus, a building owned by the newspaper proprietor and publisher of, among other titles, *Bildzeitung,* which became an emblem of capitalism as its signs provocatively beamed across the Wall to Leipzigerstrasse in the East. Two kilometres away, Kurfürstendamm with its cafés, showrooms, department stores and cinemas continued the Western dream of consumerism, in what was for its critics a bland and undistinguished normalcy.[22]

On going through the Wall, one encountered a completely different place, all the more curious because the two cities were geographically adjacent while being temporally and spatially extremely different. The sweet sharpness of the smell of brown coal (lignite) acted as a metaphor for East Berlin, optimism and sadness combined in a fragile relationship through which people's connection with their man-made and natural environment was destined to become crucial in the last twenty years of the century. The part played by material artefacts in the construction of political difference was palpable. This was shown in all the senses: through sound, for example, roads appeared quiet after the car-oriented West, their surfaces composed of different materials, and they were occupied predominantly by small, bright blue and cream Trabants and Wartburgs, cars that spoke of a future still to be realized. Their futurist styling seemed anachronistic in Unter den Linden, the historical core of the city where the most significant buildings were intact, but as they flashed past other visions of the future – the TV

Designing Modern Germany

tower (Fernsehturm) at Alexanderplatz, the Palace of the Republic – or down Stalinallee, a boulevard built for the East German workers, they looked more the part.

It was this contrast between two places, on one level both 'Germany', and the apparent role of design and material culture that provoked me to pursue this study.

**Deutsche
Werkstätten**

jetzt

Arco-Zinneberg
Palais
Wittelsbacherplatz1

BERN
HARD

1

Design Ideals, Design Reform, Design Professions, 1870–1914

Far more important than ruling the world . . . is giving the world a face. The nation to achieve this will be truly the leader of the world, and Germany must become that nation.

Hermann Muthesius, 'Die Zukunft der Deutschen Form', 1915[1]

The beginning of the twentieth century in Germany was marked by an increasing self-confidence about the possibilities for an emergent design culture that could hold its own on the world stage. During the decade leading up to 1915, when Hermann Muthesius, a Prussian senior civil servant and important commentator on architecture, design and industrial culture made this pronouncement under the title of 'The Future of German Form', he had been one of Germany's strongest advocates for promoting relations between art and industry. In part taking the model from Britain, where he had been posted between 1896 and 1904 as cultural attaché in the German embassy in London, Muthesius was one of the first of the generation to rally around the call for design reform in the new nation state of Germany. This was most clearly expressed in his important three-volume study *Das Englische Haus* (*The English House*) of 1904–5 and in his writings for the Deutsche Werkbund from 1907, an organization of which he was a founding member. Merely twenty years earlier, it would have seemed impossible for a commentator to make such a claim for Germany to hold this position. Muthesius's comment came after years of prescriptive writing about design by himself and other like-minded figures, at all levels, to help elevate the designer for industry, so that the designer's role would be acknowledged as essential for the well-being of the national economy and its success abroad. Made during the first year of the First World War, Muthesius's suggestions were therefore not out of the question, even if they would still be deemed controversial.

Lucian Bernhard, poster for the Deutsche Werkstätten exhibition at the Arco-Zinneberg Palace, Munich, 1912.

The Argument for *Kunstindustrie*

The debate on the correct education for the fine artist, applied artist and designer in Germany mounted during the second half of the nineteenth century. Underlying this was the concern to introduce a greater dialogue between the trade schools and the art academies, which evolved into quite separate institutions responsible for different forms of visual art education. Their separation was based on idealist philosophical thought, initially stemming from a distinction made by Immanuel Kant in his essay, *The Critique of Judgement* of 1790. In this, Kant distinguished two kinds of beauty, free beauty (*pulchritude vaga*), which he associated with expression in the fine arts, and dependent or applied beauty (*pulchritude adhaerens*), which he defined particularly in relation to use in architecture and design. Kant wrote:

> In architecture the chief point is a certain *use* of the artistic object to
> which, as the condition, the aesthetic ideas are limited. In sculpture
> the mere *expression* of aesthetic ideas is the main intention. Thus
> statues of men, gods, animals, etc., belong to sculpture; but temples,
> splendid buildings for public concourse, or even dwelling-houses,
> triumphal arches, columns, mausoleums, etc., erected as monuments,
> belong to architecture, and in fact all household furniture (the work
> of cabinet-makers, and so forth – things meant to be used) may be
> added to the list, on the ground that adaptation of the product to a
> particular use is the essential element in a work of architecture.[2]

The mounting interest in the new art industries – *Kunstindustrie*, as they were to be called – might achieve a reconciliation of this Kantian separation. This belief was held in a number of quarters, which should be explored to shed further light on how Muthesius's pronouncement of 1915 came to be made. It was in the 1860s and '70s that the question of the quality of Germany's industrial manufacture was first raised with increased intensity. Under the term *Kunstindustrie* fell the various skills and trades associated with the manufacture of industrial items, ranging from ceramics and glass to metalwork, textiles, furniture and woodwork. These goods could be for domestic use in the home or, in many cases, they formed the basis to equip the business and commercial enterprises that were proliferating at this time of rapid urbanization in Germany. In terms of their manufacture, by the late nineteenth century the factory system was challenging smaller-scale industries, driven by profit and replacing handwork by machine-tooling. This often undermined the previously close connection between maker, designer and finished product, with the possibility of decline in the quality of goods becoming a major issue.

For Germany, the debate began initially in its new capital, Berlin, where Hermann Schwabe, a civil servant and university professor, led the Statistics Bureau from 1865 and held a lively interest in the general well-being of the cultural life of the city.[3] Schwabe was sent to Britain as a government emissary to report on art and design education, and in 1871 he published his recommendations in the book *Kunstindustrie Bestrebungen in Deutschland* (Aspirations for Art Industry in Germany). This publication, the first of its kind, held important implications for the Deutsche Gewerbe Museum (German Trade Museum), which along with the accompanying Unterrichtsanstalt (Teaching Institute) had opened in 1867.[4] The publication formed the most complete exploration of the possibilities of educating future generations of the skilled workforce, including designers, for Germany's art industries.

Schwabe proposed a system for educational institutions that he hoped would be implemented by the government. He went so far as to offer sample curricula for students and teachers and gave advice on building up study collections and organizing exhibitions. Schwabe was well aware of developments in other countries, in particular Britain, where what became known as the South Kensington system had evolved between 1837 and 1852.

Print of the facade of the Berlin Kunstgewerbe-museum, designed by the architects Martin Gropius and Heino Schmieden, 1877–81.

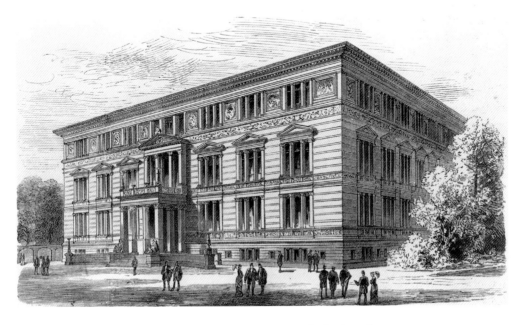

According to this model, the Government School of Design and National Art Training School (which in 1896 became the Royal College of Art) taught principles of design and what were considered the 'true principles' of ornament. An accompanying museum, in the London case the South Kensington Museum, eventually opened in 1857 and was renamed the Victoria and Albert Museum in 1899. The idea was to build collections of historical and contemporary artefacts ranging across materials and techniques. These were intended to be exemplars, object lessons in technique, use of material, artistic form and ornament, for the instruction of future generations of artisans, designers and architects.[5]

A German connection already existed through the figure of Prince Albert of Saxe-Coburg-Gotha, husband to Queen Victoria and royal consort, who, together with Henry Cole, Francis Fuller, Charles Dilke and other members of the Royal Society for the Encouragement of Arts, was largely responsible for the Great Exhibition of 1851. As royal patron, Prince Albert subsequently commissioned the architect Gottfried Semper, at the time a political refugee from Prussia, to assist in guiding the curatorial divisions of the museum, once the school's original collections had been greatly enhanced through the acquisitions from the Crystal Palace exhibition. Semper's influential scheme was to elide historical and cultural difference, organizing the museum departments instead by material. Accordingly, the first departments were Wood, Metal, Ceramics, Textiles and Engraving. Semper's major study of applied and decorative arts, *Der Stil in der technischen und tektonischen Künsten* of 1860–62 (*Style in the Technical and Tectonic Arts; or, Practical Aesthetics*) was to prove extremely important for laying down the intellectual foundations for a theory of the applied arts. According to Michael Conforti, Semper 'disregarded subject matter, which had been the foundation of academic criticism since the sixteenth century', focusing instead on 'the symbolic nature of individual motifs in objects and the transformation of their meaning in varying situations of production and cultural environments'.[6]

True to his age, Schwabe divided the education of the artist and designer into clear stages. Evolutionary models of thought were popular since the publication in 1859 of Charles Darwin's highly influential *On the Origin of Species by Means of Natural Selection; or, The Preservation of Favoured Races in the Struggle for Life*. In this, a theory of humankind was cast in developmental steps from the 'primitive' to the sophisticated or civilized, and in many systems of classification, including theories of ornament, similar models were proposed.[7]

In this respect, Schwabe's argument and curricula were no exceptions. For instance, he ran through the essential ingredients for preparing an art

Gottfried Semper, *Der Stil in den technischen und tektonischen Künsten*, originally published in 1862. This page shows the ceiling decoration from the Temple of Theseus, Athens.

Designing Modern Germany

Taf. V.

Ein Feld der Decke des Theseustempels zu Athen.
(Halbe Gröfse d. O.)

Druck v. Gebrüder Obpacher. München.

handworker in the knowledge of design applied to a variety of materials. Drawing was the primary skill, taught first in 'principles of ornament', then plant and animal form. This was followed by exercises in applied forms for the design of objects, intended for all areas of the art industries. The method was no doubt developed in the knowledge of Owen Jones's important study, *The Grammar of Ornament* (1856), through which an accomplished designer could develop a lexicon of ideas that would then be 'applied' to the material in hand.[8] A second level of drawing, Schwabe suggested, could lead the student from the linear and two-dimensional to rendering three-dimensional form, introducing the treatment of shading and colour and the ability to depict the complete object in preparation of its realization. Third came lessons in modelling from the human form. It is important to note that in all of this, 'design' was considered to be an exercise on paper, undertaken in a classroom, often following the exact instruction of the master, removed from actual materials of manufacture. Students were therefore expected to take their new knowledge back to the workshop or factory and apply the lessons learnt in the activity of making.

At the time of Schwabe's writing most students were men. It was only in the 1880s that separate art schools for women were opened in Germany, allowing opportunities to study all aspects of art and design, including in

Students in the metal workshop at the Berlin Kunstgewerbeschule, c. 1910, showing the importance of learning through making.

Designing Modern Germany

the life room. This growth was noticeable when distinctly more middle-class women became known in their own right in the early 1900s as important craftswomen, engravers, book artists, embroiderers, weavers and potters. On the education of women, in the 1870s Schwabe could offer only the following comment: 'Classes for women are an integral part of drawing school, although their introduction leaves something to be desired. Where they are introduced, they should be considered supplementary to the rest of the drawing classes.'[9]

Since classes were intended for those who were employed during the day, many took place in the evenings, and others on Sundays. The latter were organized, Schwabe noted, particularly for craftsmen in the construction and machine-building trades. A special group of classes for composition and the applied arts covered elementary and ornamental drawing, painting and drawing after the plaster cast and figurative drawing, with lectures on anatomy and proportion. Again, following the examples of London and, more recently, Vienna, where director Rudolf von Eitelberger had established the Österreichisches Museum für Kunst und Industrie (Austrian Museum of Art and Industry) in 1862 on South Kensington lines, Schwabe proposed the formation of a collection of exemplary objects. His description ran:

> This now fills four halls, of which the last one opened in July of this year. It contains carvings made of various materials, furniture and a collection of plaster casts, which have already increased in number to about 600; roughly 130 of these, which are particularly suited as exemplars for education, are cast and sold cheaply in the museum. The remaining three halls feature especially wickerwork, textiles, lace, blown and cut glass, porcelain and clay goods, mosaics, enamelled and lacquer work, as well as cast and wrought iron as exemplary or historically interesting pieces from various countries and time periods.[10]

This ambitious list was intended to supplement the existing collections of the museum, at first known as the Deutsches Gewerbe Museum (German Trade Museum). By 1880, growing in importance, the museum moved to a neo-Renaissance building designed by Martin Gropius, itself modelled on the South Kensington Museum, under the leadership of its renowned director Julius Lessing. In 1885 it was renamed the Königliches Kunstgewerbe Museum (Arts and Crafts Museum of the Royal Collections). Although Berlin was the first German city to take up such an initiative, other cities soon followed by founding museums dedicated to the applied arts, notably Hamburg, Frankfurt am Main, Leipzig, Nuremberg and Munich.[11]

In order to convince his audience of politicians and senior civil servants, Schwabe made predictions of the number of visitors such a museum might attract. Initial comparison was made with London, where the annual visitor figure for the South Kensington Museum in 1869 was thought to be 800,000, while in Vienna it was approximately 108,000. The Berlin museum, which was, as Schwabe stressed, still a teaching rather than a public institution, could claim only the exact figure of 11,757.[12] Important for his mission was the list of possible venues for travelling exhibitions, made up of art and trades schools in smaller towns and cities across Germany. It was through such a programme that educating the taste of the public would be fulfilled. He wrote:

> However, the German trade museum has taken another important step. In order to generalize the beneficial effect of its aspirations for industry, it has also founded a touring museum and has already exhibited in several cities. There is no need to prove the degree to which education is furthered, the establishment of local museums encouraged, or the visitor's taste improved, if the acquired, exemplary treasures of art are made mobile and a selection of art objects is circulated amongst provincial schools.[13]

Schwabe concluded that to inform the taste of the people would lead to the overall improvement of manufacture by the German nation. His comments, however, fell on sensitive ears, since Prussia was at this point engaged in the Franco–Prussian war, and a victory would lead to the unification of Germany in preparation for such a national venture. Developing a negative, competitive contrast with France, he continued: 'What we Germans have done for the world with the Reformation, France has done for the modern world with the Revolution.'[14]

Schwabe then used an argument that would become a leitmotif in subsequent histories of German decorative arts. At its core was a dismissal of the French preoccupation with 'les Styles', the historical traditions of style associated with the court and the tendency towards emulation of luxury rather than innovation among its *artistes-décorateurs*. Invoking the prominent commentator on design, Jakob von Falke, Schwabe wrote:

> If it is so in the spheres of the higher arts – how is it then in the field of the art industries? Everywhere there is an inconsistency of taste, a mixing of styles without principle, poor imitation, copyist-like naturalism. Falke, the most competent judge in this matter, rightly says

Designing Modern Germany

that French taste is non-taste, that trimming and appearance have replaced art, and that taste has become the slave of the available fashion, which has separated from beauty.

He continued:

What is really remarkable about the French goods of the 'industrie de luxe' [luxury industry], as they very pointedly call it, is not the composition, but the outer element of colour, the 'savoir vivre' of every object, one could say its make-up. And fine feathers do make fine birds, albeit not men.[15]

As Schwabe would have been all too aware, an exact alternative was still to be realized for Germany. It was not the first such incitement, but it was certainly one that would be repeated during the century to follow.

Another perspective on the historical interest in the applied arts was offered by Julius Lessing, an art historian, who, as a journalist, reviewed the great exhibitions of Paris (1867 and 1878) and Vienna (1873) for the German press. His journalistic activities possibly proved strategic as self-promotion; they were certainly noticed, for, in 1872, having organized two exhibitions of the applied arts, Lessing was appointed as director of the collections of the Deutsches Gewerbemuseum in Berlin.[16] He wrote an extended commentary on an exhibition drawn from collections of historical arts and crafts objects at the *Ausstellung älterer kunstgewerblicher Gegenstände* (Exhibition of Older Arts and Crafts Objects), held in the Royal Arsenal on Unter den Linden in September and October 1872. This consisted of twelve rooms arranged 'historically and technically', and proved formative for subsequent thinking about the classification of objects in German collections. The rooms were in part laid out according to the historical period, styles and movements already employed in early art history, such as the medieval, Gothic and early, high and late Italian Renaissance. They were also in part organized according to Semperian principle, by material, as in bronze, silverware, ivory, lace and porcelain. A third classification was by genre, as in jewellery and weaponry. Particularly significant for the future inspiration of generations of designers were the collections from China and Japan. Prophetically, in light of the wave of *Japonisme* spreading across many European countries in the 1870s and '80s, Lessing's catalogue text suggested that the Japanese work would provide inspiration for its 'fresh and natural truth'.[17]

Other non-European collections included important treasures from India, Persia and Turkey. The major art manufacturers of Europe, Meissen,

Sèvres and Wedgwood, were also represented. As Lessing explained, the exhibition drew from prominent palace collections, among them the royal collections at Potsdam, Monbijou and the Royal Palace in Berlin, along with important public collections and a number of individual collectors, including gifts from the manufacturers themselves. For instruction in skills, technical sections concentrated on Venetian and German glass, ivory, bronze, iron and copper metalworking. German historical periods were identified with the age of Friedrich I and Friedrich the Great, and ended with the age of Friedrich Wilhelm III and the architect Karl Friedrich Schinkel. In this way, the history of German Arts and Crafts was put in place in important collections that young designers would encounter, learn from and often react against in the years to come.

The Berlin Trade Exhibition of 1896

Another exhibition with a more straightforward commercial purpose, which offered a direct encounter with contemporary manufacture rather than collections of historical artefacts, took place in 1896. Prompted by an earlier Berlin Trade Exhibition, Die Vereinigung 1879 (The Association, 1879) formed to propose Germany's first international exhibition. In fact, the Berlin Trade Exhibition became a celebration of the capital's industries, under the symbol of a hammer held by the hand of labour, rising out of the earth to create a new city.[18] It took place in the purpose-built site of the Treptower Park in the east of the city. Covering all areas of industrial manufacture and food production, the displays were so wide-ranging that they also included sections on education and social development, sport and recreation, health and welfare. Of particular mention were the sections on chemistry, photography and scientific instruments, fields of specialist manufacture for which Germany was developing a world reputation. For amusement as well as edification, a model of a Norddeutscher Lloyd ocean liner *Bremen* was moored on the River Spree for the public to explore, and water buses ploughed their way on excursions from the city, along with an elevated railway. In tune with the expectations of visitors at interna-

Photograph of the main entrance to the *Berliner Gewerbeausstellung*, 1896.

Designing Modern Germany

Cover of the catalogue for the *Berliner Gewerbeauss-tellung* in 1896, showing the design by Ludwig Sütterlin.

BERLINER GEWERBE-AUSSTELLUNG.
1896.

OFFICIELLER
HAUPT-KATALOG
Illustrirte Prachtausgabe.

VERLAG VON RUDOLF MOSSE
Druckerei des Berliner Tageblatt.'

tional exhibitions, special effects included 'Alt Berlin', a nostalgic recon-struction of half-timbered and gabled dwellings, with streets and squares for performances and restaurants, beer halls and cafés. An evocation of the streets of Old Cairo acted as a piece of exoticism, along with a panorama of the Alps. The layout of the entire exhibition was said to have been inspired by the Paris Exposition Universelle of 1889, and the facade of the main building by architects Hans Grisebach, Karl Hoffacker and Bruno Schmitz was reminiscent of Trocadéro in the French capital. Visitors could enjoy coffee roasted in a Moorish kiosk, tea served in a Chinese pavilion, read newspapers printed by specially installed presses, and smoke cigars or cigarettes made on site. Categories within the industrial section included textiles, clothing, wood, porcelain, metal, graphic and decorative arts and the book industry, engineering, paper industry and electro-technology. The Berlin Trade Exhibition marked a crucial moment in the history of German design since it took place immediately prior to the development of a self-conscious reform movement and its displays of material excess were no doubt cause of such consternation among some. That it reached a wide audience was clear: to make good the costs an estimated 48,000 people visited daily.

In terms of artistic effect, there was little to suggest that the selection of the Berlin 1896 exhibition was aimed towards the promotion of coherent styles or a particular aesthetic preference, or that this drove individual exhibitors. Instead, the message of the exhibition and accompanying catalogue was that all tastes could be catered for amidst the general competence of manufacturers. It was seen as a distinct commercial advantage to offer the market a varied range of products and historical styles. Commentaries on furniture design, for example, indicated that 'design' in most cases consisted of a response to the commission by the individual consumer. One furniture manufacturer boasted of being able to cater for every taste and offered skills in the reconstruction of all historical styles.

The director of the Berlin Kunstgewerbe Museum, Julius Lessing, commented on the unnecessary challenge presented to specialist handworkers by pandering to popular taste. He wrote that in order to fulfil the customers' expectations, 'The craftsman must get to know the old art forms, be introduced to the architectural and ornamental rules of style, he must draw the classical orders, plants and animal forms in the form of the Renaissance, rococo and so on.'[19] This he saw as unnecessary, and instead he advocated a more defined design curriculum.

An advertisement for Emil Lefèvre, the city's largest curtain and carpet outlet, from the catalogue of the *Berliner Gewerbeausstellung*, 1896.

Designing Modern Germany

In his essay on the Berlin Trade Exhibition, Georg Simmel, the leading social theorist, remarked on the ambition to raise Berlin in status from city (*Groszstadt*) to metropolis (*Weltstadt*) by presenting the products of one city as a plethora of objects. Simmel noted that, as a form, the exhibition gave the objects on display 'a shop-window quality', which he called a 'super-additum'. He went on: 'The exhibition with its emphasis on amusement attempts a new synthesis between the principles of external stimulus and the practical function of objects, and therefore takes this aesthetic superadditum to its highest level.' He then suggested: 'The banal attempt to put things in their best light, as in the cries of the street trader, is transformed in the interesting attempt to confer a new aesthetic significance from displaying objects together – something already happening in the relationship between advertising and poster art.' This recognition of 'the dialectic of the commodity', whether in commercial exchange, at exhibition or graphically reproduced on the pages of magazines, became a point of fascination and preoccupation for many designers of the next generation.[20]

Arts and Crafts Reform

An important theoretical impulse that helped to shape the voice of German design criticism in these years came from the writings of the British Arts and Crafts movement, most prominently William Morris and John Ruskin. Both argued that it should be natural for the artist or designer to move from architecture, painting and sculpture, areas that had been elevated to the status of the academy in the eighteenth century, to embrace the applied arts and design. Morris tellingly called these 'the lesser arts' in his riposte to those who held the design of ordinary goods for the home and for utility as lower in the aesthetic hierarchy. Adding a moral dimension, Ruskin, Morris and their followers praised 'honest' craftsmanship and stood against the 'evils' of industrialization. Their embrace of hand-working skills, threatened by extinction in the face of industrial capitalism, bore influence across central Europe. As a socialist and political activist, Morris's arguments were grounded in his reading of Karl Marx and Friedrich Engels, and he persistently addressed the question of the political economy of design. Nevertheless, as research into his business practice has shown, Morris also found it difficult on occasion to reconcile his principled design ideals with the realities of running a company for profit.[21] His insistence on hand methods made the goods produced by Morris, Marshall and Faulkner and the later Morris and Company expensive and out of reach of the honest worker whom the designer addressed. Undoubtedly, the most important Morrisian

INTERNATIONALE · KUNST · AUSSTELLUNG · TURIN · 1902
ENGLISCHE · ABTEILUNG

DEUTSCHE · KUNST · UND · DEKORATION

DE · SIGN   HANDI · CRAFT

VI. JAHRG. HEFT 5 ·   · EINZELPREIS · M. 2.⁵⁰

· FEBRUAR · 1903 ·

Johann Vincenz Cissarz, cover of the special issue of *Deutsche Kunst und Dekoration* (February 1903), devoted to the English section of the Turin exhibition. It depicted the symbolic meeting of 'Design' and 'Handicraft'.

legacy was the significance attributed to design for the everyday and the belief in the value of making.

The writings of Morris and Ruskin were available for readers in Germany immediately on their publication in Britain, but, significantly, they were also translated into German in the late 1890s and early 1900s, at the height of interest from the next generation of artists and designers inspired by their example. For instance, the anthology of lectures that Morris gave in Birmingham, London and Nottingham between 1878 and 1881, originally published in 1882 as *Hopes and Fears for Art*, appeared in 1901 as *Kunsthoffnungen und Kunstsorgen.*[22] Ruskin's work also became available in translation. *Die Sieben Leuchter der Baukunst* (*The Seven Lamps of Architecture*) was translated by Wilhelm Schoelermann of Dresden in 1900, while *Grundlagen des Zeichnens* (*The Elements of Drawing, in Three Letters to Beginners*) and *Praeterita: Ansichten und Gedanken aus meinem Leben* (*Praeterita: Outlines of Scenes and Thoughts, Perhaps Worthy of Memory in My Past Life*), the autobiography of John Ruskin were published in 1901 and 1903 respectively.

As further testimony of the infiltration of these ideals, in 1903 the periodical *Deutsche Kunst und Dekoration* published a special issue on the British Arts and Crafts designers following their success at the Turin international exposition. The cover encapsulated the message of the works on display: the new design would be the result of collaboration between craftsman and designer – hand and brain. As we have already seen, Schwabe and his contemporaries considered the principles of drawing essential for artistic creation, a view shared with the British Arts and Crafts reformers. Importantly, they stood against the current mid-nineteenth-century fashion for historicism and eclecticism prevalent in most European cities as the style for interiors and architecture. Some German designers of the next generation took their ideas wholesale, while others modified them. 'Simplicity' was preferred to over-decoration, while 'truth' to the inherent properties of materials was favoured above disguise behind surface decoration or applied ornament. It was an aesthetic of reaction that could really be understood only in relation to what it sought not to be. To some contemporary eyes this appeared shocking. Wood surfaces were left untreated, avoiding the elegant marquetry or expensive veneers of conventional furniture. Joints were exposed and hinges were treated as a necessary part of the design and remained revealed. Natural methods for textiles were preferred to the latest aniline dyes. Hand techniques were used for woven cloth when possible, to avoid the sweated labour of industrial mills, and embroidery was given importance as a female activity for the home. All areas of artistic production were susceptible to this outlook, from hammered metalwork to hand-thrown pots, and books were designed using typefaces drawn from medieval sources.[23]

In all of this, the roles of women could be as makers of the home and active partners in the creation of environments, and also as muses, garbed in appropriately artistic dress, in what might be considered an objectified ideal. Reform dress became symptomatic of a wider movement to remedy German society as part of the *Lebensreformbewegung*. The loose-fitting garments were a reaction against the perceived damage caused to women's bodies by corsets and tight bodices, yet they also gave predominantly male designers a blank canvas to decorate their women while offering an

'The modern art principle of women's dress'. An article from *Deutsche Kunst und Dekoration* in 1902 shows two aesthetically dressed women in the Berlin apartment of Henry van de Velde.

alternative to Paris fashions. They were famously exhibited at the *Ausstellung moderne Damenskostume* (Exhibition of Modern Women's Dresses) of 1900 in Krefeld, heart of the German textile industry, as well as the Berlin fashion show of 1902, under the title *Reformkleidfest* (Reform Clothing Festival).[24]

Designing Modern Germany

The Workshop Movement and *Jugendstil*

In the catalogue of 1896 for the Berlin Trade Exhibition, one of the most flamboyant advertisements for a furniture company had announced its services as being able to provide 'Rococo, early and late Renaissance, Regency, Empire Style, Baroque, Chippendale as well as the thoroughly modern style – in oak, walnut, mahogany, ebony, bamboos, all used in a variety of forms'.[25] This amounted to a heady, eclectic mix. It was exactly this situation, in which a furniture manufacture provided everything the customer could require, that caused such consternation among members of the design community. One direct response was to distance themselves by forming more specialized design partnerships in the form of workshops, a move that culminated in the first modern design movement in Germany – *Jugendstil*.

In Munich, the Vereinigte Werkstätten für Kunst im Handwerk (Associated Workshops for Art in Craftwork) formed in 1898 under the leadership of the painter Otto Krüger, and included architects, painters and craftsmen, among them August Endell, Peter Behrens, Bernhard Pankok, Bruno Paul, Richard Riemerschmid, Paul Schultze-Naumburg and Hermann Obrist. In many respects, the decision to exhibit as a group followed the immediate precedent of the Munich Secession, a group of fine artists who withdrew from the city's academy to distinguish themselves as more avant-garde and concerned with the new styles of modern painting, especially those coming from Paris. Another contemporary inspiration, directly related to the applied arts, was the Guild of Handicraft established by C. R. Ashbee in London in 1889.[26]

In Dresden, a similar association, originally known as the Dresdener Werkstätten für Handwerkskunst (Dresden Workshops for Arts and Crafts) formed a year later. The two would amalgamate to become the Deutsche Werkstätten für Handwerkskunst in 1907. The workshop was organized by Karl Schmidt, a carpenter and handworker craftsman, recently returned from England, where he enthused about the Garden City movement. He was joined by Ferdinand Avenarius, who promoted the cause through his writings in the journal *Kunstwart*, and together they started to work with painters J. V. Cissarz and Ernst Walther, sculptor Karl Gross, and, among others, Hanns Schlicht, Max Rose, Otto Gussmann, Wilhelm Kreis, Otto Fischer, and Erich and Gertrud Kleinhempel. With modest beginnings, by 1899 the Dresden workshop listed eighteen employees, whereas at the time of their much-acclaimed contribution to the Brussels exhibition of 1910 this had increased to a workforce of five hundred.[27]

The aim of the Workshops was to produce artistic yet affordable goods, ranging from furniture to other designed artefacts for the home, in a variety of materials. In the first years, designs showed the longstanding legacy of craft traditions, and they could range from Rococo and Biedermeier to the neo-Classical. Soon, however, in stylistic terms the workshops became synonymous with *Jugendstil* (Style of Youth), characteristically explained as the German variant of art nouveau. The immediate source for this name was the Munich-based art magazine *Die Jugend*, which, along with *Pan*, promoted the move from the fine and graphic to applied arts in their pages. Particularly, their designs drew on natural ornament, especially plant forms, with abundant use of the lily and rose as a motif, and the organic whiplash line so familiar from French and Belgian decorative arts of a few years earlier. Examples of the latter were displayed by the most famous promoter of art nouveau, Samuel Bing, at his Maison d'Art Moderne in Paris. As a further timely catalyst, Bing also organized an influential exhibition of part of his collections in Dresden in 1898.[28]

Fritz Rehm, poster for *Ausstellung für Angewandte Kunst* (Exhibition of Applied Art), Odeonsplatz in Munich, 1909. The stylized treatment of ornament and lettering was characteristic of the Werkstatt movement.

Designing Modern Germany

Colours of the *Jugend* designers were in part inspired by a range of the decorative arts of Japan and China that could be seen in museum collections and were also available in small galleries for collectors, such as Bing's. Exotic woods were combined with the indigenous; and the application of inlays, decorative panels, intarsia and marquetry meant that the items of furniture still remained precious. By around 1905, at a broad level, the dominant aesthetic tendency had moved from the organic to stylized geometrical decoration. Such a geometric 'turn' no doubt showed another influence, namely Vienna, where the Secession founded in 1897 and the subsequent Wiener Werkstätte from 1903 formed many parallels with and inspiration for German developments.[29] Through shared language and relative proximity, a close association between Vienna and the cities of Munich, Dresden, Berlin and Darmstadt encouraged an alternative axis of cultural exchange to Paris, through which Austrian designers contributed to the flourishing of German design.

At the workshops identifiable groups of designers joined in a common purpose, even if not initially always sharing a style. Together, they could find the resources to promote themselves, exhibit and commission designs for posters, and thereby gain more attention than if on their own. In contrast to their British Arts and Crafts precedents, members of the German workshop movement incorporated machine tooling wherever possible, while maintaining high levels of craftsmanship. Through this, they hoped to reach the intended market of middle-class consumers who were developing a taste for artistic manufacture in affordable designs. Commentators praised the workshops for offering individual craftsmen the opportunity to be responsible for particular stages in the production of items, while remaining aware of the finished result. This was something large-scale industry could not do, for instance, and the workshops avoided the extreme division of labour when skills were outsourced or based on the monotonous regularity of the more commonplace factory system.

To take one example, Richard Riemerschmid's work was first noticed at the Dresden Arts and Crafts exhibition of 1899, where his integrated composition for a music salon encompassed the ideal of the 'total work of art', the *Gesamtkunstwerk*. This idea, which originally developed in the writings and operas of Richard Wagner, was adapted for the applied arts to encourage the formation of an ensemble of furniture in an overall decorative scheme. A unified aesthetic was applied across objects of different techniques and media, to create the equivalent of musical harmony. Importantly, it elevated the designer to the status of principal artistic co-ordinator of an ensemble.[30]

After only two years, the designers of the Vereinigte Werkstätten contributed to the German pavilion at the Paris Exposition Universelle of 1900. This proved a great success for Pankok, Paul and Riemerschmid, who each received a *Grand Prix* for their entries and went on to use exhibitions strategically in their further promotion. The works of German designers subsequently were seen at the universal exhibitions of Turin (1902), St Louis (1904) and Brussels (1910), as well as the many specialist arts and crafts exhibitions that were to be held in the art cities across central Europe up to 1914. A final distinguishing feature was that the workshops took responsibility to link the manufacture of design lines with their sales. Great attention was paid to the identity of the workshops: they advertised in the specialist press and commissioned modern designs for trademarks, posters, brochures and advertisements. Their later formation than British precedents meant that they could establish close connections with poster designers who were developing strongly distinctive graphic styles. Eventually known as the 'Berlin school' of poster design, the style depended on strong decorative designs in saturated colours that combined brand names with iconic images.[31]

Richard Riemerschmid, 'Room for a Music Lover', designed for the Vereinigte Werkstätten, Munich. It was exhibited at the 1899 Dresden German Art Exhibition. Riemerschmid received a Grand Prix at the Paris Exposition Universelle the following year for another scheme.

Designing Modern Germany

The first texts on the psychology of advertising and marketing opened up new ways of thinking about strategies for selling.[32] Prominent in this was the idea of the 'mark', the distinctive trademark or logo that gave a company or group an identity and the customer a guarantee of craftsmanship and aesthetic quality. Hermann Muthesius extended this idea, noticing how even the name of the designer could act as a sign in itself equivalent to an author or composer. Developing a contrast between the Munich and Dresden workshops, Muthesius further commented:

> However, they (the Dresdener Werkstätten in comparison with the Vereinigte Werkstätten) showed a certain improvement in terms of political economy as they did not, as was initially the case in Munich, make the artists commercial partners of the business, but set them into a contractually arranged relationship to the production site, similar to the customary agreements between author and publisher in literary productions. In both cases, however – and in this the new workshops fundamentally differed from the old ones – the names of the designing artists stood at the top of what was produced, just as in literature the name of the author marks the book and stands above that of the publisher.[33]

Design Promotion through Magazines

Commenting from the vantage point of 1920s and '30s Germany, the cultural philosopher Walter Benjamin identified an altered preoccupation with the domestic interior that he associated with late nineteenth-century life. In particular he counterposed private and public space. He wrote:

> Under Louis-Philippe the private citizen enters the stage of history . . . For the private person, living space becomes, for the first time, antithetical to the place of work. The former is constituted by the interior; the office is its complement. The private person who squares his accounts with reality in his office demands that the interior be maintained in his illusions. This need is all the more pressing since he has no intention of extending his commercial considerations into social ones. In shaping his private environment he represses both. From this spring the phantasmagorias of the interior. For the private individual environment represents the universe. In it he gathers remote places and past. His drawing room is a box in the world theater.[34]

While Benjamin suggested that the separation between the public and the private sphere was important at this time, paradoxically, the publication of designs for domestic interiors placed the previously private or domestic interior on a prominent level of public awareness: how people lived and their attitude to their everyday surroundings could be said to have become a subject to increasing process of commodification. Styles could be purchased, and complete interiors commissioned, thereby entering a fashion system. They could be seen to belong to an era, come into and, more importantly, go out of fashion.

Germany became distinctive for the number and ambition of publications devoted to the interior. Specialist magazines and books started to abound in the last decades of the nineteenth century and the beginning of the twentieth. As an example, among the founders of modern art publishing in Germany, the figure of Friedrich Bruckmann was important. Bruckmann had studied at the Sèvres porcelain manufacture and on his return to Bavaria established his own factory. His first publishing company, Verlag für Kunst und Wissenschaft, began in Frankfurt am Main in 1858. Most significantly, in 1885 he published the first German art magazine, *Kunst für Alle*. Bruckmann Verlag was taken on by his sons, Alfons and Hugo, who turned their attention to design and the decorative arts with the Munich-based journal *Dekorative Kunst*, which began publication in 1897. This proved an influential vehicle for the prominent critic Julius Meier-Graefe, who promoted new artistic developments in design in France, Belgium and Britain, along with Germany, on its pages.[35]

Another important figure for the rising profile of Germany in the world of art and design publishing was Alexander Koch of Darmstadt, who was responsible for the country's first magazines dedicated to interior design. Koch's *Innendekoration* started publication in January 1890, while his *Deutsche Kunst und Dekoration*, which also focused primarily on interiors, began in October 1897. In many respects, the latter represented Koch's greatest undertaking and ran for 35 years until 1932.[36]

As a young man, Koch had worked for the type foundry and printer Flinsch of Offenbach am Main. His first magazine was *Tapeten-Zeitung* (Wallpaper Magazine), which was initially a trade journal that moved during the late 1880s from addressing the concerns of the producer to those of the consumer. Koch's own drawing skills and experience of typography meant that he took an active interest in the design of the journal and he subsequently commissioned many prominent designers of the *Jugend* generation for his later projects. Throughout his long career Koch used books and periodicals as a source for thematic publications promoting ideas about interior design. He

Illustrirte kunstgewerbliche Zeitschrift für
Innen=Dekoration
(Ausschmückung u. Einrichtung der Wohnräume)
Herausgeber: Alexander Koch
Kunst-Verlag Darmstadt

Inhalts-Verzeichniß des Jahrgangs 1890.

Frontispiece of the first
issue of *Innendekoration*
in 1890, edited by the
Darmstadt art publisher
Alexander Koch.

co-wrote with Hermann Werle *Das vornehme deutsche Haus* (The Refined German House) of 1896.[37] With its subtitle of *Innenräume, Möbel und Dekorationen* (Interiors, Furniture and Ornament), the book consisted of a portfolio of drawings by the architect Werle, presenting the interior through expansive illustrations. Aimed to inform on matters of taste, to instruct and inspire, in such a volume the text was confined to the captions, pitched internationally in German, English, French and Spanish.

After 1890 Koch's range encompassed illustrated design magazines, while his broader notoriety grew as he became the official publisher of the design reform movement in Darmstadt. The town, situated in the duchy of Hesse, was one of several places to develop an identity as an 'art city' at the time. The beginnings of the Darmstadt *Jugendstil* are usually associated with the Grand Duke Ernst Ludwig's commission of the British designer Mackay Hugh Baillie Scott in 1897 to equip two of the private rooms of the New Palace, and his subsequent invitation to the Austrian Joseph Maria Olbrich and a group of eventually 23 other artists, designers and architects to live and work on the site of the Mathildenhöhe artists' colony.[38] There, the collection of houses, museum and other purpose-designed buildings were opened to the public during four exhibitions between 1901 and 1914, aimed to promote the model way of life to the public.

One special issue of the magazine was devoted to Haus Behrens, one of the villas designed for the artists' colony, and showed the in-depth, monograph treatment of the full aspects of a house that could be given in such a journal. At the time, Koch and Peter Behrens were collaborating on the Turin International Exhibition of 1902, where the designer installed a version of Koch's editorial office, as well as displaying designs for jewellery and other metalwork. Koch invited the architect to design the entire issue. Behrens employed his own typeface and ornamental devices throughout the design. The house was depicted photographically and in a drawing as well as an architectural plan and a cross-section. Further details were given of room arrangements, the garden and even apparently minor details such

as door handles. The unity of female form, design and the interior was again stressed in the artistic photograph of Frau Behrens in one of the rooms, fashioned in a variant of a *Reformkleid* to her husband's design. As an editor, Koch's most significant skill was shown in linking the book, the exhibition and the magazine in an editorial continuum.[39]

An editorial strategy that Koch shared with other magazines such as *The Studio* and *Art et décoration* was to run competitions for amateurs and professionals in his magazines. No doubt these competitions were aimed to attract readers and subscribers, as well as to generate editorial content; female readers were especially targeted. They began with a poster design competition to announce the journal, as well as the competition *Wie können unsere Frauen zur Ausschmückung der Wohnräume beitragen?* (How Can Our Women Contribute to the Decoration of our Living Rooms?), which ran between 1891 and 1906 in *Innendekoration*. A second competition held in 1896 and 1902 was for *Einfache und Billige Wohnung* (Simple and Cheap Dwellings), an area of design activity in which Germany was to gain prominence. The most prominent competition, however, announced in March 1901, was for *Ideen – Wettbewerb für kunstlerich eigenartige Entwürfe für ein herschaftliches Wohnhaus eines Kunstfreundes* (Ideas for Artistic and Original Designs for a House for an Art Lover), which drew responses from a range of internationally based designers. The

Peter Behrens, design for Alexander Koch's office, manufactured by Ludwig Adler of Darmstadt. The room was displayed at the Turin International Exhibition of Modern Decorative Art in 1902. *Deutsche Kunst und Dekoration*, January 1902.

Peter Behrens, metalwork designs for a buckle, brooch and pendant made by Wilkens and Sons, Hamburg, 1902. *Deutsche Kunst und Dekoration*, January 1902.

Designing Modern Germany

results were published in *Deutsche Kunst und Dekoration*, and also featured in the celebrated portfolios *Die Mappenwerke – Haus eines Kunstfreundes*.[40]

The German Werkbund

Interior design, the graphic arts and design publishing were not the only areas in which Germany was seen to excel at this time. The early 1900s were also marked by an awareness of the full force of industrial design. Central to this was the German Werkbund, an organization founded in Munich in October 1907 by a group of twelve manufacturers and twelve designers. Among its founder members were Peter Behrens, Hermann Muthesius, Bruno Paul and the Viennese architects and designers Josef Hoffmann and J. M. Olbrich, who were resident in Germany at the time, along with the chairman, architect Theodor Fischer. The aim was to bring together industrialists, retailers and designers, who, together, could improve the quality of German goods for the home and export market.[41]

Along with meetings where the urgent issue of encouraging industries to employ designers was discussed, the Werkbund initiated some of the first exhibitions of modern industrial design and developed specialist publications, among them the important *Werkbund Jahrbuch* (yearbook), of 1912–20, and *Das Deutsche Warenbuch* (literally, Book of German Wares) of

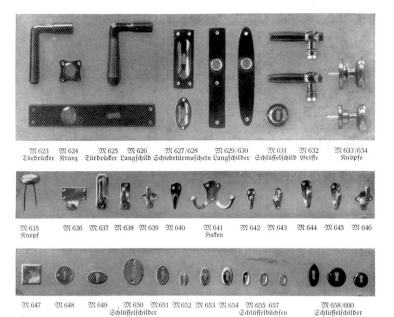

Deutsches Warenbuch, first published in 1915. The photographic presentation of objects set against a plain background emphasized their formal properties and became an established method for much product design photography.

ℜ 112   ℜ 113
Armlehnstühle
     ℜ 114

1915. The latter served as a register of approved designs considered to meet the criteria of good design, with their price and retail outlets listed, all aimed to help the consumer. The goods were placed against a plain background and presented in clear, objective, black-and-white photography that emphasized the formal properties privileged by the Werkbund.

The wider social and political purposes of the Werkbund were design reform, aesthetic education and the encouragement of well-designed goods. It offered serious commentary on advertising and publicity, and ranges of consumer goods, as well as products of heavy industry and architecture itself. A model organization of its kind, its influence was felt in the German-speaking world with the formation of the Austrian Werkbund in 1912 and a Swiss branch in 1913, while a group of British visitors to the Cologne Werkbund exhibition of 1914 returned to establish the Design and Industries Association the next year, taking direct inspiration from it.[42]

The particular debate that engaged the Werkbund was how design should adapt to industrialization. All members agreed that they needed to stand against what were by then considered backward-looking Arts and Crafts principles, but beyond this opinion was split over the exact path to modern design. Two primary concepts informed the debate: *Typisierung* (standardization) and *Durchgeistigung* (spiritualization). How or whether they could be reconciled was open to question. First came the view that standardization was a natural consequence of industrialization. By accepting this, the Werkbund could promote 'type forms' for objects that had reached their optimum form, such as those selected in their own exhibitions and publications. These they saw as escaping the over-individualization of objects from previous eras. Unnecessary ornament was avoided, and the quality of *Sachlichkeit* (objectivity) could be achieved through adopting a rational approach to form-giving, guided by the requirements of engineering and technology, which were deeply respected. The major advocates of this point of view included Hermann Muthesius, as in the essay *Das Formproblem der Ingenieurbau*. The culmination of such thinking was realized, in part, by the foundation of the Normenausschuss der Deutschen Industrie (German Industrial Standards Organization) in 1917, which went on to publish agreed standards for all manner of industries.[43]

Often seen to be at variance with this acceptance of *Typisierung* was the wish to instil industrial goods with properties of a spiritual nature, a point of view expressed by other members of the Werkbund, among them Henry van de Velde, then director of the Weimar Academy of Art. The concept of *Durchgeistigung* could encompass a number of attitudes. On occasion a commentator such as Werner Sombart appealed to the need to instil industrial goods with values and qualities that could become associated with a national spirit or character. Others, such as van de Velde himself, applied the concept more straightforwardly to reinforce the importance of the artistic contribution of the designer to the visual appearance of industrially produced goods.[44]

While such design philosophical debates occupied many of the texts published by the Werkbund up to 1914, on a more practical level its other activities meant that public awareness of design and the designer was raised in a number of ways. For instance, in its mission to promote its values, regional competitions for the best shop window displays were held. In these, simplicity and clarity were valued above straightforward accumulation in arrangement. The Werkbund promoted the power of the trademark, packaging and the well-designed poster advertisement, often through selections made for travelling exhibitions. Between 1902 and 1914 the Deutsches Museum für Kunst im Handel und Gewerbe (German Museum for Art in Trade and Industry), founded in Hagen by Karl Ernst Osthaus, an active Werkbund member, proved that modern 'design for industry' could also be a subject equal to the fine arts and worthy of museum display. Osthaus built up a remarkable collection of applied arts and design, formulated new ideas for their display in touring exhibitions, as well as in a purpose-built museum in his home town of Hagen in north-west Germany, and established an important photographic archive with the intention of promoting the serious study of architecture and design.[45]

An exemplary form of collaboration between industrialist, retailer and the designer was the case of Kaffee Hag, the Bremen-based coffee distributor that entered German and foreign markets as a branded good with its distinctive identity at this time. In 1906 Ludwig Roselius, the company's director, introduced a caffeine-free coffee, which he sold under the trademark Kaffee Hag, an abbreviation of Kaffee-Handels-Aktien-Gesellschaft. He commissioned the leading poster artists Ludwig Hohlwein of Munich and Lucian Bernhard of Berlin to draw the public's attention to the product on the street and shop through fashionable designs. Most importantly, and the aspect that found most approval from Werkbund figures such as Osthaus, Roselius asked the designers Alfred Runge and Eduard Scotland to design distinctive tins, packets, cups and saucers, signage and point of display material that gave what was previously an indistinguishable product a modern graphic identity that would encourage loyalty from the customer and enhance the appearance of the interiors of coffee houses and grocers shops alike.[46]

Alfred Runge and Eduard Scotland, design of packaging for the Kaffee Hag company of Bremen, between 1906 and 1910. It fulfilled the recommendations of the Werkbund circle for a clear, well-designed corporate identity.

Peter Behrens and Bruno Paul: Two 'Model' Designers

The example of two designer members of the Werkbund clarifies further the possibilities of the organization. Peter Behrens was most celebrated as Germany's first industrial designer and an important influence on what was later known as corporate design. He trained as a painter in Karlsruhe in the late 1880s before settling in Munich, where he became associated with the Munich Secession, in the company of Max Slevogt, Lovis Corinth and other artists of the Freie Vereinigung Münchener Künstler (Free Association of Munich Artists). In 1897 Behrens was also one of the founder members of the Vereinigten Werkstätten für Kunst und Handwerk. As his career grew, he embraced the applied arts, design and subsequently architecture. Some of his first designs for book arts, textiles, ceramics and glass and furniture were displayed at the Künstlerhaus in Zurich in 1897 and also at the important Glaspalast exhibition in Munich of 1899.[47]

After a short period in the artists' colony of Mathildenhöhe in Darmstadt, in 1903 Behrens was called to become director of the Düsseldorf Arts and Crafts School. In 1907 he then established an architectural office in Neu-Babelsberg, in the far south-west suburb of Berlin, where at different stages Walter Gropius, Le Corbusier and Mies van der Rohe worked in junior capacities. Most importantly for the future of German design, Behrens was appointed in the same year to the major electrical company AEG (Allgemeine Elektricitäts-Gesellschaft) as an architect and 'artistic director' (*künstlerischer Leiter*). The company had been founded in 1883, originally as Deutsche Edison-Gesellschaft für angewandte Elektricitäts (DEG). The

Designing Modern Germany

name was changed under its modernizing director, Emil Rathenau, in 1887, a point that marked its transition from manufacturer of electrical light bulbs to major conglomerate, producing a range of electrical equipment on a mass scale. By 1907 its capital stood at 100 million marks and it had 32,000 employees. Rathenau was aware of the approach taken by American companies to cartels and corporate organizations, and the importance that 'publicity' and a coherent identity could have on the wholesaler, retailer and individual consumer. Accordingly, Behrens's design scheme was expected to involve everything from the company stationery and internal printed matter to advertising and publicity, and from AEG goods themselves to its buildings and workers' housing, in the form of the garden-city suburb of Berlin Hennigsdorf. Significantly, Behrens's success stemmed from combining tradition and modernity. For the major turbine hall in the Wedding district, for example, the designer used the latest technology of structural steel frames, which he left exposed to reveal their innovative use. Yet commentaries also noticed how the building's references to Schinkel's classicism in its proportions elevated what had been considered a functional industrial building type to the level of *Fabrikkunst* – a factory art.

On 29 August 1907 a journalist in the *Berliner Tageblatt* wrote: 'No longer can there be doubt that the future of the industry also belongs to the field of art, and that our times rush towards a method of production, which they are most agreeable to, towards industry, as long as it concerns works of the applied arts.'[48] In the case of product design, Behrens's office oversaw the redesign of electric lamps, many for industrial use on Germany's expanding railway, tram and shipping networks, and for industrial and retail buildings, as well as for the home. Then there were small motors, electrical heating equipment, and kettles, fans and clocks and sundry electrical items for commercial

Peter Behrens, model for the AEG turbine hall in Berlin-Wedding, 1908.

or domestic use. What made Behrens's contribution so remarkable was his ability to move from the graphic depiction, as in a piece of publicity, to its full realization as an AEG product. His approach to corporate design, acknowledging how an artefact conveyed a message about a company that the consumer identified through product recognition, would hold sway for the rest of the century. In terms of print identity, Behrens had already designed the typeface Behrensschrift in 1902, before arriving at the AEG. This modern script had elongated, cursive 'German' qualities of black-letter Fraktur, while also appearing fashionably *Jugendstil* in character. By contrast, for AEG, Behrens employed his version of a Roman typeface (Behrens Antiqua) that was elegant and refined. Importantly, through its neo-Classicism, it brought an international rather than a national association to bear on the designs, rendering them at once legible across German borders and less culturally specific.[49] With this approach Behrens oversaw the publicity of the company, designing the trademark, the company brochures and the prestigious showrooms, where examples of the AEG range were displayed in the window and in specially designed vitrines in the reception areas.

Like Peter Behrens, Bruno Paul was another prominent Werkbund figure, equally important for German art and design, but in the area of furniture and interior design. After studying at the Dresden School of Applied Arts between 1886 and 1894, Paul joined the artistic circles of Munich. Through the contribution of his many satirical drawings his name became especially associated with the journal *Simplicissimus.* Paul was appointed director of the School of the Applied Arts in Berlin in 1907, a position he held through its transformation to the United State Schools for Free and Applied Arts (Vereinigte Staatschule für Angewandte Kunst) and up to 1933, when he was dismissed by the National Socialists.[50]

If the international exhibition activities of the German Werkbund provided one prominent way for the products of German industry to become recognized and communicated to a wide audience, another direct way was in the currency of products themselves. In this, Paul's example is instructive. Transatlantic ocean liners, another product of total design, offered industrial design-

Peter Behrens, interior of the AEG showroom in König-grätzer Straße, Berlin, 1910.

Designing Modern Germany

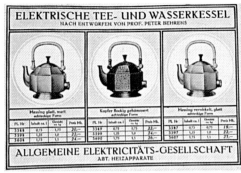

The publicity brochures designed for AEG by Peter Behrens in 1908 revealed his overarching principle of composition applied to both graphic and product design.

ers, applied artists and interior designers a practical and very public way for their work to be appreciated. The task in hand mirrored the contemporary set of Werkbund debates about how the designer could be strategically employed as a conduit to link design, industry and, in this case, an elite public, who could afford to travel on transatlantic liners. Even if short-lived, the airship formed an interesting contemporary parallel mode of transport and a similar platform for design expression.[51]

The challenge that the liner presented to the designer was as an engineered environment that required the careful and safe negotiation of space. The Norddeutscher Lloyd line under Dr Wiegrand approached the Vereinigte Werkstätten für Kunst im Handwerk following their successful installation of artists' rooms, exhibited in Dresden in 1906. Ten selected designers were asked to submit ideas, and from them Bruno Paul was chosen. By this time, Paul already held an established reputation as a designer interested in *Typenmobel*, production of furniture based on ideas of standardized units. The decorative paradigm for liner design in the period of their expansion in the second half of the nineteenth century was the luxury hotel. Directors attempted to create the comfort and service of a 'home away from home' for their wealthy passengers, with attention to elegant surfaces, wood panelling, soft carpets, upholstered furniture and chandeliers. Most of all, the emphasis was to create an illusion, to disguise the character of the ship. By contrast, Paul's designs retained the previous concern for luxury, but combined this with a new approach to conception of space and the function of decoration that acknowledged that the liners were system-built structures: their origins were in industrial manufacture and were not, therefore, those of more conventional architecture. Paul would go on to design four ships altogether between 1907 and 1909.

For the ship *Prinz Friedrich Wilhelm* of 1908, on the fiftieth-year jubilee of the company, Paul designed the main public rooms, which aimed to

serve 600 passengers, as well as the cabins of 2 to 2.5 metre surface area.[52] He took the motif of the square and circle as a basic design unit. This was then applied to the metalwork grilles for the doors and windows, particularly effective for the skylight over the dining room, which allowed more daylight to enter the interior lower spaces than usual. The overall panelling of the hallways and staircases, while elegant and restrained, was organized to reveal the underlying structure of the ship's engineering. This elegance was continued in the designs for furniture, both for cabins and public dining and sitting areas. Most unusual for a room associated with dark, 'masculine' colours was the dining room, where white-lacquered panelling was punctuated by black and green leather-covered columns. In a special supplement of the periodical *Dekorative Kunst* of 1908, the critic Emil Waldmann applauded Paul's solution:

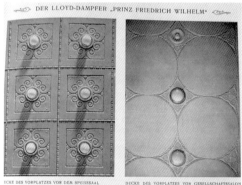

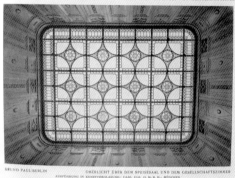

By combining grained and patterned wooden surfaces, light and dark, lustrous and matt woods, Bruno Paul creates, almost without any ornament, but only with geometric borderlines or accentuated geometric intarsia, 'patterns' of never-ending appeal. Colour is of course essential here, it is in fact often the main carrier of the mood of an entire room. Thus far Bruno Paul has been reserved in his harmonies and discrete in tone as well as full of nuances. Now he more often juxtaposes strong colours and thereby grows more sonorous in his expression.[53]

Bruno Paul, designs for the interior of the Norddeutscher Lloyd ocean liner Prinz Friedrich Wilhelm, 1908.

Designing Modern Germany

The overall systematic approach, while forming a favourable impression on the company's director, also met the approval of commentators in the circles of the Werkbund. It proved influential as an approach to interior design that could be applied to other situations, notably by August Endell and Walter Gropius for their celebrated designs for railway carriage interiors a few years later. Even more significantly, although not for its style, were the implications of designing for limited space that would become a priority in the 1920s, in the minimum dwellings for social housing discussed in chapter Two.

The Department Store and the German Consumer

When one hears in a family today 'We are going to Wertheim' this does not necessarily mean we need something particularly important for our household, but rather one speaks of it as an excursion such as one makes to a beautiful place in our near neighbourhood. One chooses an afternoon when one has a lot of time, arranged if possible with acquaintances. On arriving in the Leipzigerstrasse, one is firstly fascinated by the shop windows, then one enters the ground-floor rooms, looking at the most diverse displays, buys something perhaps here and there, then one goes by lift to the first floor and if possible takes a cup of chocolate and an obligatory piece of tart or apple cake. . . . Time flies while looking at the most diverse textiles, the 'toilette' of the sales ladies, or through conversations and other things, and when one suddenly notices the hour, it is high time to go home.[54]

Gustav Stresemann's perceptive account of a visit made to the Wertheim department store, written in 1900, describes an experience that became familiar to most people in the Western world in the twentieth century. His anecdote gains all the more weight when we learn that as well as being an acute observer of modern life, Stresemann, a liberal politician and statesman, was to become both Chancellor of Germany and Foreign Secretary during the Weimar Republic.

The department store entered literature as early as 1883, with the publication of Emile Zola's novel *Au Bonheur des Dames* (*Ladies' Delight*), which gave an account of a young provincial shop-girl's ordeal in adjusting to working in cosmopolitan Paris.[55] In this story, Zola identified elements that would fascinate subsequent generations of commentators, critics and historians of the emergence of modernity. The new commercial enterprises opened possibilities to construct environments of amassed distraction, often thought of as 'cathedrals of consumption' or 'phantasmagoria', already alluded to by Georg Simmel in his commentary on the Berlin exhibition.[56] They were marvelled at by some for their opulent displays of mass-manufactured goods, yet reviled by others for the elaborate ways in which the emerging science of retail psychology disguised their more blatant commercial purpose of persuading customers to buy.

The architectural design of German department stores first claimed international attention in the early 1900s. As modern variants on the original, they seemed to combine the luxury of their French predecessors with the physical scale and economic ambition of their American counterparts. It was commented that the department store could take the place of the market hall and the arcade, becoming 'a town within a town'. Their design was praised for combining new construction methods and materials such as iron, concrete and glass to develop a modern form of decoration. When it opened in new buildings designed by Alfred Messel in 1903, Wertheim in Leipzigerstrasse, Berlin, was understood to be the largest and most modern department store in Europe. It became the subject of an extended commentary by Paul Göhre in his book *Das Warenhaus* of 1907, which dealt with its complex modernity.[57]

Describing the exterior of the building, Göhre remarked on the lack of signs, advertisements and lighting effects on the building's exterior. In

The Wertheim department store, designed by architect Alfred Messel, was claimed to be the largest department store in Europe when it opened with a one-hundred-metre-long shop facade, *Mode-Katalog*, 1903–4.

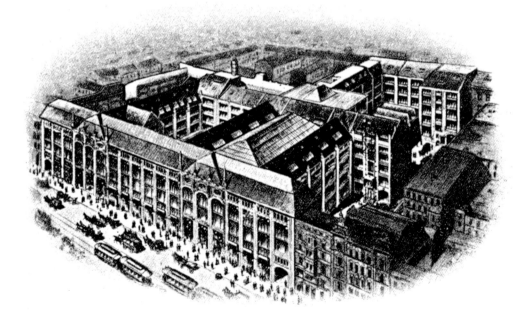

Designing Modern Germany

place of these, the architect Messel ensured that the built form and large display windows were sufficient to announce the shop to the passer-by. Describing the impact on entering, Göhre echoed the language of Zola and other writers before him:

> He who enters the Wertheim department store for the first time, receives the impression of crushing crowds. People in continuous floods at almost any time of day, always a row of sales stands, an ocean of goods, on display; stairs, lifts, floors, visible like the ribs of a skeleton; assembly rooms, courtyards, halls; corridors, corners, offices; narrowness and breadth, depth and height; colours, lustre, light and noise: an outrageous muddle, apparently without plan and order. Of course, whoever looks for goods will reach the correct place the very first time as well; receptionists in black suits, positioned at the entrances, show the way and direction; every salesman, every saleswoman quickly provide precise and clear information. Whoever wants to gain an overview and insight into the store and its machinery, however, will require more frequent visits, almost a proper study.[58]

Interestingly, Göhre interpreted the whole environment as a living organism that needed to be controlled. An important psychological impact was made by the central hall, which was lit by skylight during the day and lamps and candelabra by night. This was made possible through the use of modern cantilevered arches that supported the balconied galleries.

Göhre toured the building, starting on the top, fourth floor where the photographic department for customers and offices for personnel and services were located. The latter included workshops for carpenters, painters, electricians, tailors and costumiers, upholsterers, bookbinders, locksmiths, glaziers and polishers. The dining rooms for staff were combined with a roof terrace for summer relaxation, and here Göhre drew the analogy between the store and an ocean liner, calling its entirety 'a triumph of modern, business organization and human labour'.[59] As far as its displays were concerned, Wertheim employed a 'director of decoration', with two artists responsible for window display and furniture display and the third, a sign painter, who looked after the entire interior arrangement and 'tasteful' use of packaging. At its height in 1905, the store employed a remarkable 3,500 staff.

Wertheim had two main competitors in Berlin, Hermann Tietz and Firma Jandorf, which Göhre put on a sliding social hierarchy. At the top, Wertheim appealed to the 'gute Gesellschaft' or high society; by contrast

Tietz was directed towards the 'guter behaglicher Mittelstand', the respectable middle classes, while Jandorf aimed its services towards the 'besserer Berliner Arbeiter', the better-off Berlin working classes. This, Göhre suggested, was reflected in the different approaches the stores took to shop display and decoration:

> It is also more than enough with the decorations of the shop windows: at Wertheim exquisite artistic taste, at Tietz the most elegant effects. Jandorf-Spittelmarkt however, aesthetically seen, cannot keep up, neither with Tietz, and even less with Wertheim. There is nothing but goods, goods, goods, which together with the shoppers, fill the small, narrow rooms almost to suffocation, and namely goods which are as much devoid of beauty as is the store in which they are piled up to be sold.[60]

He concluded his appraisal of Wertheim in these positive terms:

> There is no haze of sausages and beer, no tobacco and cigarette smoke, no disorder of all sorts of loud instruments in use, but merely a consistent, fading humming, talking and calling, here and there

Photograph of the central hall of the Berlin Wertheim department store, where handkerchiefs, gloves, capes and umbrellas were sold. It incorporated galleried landings overlooking an atrium with an elaborate decorative scheme, frieze and the monumental sculpture 'Work' by Professor Ludwig Manzel. (Photograph from *Mode-Katalog*, 1903–4.)

Designing Modern Germany

Cover of *Deutsche Kunst und Dekoration*, Wertheim special issue, March 1903.

Mackay Hugh Baillie Scott, design for a ladies' room as displayed at the Wertheim artistic furniture exhibition of 1903. *Deutsche Kunst und Dekoration*, 1903.

chiming, bright lights and the delicate scents of perfumes, fruits, fresh lacquer, flowers, chocolates, coffee, teas and soaps. Moving around happily – cleanliness. Add the youth of most salesmen and saleswomen: there is a desire to buy. The goods of modern culture surround us in richness and beauty.[61]

Returning to the promotion of modern design, in his journalism the Darmstadt editor Alexander Koch had already drawn analogies between the magazine and the shop window. This came to fruition in one respect, in a special issue of *Deutsche Kunst und Dekoration* in March 1903, which featured all the furniture available at the Berlin Wertheim store in that year. Wertheim's furniture and interiors department dedicated a large space to an exhibition of a sequence of twenty rooms, available to order, including several dining rooms, a children's bedroom, a ladies' day room and a man's office. According to Göhre, the installations, while adding to Wertheim's prestige, did little in terms of bringing in profit since they were not a commercial success. He noted that the designs of Germany's most high-profile Arts and Crafts architects cost 200,000 marks to install and were reported to have returned a mere quarter million.[62]

The Cologne Deutsche Werkbund Exhibition of 1914

This chapter opened with Hermann Muthesius ascribing a place on the world stage to Germany for, in his words, 'giving it a face'. A year earlier, in 1914, he had drawn attention to the possible future directions of German design as one of the two major protagonists in what became known later as the 'Werkbund debate', subsequently described by Frederic Schwartz as 'a *locus classicus* in the history of modern architecture in the West'.[63] In many respects, it was also to be the culmination of discussion about appropriate industrial design, with Henry van de Velde championing the designer-artist, Muthesius the designer-engineer. As suggested by the satirical drawing of Karl Arnold published in *Simplicissimus*, this left the designer-maker to continue without 'design' at all.

The setting for this exchange was the lecture theatre, designed by Van de Velde at the exhibition, held on the banks of the Rhine facing the city of Cologne. Originally planned for May to October 1914, the event was forced to close early because of mounting hostilities and the outbreak of the First World War on 1 August. Nonetheless, it received considerable press attention. The various pavilions and their architects gained much acclaim, and many photographs of the goods on display went into the publication *Das*

Von der Werkbund-Ausstellung   (Zeichnungen von Karl Arnold)

van de Velde schuf den individuellen Stuhl — Muthesius die Stuhl-Type — und Schreinermeister Heese den Stuhl zum

Deutsche Warenbuch in the subsequent year. A symptom of the sensitive political situation, the first exhibition poster, designed by Peter Behrens and depicting a heroically mounted figure bearing a torch, was replaced by a totally typographical design by Fritz Ehmcke, which was believed to be less susceptible to nationalist interpretation.

The main buildings were designed by leading architects and included Peter Behrens's Festhalle, Theodor Fischer's main hall, Wilhelm Kreis's tea-house and Adelbert Niemeyer's main café, with interiors overseen by Villeroy & Boch. Most were executed in restrained, neo-Classical styles, the buildings made in plaster and wood to imitate stone, typical of many world exhibitions. In the main hall, twelve rooms were dedicated to the 'twelve apostles of German form'. These were Van de Velde, Obrist, Pankok, Endell, Behrens, Riemerschmid, Paul, Martin Dülfer, Hoffmann and Niemeyer, as well as the deceased Eckmann and Olbrich. The pavilions that claimed greatest public and critical attention were those that looked to the future in their design. Van de Velde's theatre was praised for its dramatic expression, equivalent to the mysticism of Maeterlinck, Gothic rather than Baroque, 'This architecture is a battle, to carve a space from the cosmos through curves'.[64]

By contrast, Walter Gropius's model factory had a central entrance flanked by figurative sculptural reliefs and was neo-Classical at core, but it

DEUTSCHE WERKBUND-
AUSSTELLUNG
KUNST IN HANDWERK,
INDUSTRIE UND HANDEL∙ARCHITEKTUR
MAI CÖLN 1914 OCT.

was the two spiral staircases at either end of the front facade, encased in glass, and the free-standing glass wall on the rear of the building exposing the cantilevered structure underneath, particularly at the corners, that claimed attention. The building was heralded as introducing a new style. In striking contrast with the rectilinear assuredness of the model factory was the much smaller, jewel-like pavilion by Bruno Taut for the German glass industry; crystalline in its structure, made of faceted glass, it manifested Taut's desire to find an expressive architectural form.[65]

The reviewer for *Deutsche Kunst und Dekoration* was Koch himself, who concluded that the exhibition was testimony to the influence of the engineer on the contemporary urban environment and also on works of art.[66] The Cologne Werkbund exhibition was Germany's most definitive manifestation of design this far into the century. Prior to it, further ideas for a German international exhibition had also been discussed following the failed attempt in 1896. In 1910 Alexander Koch had already written of the need for a major exhibition in his polemical essay *Eine Deutsche Ausstellung?* Despite an awareness of the dangers of what he called 'exhibition fatigue', Koch nevertheless proposed a celebration of fifty years of the German Reich in 1921, which called 'a national obligation of honour' and a 'cultural performance on a grand scale'. He continued:

> Every year the number of foreign visitors seeking to study German character, German institutions, German trade and exchange, and, through this, German life, increases. Our industry, our municipal institutions, social welfare, our hospitals and schools have become permanent objects of study for the representatives of other nations.[67]

Koch wrote that this proposed exhibition of the German Empire should certainly offer a 'city',

> not a romantic old town with so-called picturesque corners, but a modern city with all the achievements of technology, of hygiene, of architecture, of administration and transport, a construction in which the sites of education, of leisure, of entertainment should be just as much represented as those for the provision of water, light and food.

He listed what it should contain:

> Schools, churches, administration buildings, a market hall, hospital, museum, theatre, concert hall, Orpheum, circus and so forth.

Bruno Taut, photograph of the staircase leading to the dome of the Glass Pavilion at the 1914 Cologne Werkbund exhibition, revealing its crystalline structure.

Exhibition halls, a park, gardens, fountains, baths, a stock exchange, banks, retail shops, a post office, various kinds of public transport and everything a modern urban developer must think of.[68]

Koch's vision of the complete city, no doubt in part prompted by his awareness of developments abroad, although reflecting his distinctive thoroughness, would not be realized in the remaining years of the empire. And when the proposed date of 1921 arrived, it was firmly out of the question. In many respects these ideas would take on a more radicalized form in the 1920s, when housing estates for the dispossessed working classes became a priority. Furthermore, Koch's evocation could also be said to have formed a blueprint for the towns and cities of future planners of the Federal Republic and Democratic Republic much later in the century.

2

Experiment and Tradition in Design, 1917–33

The British poet Stephen Spender spent much time in Germany of the Weimar Republic in the late 1920s and early 1930s. His autobiography offered a sympathetic outsider's view of the movement of *die neue Wohnkultur* (the New Living Culture), which was strongly Modernist in outlook. An important characteristic of this new way of life, which appears in this extract and for which the word 'Weimar' became shorthand, was an apparent lack of things and a general wish to rid life of the unnecessary:

> Dr Jessell had introduced me to several of his friends. Gradually I found myself detaching myself from him and spending more and more time with them. The two I liked the most were called Joachim and Willi. Joachim had a large studio flat, of which he was extremely proud, on the outskirts of Hamburg. One night he invited my host and me to a party.
>
> We climbed up four flights of stairs and I found myself in a large simple, airy room, like an attic, lit by a skylight and by slits of windows looking over Hamburg. The room was L-shaped, so that one part of it could not be seen from the other. At each end were beds which were mattresses, and bare Modernist tables and chairs made of tubes of steel and bent plywood. The main part of the room formed a large space which had been cleared for dancing. The room was lit by lamps of tubular and rectangular ground glass.
>
> We arrived late for the party. The other guests were already there. Joachim was tall, with a rather Mexican appearance, a sallow complexion, black eyes, raised, sensual, expressive nostrils, brushed back hair. As soon as he saw me, he took my arm and showed me all

Marcel Breuer and Gustav Hassenpflug, design for the gymnastics studio of Hilde Levi, Berlin, 1930.

the objects in the room: the bowl of rough-cut glass, the Mexican mat, the Modernist crockery, and the massive books printed in heavy clear-cut modern types which indented the rag-paper pages.

He talked in English with a faint American accent, telling me he had bought these books shortly after he had left school, but that he didn't read much now. He liked beautiful things, but he preferred 'living' to having things. Living was bathing, friendship, travelling, lying in the sun. 'I like the sun mostly and doing things with my friends: not reading.' I admired a drawing pinned on the wall. He said that he had done it long ago but that now he had given up drawing. He did, however, take photographs, and giving me a handful from a shelf under the Finnish table, he strolled off to greet other arrivals.[1]

Those objects that are mentioned, however, appear to be specific and act as icons for a world view that, paradoxically, was full of meaning. In this way, Spender comments on modern European artefacts, such as a Finnish table and a non-European Mexican hat. Such juxtaposition was in itself symptomatic of a modern outlook, to find 'primitive' or authentic qualities located in other cultures and appreciated for their formal properties, out of context. Photography is mentioned as a newly modernized form of visual record, and there is a sense of sexual independence alluded to in the preoccupation with body culture, the sun and nature.

Not in Spender's account, but nonetheless important as a context for wider Weimar society, was the continuing migration of people to the cities. Spender belonged to the educated middle classes, but it was the emergence of another sector of society, the new lower-middle class of urban workers known as *die Angestellten* (employees), that prompted a particular fascination in the Weimar press. Most famously, their status was commented on by the writer Siegfried Kracauer, journalist and cultural theorist, who described their potential classlessness, sexual ambiguity and evident challenge to accepted social demarcations.[2] On the one hand, Kracauer was fascinated by the mass identification among such people through new media and what he saw as their distracted rootlessness. Yet he was also appalled by the preoccupation with what he saw as trivial commodities, catering to the taste of the 'little shop girls', which he so unsympathetically dismissed.

Changes in accepted gender conventions, for women in particular, were emblematic of the new-found modernity of the Weimar years. The 'New Woman' in Germany was in part indebted to a model of modern woman who had come to inhabit the larger cities of the United States of

Designing Modern Germany

America during the preceding years.[3] On the founding of the Weimar Republic in 1919 came German women's suffrage. With a population of more women than men as a result of war losses, many new possibilities for women to enter education and the labour market arose. Combined with moves to legalize birth control, women's position altered considerably. The new outlook was expressed outwardly by a new look: bobbed and cropped hair, flat-chested dresses, short skirts, stockinged legs and the conspicuous wearing of make-up. Importantly, with political enfranchisement and changing social roles, women were actively vocal in the movement for the new way of life, and more women were to enter design professions as part of this.

Symptomatic of the general mood of the times was an article that appeared in the popular press in 1929, 'Das Heim einer Junggesellin' (The Home of a Young Employee) of October 1929. This was concerned with how to design homes for the new population of young independent people. The text, by a journalist simply identified in fashionable lower-case font as 'e. cz', opened with the theme of America. Many of the preoccupations of the period were identified in this article, part of which read:

A luxury studio apartment as discussed in the article 'Das Heim einer Junggesellin' (The Home of a Young Employee), 1929, with a space-saving alcove, curtain for the bed and purpose-built fitted cupboards.

Berlin is the most American city in Germany, according to visiting Americans. New facilities that ease and make convenient the lives of afflicted and rushed city dwellers constantly appear and confirm the American verdict. There are not only fast restaurants, escalators and automats of every kind. Living is reformed too, and becomes more

comfortable and pleasant. Architect Hans Scharoun has built a house on Kaiserdamm which enables single people, bachelors and bachelorettes who detest bed-sitting rooms, to possess a home and still, only one room. Many one-room apartments comprise a HOUSE. Whoever thinks that such one-room apartments can be neither practical nor beautiful should take a look at the charming apartment decorated by interior architect Toni Mayer-Crailsheim, pictured here.[4]

'The New Living Culture'

The 1920s was a period of radical cultural experiment that in many cases was more pronounced in Germany than in many other countries. As commentaries across the arts have suggested, the particular set of circumstances, including defeat in the First World War and extreme monetary inflation, combined with liberal reform in politics and an intensity in technological modernity, for many led to an accelerated and radical lifestyle. Design was no exception in this: in fact, it could be argued that it came to the fore as one of the most experimental and active ingredients through which the new way of life could be defined.

The extreme human disaster of the First World War created a rupture and a sense of 'before and after' in German history, which in turn created a discernible generational divide. While designers of the first decade of the century had developed a strong sense of a national culture, as revealed by the various debates in Werkbund circles, the next generation would turn to internationalism as their context and ambition. Until the stabilization of the German economy after 1923, the political and social turmoil of the immediate post-war years allowed for experiment in artists' studios and the design schools alike. Indeed, the release from practical considerations of seeing designs through to production has earned this period the identity of laboratory years.

The leading concept among Modernists in the 1920s in German-speaking countries was that of *die neue Wohnkultur*, already encountered in Spender's account, which can be loosely translated as 'the new living culture'. Through this, it was optimistically believed that design could lead to a better material and social world, by embracing abstraction in artistic composition and standardization of machine production. Germany, and in particular certain cities such as Berlin and Frankfurt am Main, became sites for this movement and attracted international groups of designers. Variants of the new style were developed in each media, as examples of *das Neue Bauen* and *die Neue Typographie*, as designs for furniture, glass, ceramics and

Designing Modern Germany

textiles show. In all cases, the prefix *neu* suggested a fresh approach, often informed by sets of principles, even manifestos, that took the form of radical restatements of position.

The above article appeared in a newly launched magazine, *die neue linie* (the new line, lower-case in original), which started publication in 1929. Its contents are worth dwelling on since they provide an interesting insight into the concerns of the modern reader and what had been achieved by way of further introduction to the Weimar years. All was to be thoroughly challenged by the rise of Hitler in 1933. *Die neue linie* was issued monthly and addressed the assumed needs of the New Woman: her fashion, leisure time and cultural as well as professional activities. It would be her guide in most aspects of life, whether motoring, holidays, weekend pursuits, sports or general well-being and health. Its modernity was clear from the covers. The art director was Herbert Bayer, newly independent from his commitments at the Bauhaus, who was establishing himself as a successful designer for publishing and advertising, largely for Dorland agency in Berlin. Bayer's hallmark was the lower-case masthead for the words 'die neue linie', which appeared in his novel 'universal' typeface, created in 1926. As well as his own designs, Bayer invited his former colleague László Moholy-Nagy and the popular Berlin fashion illustrator Otto Arpke to entice readers with their covers.[5] The editorial in the first issue identified the magazine's intended audience:

Madam,
You and we are standing at a point, from which 3 paths go out into the world:
On one path, men and women with heads and wigs march and strike up the tune of the 'good old days'.
On the other path, snobs wander and proclaim with a frown that in Paris, one now extends one's eyelashes with the legs of flies and that Gloria Swanson should be the ideal of every lady.
Madam, you sense as we do, that the 'good old times' have irretrievably passed, and that a lady does not acquire her ideal from Hollywood. You know that there is a third way, that of the true lady.[6]

According to this 'third way', *die neue linie* would offer twelve pages of fashion per issue, a short story and reports on newly released films, all established elements in popular magazines of the time. It was the style of its illustrations and the kinds of article that the magazine seemed to push that distinguished its commitment to Modernism. It was not dogmatic, so, for

die neue linie

mai 1931

heft 9 · mai 1931 · preis 1 mark · verlag otto beyer leipzig / berlin

instance, humorous touches appeared, as in 'Kleine Dinge Beleben unsere Umwelt' (Small Things Animate our Environment), which was a page of photographs of ceramic hens by Blaues Haus, Berlin. Nevertheless, many of the illustrations came in the form of the new photography, with distorted viewpoints, sharp angles, long shadows, views taken from above and below, silhouettes and abstract compositions. A case in point was a short photo-essay, 'Die Schatten werden länger: die Berliner Schauspielerin Ellen Frank am Strand von Sellin' (The Shadows Become Longer: The Berlin Actress Ellen Frank on the Beach at Sellin).[7]

Advertisements in *die neue linie* consisted of promotions for fashion-able perfumes and soaps, BMW and Mercedes automobiles, the State Majolica Manufactory (SMM) of Karlsruhe, Junkers water-heaters and Singer sewing machines. They implied a targeted aspirational reader among the wealthier middle classes. An apparent emphasis on health fitted the broader social phenomenon of the physical body culture, so much the fashion in late Weimar Germany, with articles such as 'Gesundes Siedeln und Wohnen' (Healthy Dwelling and Living), which showed the newly exhibited Modernist housing estate of the Breslau Werkbundsiedlung, while straightforward advice was offered in 'Die Letzten Sonnentage im Freien' (The Last Summer Days in the Open Air) and 'Erhalte dich Gesund' (Keep Yourself Fit), which showed exercises that one could do for ten min-utes a day. Great attention was paid to seasons, not just in clothing, but also in consumer advice, tips, travel articles and even short stories. In December 1929 the Christmas issue revealed winter fairy tales illustrated by pho-tograms by the avant-garde film-maker Oskar Nerlinger, and this was followed, to help the uninitiated, by 'What Is a Photogram?' to explain the camera-less technique.

Decorating advice encouraged the reader to adopt modern ideas, and through this *die neue linie* presented one of the first opportunities to intro-duce a wider magazine-reading public to the designs of the Bauhaus. Articles appeared such as 'Das Geheimnis der gutbeleuchteten Wohnung' (The Secret of a Well-Lit Apartment) and 'Deutscher Geist in Paris' (A German Spirit in Paris) on the Werkbund exhibition by Walter Gropius, Herbert Bayer and Marcel Breuer at the Grand Palais in Paris in 1930, while Gropius's Dessau house was featured in the article 'Wie wohnen wir heute?' (How Do We Live Today?) and illustrated with photographs by Lucia Moholy-Nagy. Another strong theme in the magazine was the independence given to women by driving, including in November 1930 'Der Wagen den die Dame Fährt' (The Car that the Lady Drives), which recommended the purchase of a 10/50 PS six-cylinder Wanderer Cabriolet, the 2.5 Litre Brennabor Juwel or the Opel

Cabriolet (January 1930), 'Ein Auto Erlebt die Natur' (A Car Experiences Nature) and even advice on what to wear when motoring.

As the magazine went into the early 1930s, it showed an increasing pre-occupation with the cult of the Mediterranean. This could be understood as simply a form of escapism, in pursuit of holidays and leisure, or interest in the politically risqué, as in 'Wie wohnt Mussolini' (How Mussolini Lives) in March 1930. As we will see in chapter Three, Modernism's relationship to neo-Classicism was to be renegotiated, partly as a consequence of changed political times, in many more fundamental ways.

The Bauhaus: Developments in Design Education

If between 1907 and 1914 the German Werkbund, discussed in chapter One, epitomized more than an organization for the promotion of design in industry, since it captured the wider national imagination in its projects to characterize the spirit of the age, the same could be said for the Bauhaus in the Weimar period. Neatly, the school's years of existence in Germany from 1919 to 1933 matched those of the Republic.

The individual institutional story of the Bauhaus has been told a great many times. A design school with a limited yet extremely influential cast of characters, a well-documented curriculum, and many extant works by staff and students, it lends itself to history-making in ways that other cultural forms frequently elude. This is not to disparage the school's significance, for more than any other entity of the Weimar years, it encapsulated the desire to design a better world, to increase international communication through design and to use the modernity of materials, techniques and forms to pro-mote an egalitarian, democratic society. This suggests that aspects of its development must be told in the context of a wider history of German design.[8]

In 1919 Walter Gropius, by then an established architect aged 36, was appointed as the director who would lead the merging of the Hochschule für bildende Kunst (Weimar Art Academy) with the Grossherzogliche Kunstgewerbeschule (School of Arts and Crafts). Until 1914, the latter, under the patronage of the grand duke of Saxe-Weimar, was under the directorship of the Belgian architect and designer Henry van de Velde and was an important centre for design education. Its new formal title became Staatliches Bauhaus Weimar. The word 'Bauhaus' was an adaptation of the term *Bauhütte*, which referred to the temporary building huts that were erected by craftsmen while building the great Gothic cathedrals. Paradoxically, Bauhaus was at once an encapsulation of the new director

Gropius's romantic belief in a fellowship of artists and designers, and also a modern word that would work in shorthand when used in other languages, in ways that later would be considered a brand.

Gropius used his appointment as the opportunity to address the issue of reform in art and design education. His opening manifesto and programme should be quoted at length since it gives a full indication of his ambitions for change. It appeared as a four-page leaflet with the woodcut *Cathedral* by the Expressionist artist Lyonel Feininger, a member of staff until 1924, who remained associated with the Bauhaus until it closed. Gropius wrote:

> *The ultimate aim of all creative activity is the building!* The decoration of buildings was once the noblest function of the fine arts, and the fine arts were indispensable to great architecture. Today they exist in complacent isolation, and can only be rescued from it by the conscious co-operation and collaboration of all craftsmen. Architects, painters and sculptors must once again come to know and comprehend the composite character of a building both as an entity and in terms of its various parts. Then their work will be filled with the true architectonic spirit which, as 'salon art', it has lost.

Gropius then outlined the division between the artist, taught at academies, and the craftsman, taught at technical schools, a situation he sought to address:

> *Architects, painters, sculptors, we must all return to the crafts!* For these there is no such thing as 'professional art'. There is no essential difference between the artist and the craftsmen. *The artist is an exalted craftsman.* By the grace of Heaven and in rare moments of inspiration which transcend the will, art may unconsciously blossom from the labour of his hand, *but a foundation in handicraft is essential for every artist.* It is there that the primary source of creativity lies.
>
> Let us therefore create a new guild of craftsmen without the class distinction that raise an arrogant barrier between the craftsman and artist! Let us together desire, conceive and create the new building of the future, which will combine everything – *architecture* and *sculpture* and *painting* – in a *single form* which will one day rise towards the heavens from the hands of a million workers as the crystalline symbol of a new and coming faith.[9]

In the sense that in this 'new guild of craftsmen' he was advocating artistic expression rather than a more rigid interpretation of design for industry, the manifesto aligned Gropius at this point to the anti-Muthesius faction of the earlier Werkbund debate. In the aftermath of war in 1918, Gropius had been a founder member of the Novembergruppe, along with the artists Lyonel Feininger, Karl Schmidt-Rottluff and Gerhard Marcks, and the architects Mies van der Rohe, Erich Mendelsohn, Hans Poelzig and Bruno Taut. They associated in Berlin as the Arbeitsrat für Kunst (Working Council for Art) after the November Revolution had led to the formation of a new constitution and a liberal democracy. Their heady social and political commitment was combined with heightened emotional spirituality.[10] Understandably, Gropius's vision for the school combined current ideas of protest against accepted values in society with a belief in the heightened possibilities for art.

The initial Bauhaus programme listed the areas to be taught. Gropius's design curriculum, outlined in full in 'Idee und Aufbau des Staatliche Bauhauses Weimar' (The Idea and Structure of the Staatlichen Bauhaus Weimar), followed in 1923 and proved highly influential on future design pedagogy.[11] During these years, against substantial economic difficulty caused by unprecedented levels of inflation, Gropius managed to set up workshops and appoint master craftsman as instructors, and attract an impressive group of artist-designers as *Meister*. A significant step was the introduction of a half-year course that all students would take regardless of their subsequent specialization. The foundation course, or *Vorkurs* as it was known, was intended to introduce underlying principles of elementary form and studies of materials. The first *Meister* to lead the course was Johannes Itten, a Swiss-born artist, who went on to publish his teachings as *Design and Form* (*Gestaltungs-und Formenlehre*) much later in 1963.[12] Itten was a follower of the Mazdaznan religion, and his stress on a spiritual orientation among students encouraged instinctive responses to materials and an expressive, craft-oriented form of creativity. Increasingly, this outlook proved controversial, as well as difficult to justify to the members of the Ministry for Education and Justice of the state of Thuringia, who administered funding to the Bauhaus as a state institution. On Itten's departure in 1923 (in protest against Gropius's decision to encourage commissioned work), Gropius appointed the Hungarian-born polymath László Moholy-Nagy, who turned the curriculum of the *Vorkurs* away from an orientation in craft towards that of design for the machine. Importantly, Moholy-Nagy encouraged the investigation of the potential of new materials for industrial use, with experiments in metal, glass, plastics and photography, in keeping with the aim of finding industrial application for their design

Otto Lindig, tall lidded ceramic jug, 1922. The design showed an interest in the elementary forms of cone, cylinder and sphere.

Designing Modern Germany

experiment. These two stages of the *Vorkurs* underpinned a broader difference between the two periods of the school.

A second fundamental principle, clear in Gropius's inaugural manifesto, was the belief that students should be taught in workshops where they would be encouraged to understand the principles of form with a thorough knowledge of materials. Presented in a diagram of concentric circles, the curriculum showed how students would progress from the *Vorkurs* to join a department based on material such as glass, clay, stone, wood, metal, sound, textiles and colour, before they reached the centre, the culmination of studies after three years, which was 'building'. The school's aim in training students reflected the established idea that to realize built form as architecture was to embrace all other disciplines, yet Gropius's choice of terminology stressed the practical and experimental rather than 'architecture' per se. He wished to avoid its established academic associations.

Although the emphasis was on workshop-based learning, Gropius also appointed staff to give lectures in theory, *Formmeister*, among them the established and highly respected artists Wassily Kandinsky and Paul Klee. Kandinsky had already published the essay *Concerning the Spiritual in Art* in 1913, and he gave courses in 'analytical drawing' and 'abstract form elements', while also serving as head of the mural-painting workshop. Klee taught 'elementary design of the plane' to all students and was head of the stained-glass workshop until 1924, after which he taught design theory in the weaving workshop.[13]

In 1923 Gropius led the transition from an emphasis on 'community, handicraft and architecture' towards consideration of 'type, function and industry'.[14] By 'type' was meant *Typisierung*, reference to standards and rational systems of design. The ground for the change to this second stage was prepared by the Dutch designer Theo van Doesburg, who was invited to teach courses at the school between 1921 and 1923. A member of the De Stjil group, Van Doesburg was also a leading figure in international Constructivist circles and in many respects, like Moholy-Nagy, represented advanced ideas about possible future directions for modern design and architecture. Like others in the movement, the Dutch designer advocated the use of primary colours, white, grey and black, understood to be supra-individual and not prone to the subjectivity of Itten's earlier emphasis. In a similar way, geometry and abstraction were favoured above the recourse to natural forms typical of the early Bauhaus years. Even if the industrial and economic circumstances had been better before 1923, it seems unlikely that many of the designs were ready to go into production as intended. Instead, the real achievement by then was to have laid the foundations to

Designing Modern Germany

develop a language of forms that broke with conventional expectations of objects in many fundamental and enduring ways. Commenting on the change from craft to design, made in part to fend off external pressures, Lyonel Feininger, at the time head of the graphic printing workshop, wrote to his wife:

> But this much is sure – if we cannot show 'results' to the outside world and win the 'industrialists' to our side, then the prospects for the future existence of the Bauhaus are very dim indeed. We now have to steer toward profitable undertakings, towards mass production! That goes decidedly against our grain and is a forestalling of the process of evolution.[15]

Funding to equip new workshops was renewed by the Weimar authorities in 1922 on condition that the school would hold an exhibition in the following year. This provided the opportunity for Gropius to announce publicly the reorientation of the school in an opening lecture given in August 1923, under the title 'Art and Technology: A New Unity'.[16]

Herbert Bayer, cover of the book *Staatliches Bauhaus, 1919–1923.*

The focus of the exhibition was *Haus am Horn*, a single-storey, white, cuboid, single-family dwelling built in a middle-class suburb of Weimar to the design of Georg Muche. The model house was equipped by the various workshops. It included a modern kitchen with fitted units, up-to-date electrical equipment, Jena glass and ceramic storage containers by Theodor Bogler. A carpet with abstract design woven by the textiles department covered the central room floor. Light fittings were designed by the metal workshop, and furniture throughout the house combined the experimental efforts of textiles and woodwork staff and students, among them Josef Albers, Marcel Breuer, Alma Buscher and Erich Dieckmann.[17] An accompanying publication, *Staatliches Bauhaus Weimar, 1919–1923*, designed by Herbert Bayer and Moholy-Nagy, illustrated further products of the various departments at the school, while exhibitions, including the first on international modern architecture to be shown in Germany, were held in the school's main building.

Despite considerable efforts to demonstrate the benefits of the school, and attracting 15,000 visitors to the exhibition, the reputation for progressive aesthetic and social ideas convinced the conservative majority within the Thuringian government to vote to withdraw funding from the school, making it impossible to remain in Weimar. On the invitation of its socialist authority, in 1925 the school moved to Dessau, a city where the possibilities of linking with industry, including the engineering and aircraft company Junkers, were stronger. The purpose-built accommodation, designed by Gropius for the school, student residences and nearby series of masters' houses, added to the sense of a radical new beginning.[18]

As the workshops evolved, in part to suit the requirements of commissions, some areas proved more successful than others. Under Herbert Bayer and Joost Schmidt, in keeping with the time, the typography workshop

Hinnerk Scheper, colour rendition of the exterior of the Bauhaus buildings in Dessau, c. 1926.

Designing Modern Germany

took on advertising and exhibition design while retaining the areas of more conventional typography and book design.[19] Design for letterpress involved asymmetrical setting, employing primary colours, especially a striking use of red ink, and single-case, sans-serif alphabets, at first with what was available, then the new fonts, including Herbert Bayer's own 'Universal', a typeface designed in 1926 using the circle and 45-degree angles. Although Gropius was keen to deny that there was a 'Bauhaus style', inevitably the products acquired a similarity of appearance across the various media, informed by common design principles. Other successes included wall-paper and textile sales under the Bauhaus company name.

Bauhaus designers shared with their contemporaries an interest in redefining standard forms of furniture and evolving new industrial goods. This was the case, for example, with the tubular steel cantilevered chair, which in many respects was a variant on the traditional dining chair. The development was by no means exclusive to the Bauhaus. Ideas for a cantilevered chair were initiated simultaneously by the Dutch designer Mart Stam and the architect Mies van der Rohe, as well as by Marcel Breuer, a student and from 1925 head of the furniture workshop at the school. Among other things, this led to long and complicated legal struggles over patents.[20] The cantilever principle appealed to Bauhaus thinking because it achieved maximum support for the human body with minimum material. The technique of bending aluminium, taken from bicycle manufacture, fulfilled the wish to be modern and industrial in spirit, even if not in the actuality of manufacture because of the amount of hard work and finishing involved. Importantly, the appearance of the cantilevered chair suggested dematerialization, with the loss of the conventional four supporting legs. The result matched the aim to achieve geometric, simple transparency, and came closer to the ultimate dream of sitting on air.

It is not possible to consider all areas of Bauhaus activity in depth, but only to take one remarkable area of achievement. Marianne Brandt had studied painting and sculpture at the Weimar Academy of Fine Art and was first a student at the Bauhaus in the years 1924–6, before becoming an assistant then head of the metal workshop, its only female member. She subsequently pursued a career combining teaching and work as a professional designer. Brandt's designs for teapots, silver services and lamps, based on elementary forms and plain surfaces, encapsulated the wish to produce modern objects and became some of the most celebrated designs of the entire school. They have since been in production under licence.[21]

The Bauhaus was considered exceptional for the intensity of the educational experience and the remarkable figures it attracted as staff and students.

It also became known very quickly through its own publishing programme, first the various *Bauhaus* magazines, then the important Bauhaus books (1925–30), a series that made available the aesthetic philosophies of staff and 'fellow travellers', crucially through illustrations of work as well as texts.[22] Amidst such developments, sceptical voices also emerged. Georg Muche, who had taught on the *Vorkurs* with Itten before taking charge of the weaving workshop, wrote the article 'Fine Art and Industrial Form', which appeared in the first issue of the *Bauhaus* magazine, as well as the art magazine *Das*

Designing Modern Germany

ARCHITEKTURBEDARF GMBH

DRESDEN-A.1
WALPURGISSTRASSE 15
TELEFON: 19026
TELEGRAMME: TYPAR

W2
TISCHLEUCHTE

Entwurf: Wagenfeld
Gesetzlich geschützt

RM: 34.—

Gesamthöhe:	43 cm
Fuß: Spiegelglas, poliert	ø 14 cm
Schaft: Glasrohr	ø 3 cm
Schirm: Milchglas	ø 20 cm
Schirmring:	ø 16 cm

Ausführg. d. blanken Metallteile: messing-vernickelt, poliert

Mattierte Glühlampen vermeiden Schlierenbildungen im Schirm

Leaflet for the firm Architekturbedarf of Dresden, which supplied contemporary architects with modern designs. Here, the W2 table lamp, designed by Wilhelm Wagenfeld at the Bauhaus metal workshops, is announced with specifications set in the new typography, including the price of 34 Reichmarks, c. 1926.

Kunstblatt in 1926.[23] In Muche's opinion, there was a danger of designing objects intended for industrial production as if they were fine art. He went on to question the appropriateness of starting with considerations of outward form. Bauhaus objects could resemble functional industrial design, he contended, while actually being labour-intensive to produce and dependant on many hand skills. Muche challenged the implied necessary connection, often suggested at the time, between abstract form and the requirements of industrial design, and he concluded that fine art and design, having had a period of fruitful creativity and exchange, should go on to pursue separate paths.

Recent critique from feminist scholarship has also suggested that it was difficult for women to convince the senior members of Bauhaus staff of their equality, except in certain areas of the curriculum, such as textiles and weaving. In general, a greater number of women found opportunities to study or teach in the areas of the applied arts, subjects traditionally associated with the feminine, and in this respect, the Bauhaus mirrored the wider prejudices of society at the time.[24]

The general development of the textile workshop followed the broader school's policy, from the priorities of craft to industrial design. Gunta Stölzl was a student at the Münchner Kunstgewerbeschule (Munich Arts and Crafts School), then, on joining the Bauhaus, found the teachings of Itten and Klee most formative on her evolving approach to colour, form and, in particular, abstract composition. Between 1925 and September 1931 Stölzl was master of craft in the weaving workshop. She also ran her own weaving mill in partnership in Zurich. At Weimar, the emphasis had been on hand techniques for hangings and 'free' textiles, conceived as individual creations to be displayed as art, often in the place of abstract paintings. After 1923, and particularly in the new premises of Dessau, with, among others, Gertrud Arndt, Anni Albers, Helene Nonné Schmidt, Lis Beyer and Margaret Leischner as her colleagues, Stölzl oversaw the change to developing experimental yarns and new combinations of techniques aimed at industrial application in the weaving of carpets and furnishing fabrics, conceived as an industrial design. Instead of applied

decoration, attention was given to the integral properties of the weave. As
Stölzl explained:

> Textiles for everyday use are necessarily subject to accurate technical,
> and limited, but nevertheless variable, design requirements. The techni-
> cal specifications: resistance to wear and tear, flexibility, permeability or
> impermeability to light, elasticity, light- and colour-fastness, etc., were
> dealt with systematically according to the end use of the material.[25]

While certainly the most renowned, the Bauhaus was not the only art
school to embrace Modernism. To take other examples, the new design was

Designing Modern Germany

also taught at schools in Breslau, Frankfurt am Main and Magdeburg, where each had its own Modernist circle, often in close contact through publications, membership of exhibiting societies and joint projects.[26] During the 1920s other schools developed distinct identities for a particular branch of design, for instance, Burg Giebichenstein specialized in the modern applied arts and had close associations with the Bauhaus, while at the Meisterschule für Deutschlands Buchdrucker (Master School for Germany's Bookprinters) in Munich, Jan Tschichold and Paul Renner each taught the new typography for a stage. And at the commercial end, the Reimannschule, a privately run art school founded in Berlin in 1902, by the 1920s was offering courses in fashion, graphics and illustration, as well as training in window display and other modern requirements for the retail industry.[27]

A watershed for the Bauhaus came in the year 1928, when many of the crucial members of teaching staff left, following Gropius's own departure to pursue his architectural practice, among them Moholy-Nagy, Breuer and Bayer, who had helped define the identity of the teaching. This break led to the tendency to regard the years of the Bauhaus between 1919 and 1928 as 'heroic'.

As Gropius's successor, Hannes Meyer, an architect with Communist beliefs, turned the curriculum towards the technical interpretation of architecture and addressed mass housing for society, encouraging students to consider social and scientific criteria. Indeed, utility and questions of economy replaced the formalist preference for pure colour and elementary form. Meyer encouraged design as a collective process and stressed collaboration. The revised manifesto for the school, written by Meyer, made clear the new emphasis. He wrote: 'Building is nothing but organization: social, technical, economical, psychological organization', and he introduced students to skills and knowledge for this.[28]

The departments were reorganized under Meyer into four main areas. 'Advertising' covered typography and graphics, as well as the increasingly important field of photography, which was under Walter Peterhans. The previously known wall-painting, furniture and metal workshops were amalgamated as 'interior design'. The textiles and building (*Bau*) departments remained. The emphasis on practical knowledge gained through the workshop was retained, even if not in the exact balance.

Hannes Meyer wrote:

All of these things are products of the formula, function times economy. They are not artworks; art is composition, while purpose is function. The idea of composition of a harbour strikes us as nonsense; the composition, however, of a city layout, an apartment house . . . [?] But building is a technical not an aesthetic process, and the purposeful function of a building always contradicts artistic composition. Lent ideal and elementary form, *our apartment house becomes a residence machine.* Heating, sunning, natural and artificial light, hygiene, weatherproofing, garaging, cooking, radio reception, optimum convenience for the housewife, sex and family life, etc., are all path-breaking force vectors, the components of which are built into the house.[29]

Meyer consolidated his position by appointing his own staff from among a range of radical architects. Ludwig Hilberseimer was the most important. Meyer also invited visiting lecturers from Austria, the Netherlands, Czechoslovakia and Poland who contributed to the students' understanding of international debates. In many respects his policy could be considered to have fulfilled Gropius's aims, but the mounting conflict between Communist and non-Communist students and increasing political difficulties beyond the school made Meyer's position difficult to sustain. In 1930 he resigned, leaving Germany to continue his interests in public housing in the Soviet Union.[30]

Mies van der Rohe was appointed to succeed Hannes Meyer as director on 5 August 1930 and is generally recognized as turning the school into an architectural institute. He joined as director with an established reputation as an architect. When appointed, he had a successful office in Berlin, and in the preceding years he had been a principal contributor to the German

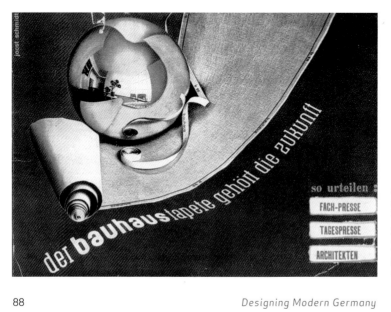

Bauhaus Wallpaper Belongs to the Future brochure, designed by Joost Schmidt, 1931. Bauhaus wallpapers proved to be one of the most successful commercial enterprises of the school.

Designing Modern Germany

Werkbund housing exhibition *Die Wohnung* (The Dwelling), which opened in 1927 at Am Weissenhof, Stuttgart, with houses and flats by Le Corbusier, Mart Stam, J.J.P. Oud, Hans Scharoun, Josef Frank, Ludwig Hilberseimer and Peter Behrens, amongst others. Mies was also the chosen architect for the German pavilion at the Barcelona exposition of 1929, for which he also designed the 'Barcelona' chair. At the Bauhaus he appointed Lilly Reich, his partner in the Berlin architectural practice, as head of interior design.[31]

Mies's reputation as a leading architect was not in doubt: more in question was his suitability as a director of what had been the most experimental design school in Germany, and his sympathy for areas outside his immediate interests. Crucially, Mies was prepared to make unpopular political decisions to remove students who had supported Meyer. He negotiated the school's destiny when the National Socialists gained control of the city of Dessau in 1932 and began to campaign for the closure of the school. All staff were dismissed and plans to destroy the buildings were prepared. As one newspaper reported:

> The disappearance of this so-called 'Institute of Design' will mean the disappearance from German soil of one of the most prominent places of Jewish-Marxist 'art' manifestation. May the total demolition follow soon and may on the same spot where today stands the sombre glass palace of oriental taste, the 'aquarium' as it has been popularly dubbed in Dessau, soon rise homesteads and parks that will provide German people with homes and places for relaxation.[32]

The announcement to close the school in Dessau was made in the summer of 1932, and Mies led the move to Berlin, where he reoriented the teaching towards Gropius's original intentions. On 20 July 1933 the Bauhaus was closed for good on the decree of the National Socialist ideologue Alfred Rosenberg. The school's reincarnation in Chicago as the New Bauhaus under the leadership of Moholy-Nagy is considered in chapter Three.

The New Frankfurt and the Modernist Interior

In 1928, at Château La Sarraz near Geneva, a group of international architects formed into the CIAM, the Congrès Internationaux d'Architecture Moderne. A testimony to the importance in which German developments were held was that its second meeting was dedicated to the 'minimum existence dwelling' and taken to Frankfurt in order to study the social housing developments that since 1926 had been the work of Ernst May and the municipal building department. *Die Wohnung für das Existenz-Minimum* (Minimum Existence Dwelling) was a model form of rational planning devised to provide an effective solution to apply to mass housing.[33] In Germany since 1918, urban populations had been growing, partly as a result of rehousing from inadequate older dwellings and partly with the continuing migration to the large cities by people in search of employment. Through measurement, allocation of space and the rational organization of furniture and fittings, it was hoped that housing authorities would be in a position to equip their populations with good, new, affordable homes. These were mainly built in large-scale housing estates (*Siedlungen*), made up of apartment blocks of four storeys, most frequently designed according to the architectural principles of Modernism. Their appearance was as long, horizontal bands of concrete-clad facades, sometimes painted white, at other times in bright colours, with windows and balconies arranged as exactly repeatable elements to stress their standardized character. Many of the estates were provided with a kindergarten for young children, schools, shops and communal laundries; they were connected to the cities by new transport networks; and, when landscaped, their initial uncompromising exterior became harmonized into a positive vision of what a democratic future could hold. The estates introduced the benefits of modern design and architecture to a broad public under the guise of a heroic form of social engineering that was not without controversy. Whether it was capitalism itself, albeit often in the form of benign socialist local government, or the new residents themselves (in the minds of those on the Left an appeased labour force) who would be the main beneficiary, was the larger political question.

While the CIAM event concentrated on Frankfurt am Main as one of the most extensive examples of social housing, parallel developments took place in other cities across Germany at the same time, among the most famous the Onkel Toms Hütte (Uncle Tom's Cabin) in Berlin Zehlendorf and Hufeisensiedlung (Horse Shoe Estate) in Britz, both the work of Bruno Taut as head architect for Martin Wagner and GEHAG, the city's building administration. At the Siemensstadt estate, a complex to house workers in the

Hans and Grete Leistikow, cover of the magazine *Das neue Frankfurt* in 1930, showing the Budgeheim estate in Frankfurt am Main.

expanding electrical industry of Berlin, the lead architects were Hans Scharoun, Hugo Häring and Walter Gropius.[34] In Breslau, in the East, *Wohnung und Werkraum* (Dwelling and Workspace) of 1929 was one example of a German Werkbund model-housing exhibition, open to the public for three months, under the direction of Johannes Molzahn.[35] In Stuttgart, another famous example of a Werkbund housing exhibition was held at Am Weissenhof in 1927. Under the exhibition title *Die Wohnung*, attention was given to middle-class dwellings, and an international array of architects were invited to submit designs, which in several cases exceeded their budgets.[36]

By the Weimar years, publications on interiors, housing and urban planning abounded. Architects and designers themselves were not shy of contributing to this proliferation. The combination of new techniques in layout design in magazines, posters, advertisements and specialist books put domestic life on a broad, modern agenda. Significantly, the graphic, typographic and photographic means employed in the Frankfurt projects sent a message of rational consumption in a graphic form that avoided the more conventional marketing strategies of the popular press. First, the *Frankfurt Register* provided a list of recommended goods intended to help in the choice of items to equip new homes, along the lines of Werkbund precedents. Secondly, *Das neue Frankfurt* was a monthly magazine addressed to professionals that carried articles on the theme of the *neue Wohnkultur*.[37] Initially designed by Hans and Grete Leistikow, then from 1930 by Willi Baumeister, it can be seen as a reaction to the developing commodity culture of more commonplace contemporary magazines, which stressed personal fulfilment or psychological gain. This was apparent in the look of the magazine: black and white instead of colour; objective rather than pictorial photography; an emphasis on information and statistical 'evidence' rather than the persuasive, seductive texts of consumer-oriented magazines. The social orientation of the Frankfurt projects was clear in the editorial content: special issues of *Das neue Frankfurt* appeared on hygiene, schools, affordable dwelling, the concept of the city and art and design education. These were matched by reviews of parallel building movements in the Soviet Union and Switzerland. In many respects the modern attitude of the project presented a set of oppositions as the mass media became more adept at providing images that captured the colour and texture of modern life. *Das neue Frankfurt* codified an aesthetic of resistance and critique.

One focus of attention in the movement for new social housing was the woman as both consumer and producer of the home. According to architectural historian Hilde Heynen, the woman of the Weimar period enjoyed new freedoms. She wrote:

She is competent and confident, knowledgeable about fashion, and interested in art and culture. Although, after marriage, she will still be the one considered responsible for the home and children, she is able to move in public life on her own in a much more self-evident way than her sisters a few decades earlier.

And Heynen added: 'In order to manage her home, she has moreover acquired Taylorist skills, which she applies in a perfect execution of all the prescriptions of home economics.'[38]

As an indication of such thinking, Bruno Taut, a major protagonist for the movement, published his own views of the future direction of housing in the book *Die neue Wohnung*, first published in 1924. This had as its sub-title *Die Frau als Schöpferin* (The Woman as Creator). As an enlightened professional, Taut wrote:

New dwellings will provide the woman with a way to improve her performance. She will adopt a new organization for her work and, with due consideration to the given circumstances, arrange to perform individual chores – tending the children, cooking, serving meals, washing up, cleaning, laundry, shopping, etc. – according to a plan. Sufficient time for going on walks and sleeping will be calculated into it, as the new home economics teaches, which amounts to the application of the Taylor System to the household . . .

The nerve centre of the dwelling is the kitchen, where the housewife's main work in a small household takes place. The small or middle-sized dwelling plays the central role in our considerations because of its prevalence; but what is right for it is easily applied to the large dwelling, leading to a better solution to the problem of servants, which is equally difficult the world over.[39]

The term 'Taylorism' was derived from the theories of Frederick Winslow Taylor, whose *Principles of Scientific Management* was published in 1911, and applied time and motion studies to factory organization. Taylor's ideas were extremely influential across Europe and the Soviet Union in the early 1920s, and were celebrated by modernizers with a range of political positions. Rationalization was not restricted to the workplace, and a number of equivalent developments in the growing area of the new science of home economics, also primarily in the United States of America, had taken place leading up to 1914. For example, *The American Woman's Home*, originally published in 1869 and written by sisters Catherine Beecher and Harriet Beecher Stowe, was one

Designing Modern Germany

of the late nineteenth century's most important handbooks of domestic advice. It provided household hints, with articles on cooking, decorating, housekeeping, child rearing, hygiene, gardening, etiquette and home amusements aimed towards middle-class American women readers. In turn, Frank Bunker Gilbreth and Lillian Moller Gilbreth extended the search for a rational approach to housekeeping and the workplace in academic studies carried out in university departments.[40] Most important for the planning of the home in the 1920s were the works of Christina Frederick, who adapted ideas of time and motion studies to food preparation, kitchen organization, and carefully analysed the path of housework, in order to arrange equipment for the servant or housewife in ways that cut down on unnecessary labour in *The New Housekeeping: Efficiency Studies in Home Management* in 1912. Frederick straddled academic and popular worlds, published in the women's magazine *Good Housekeeping*. These ideas formed the basis of Erna Meyer's *Der neue Haushalt*

A visual contrast of 'before and after' indicated how to modernize a 'worker's living room' by Bruno Taut in his book *Die neue Wohnung, Die Frau als Schöpferin*, 1926.

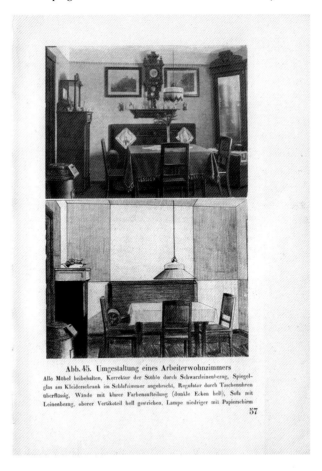

Abb. 45. Umgestaltung eines Arbeiterwohnzimmers

Alle Möbel beibehalten, Korrektur der Stühle durch Schwarzleinenbezug, Spiegelglas am Kleiderschrank im Schlafzimmer angebracht, Regulator durch Taschenuhren überflüssig, Wände mit klarer Farbenaufteilung (dunkle Ecken hell), Sofa mit Leinenbezug, oberer Vertäkoteil hell gestrichen, Lampe niedriger mit Papierschirm

57

(The New Household) of 1926, which provided German readers with an authoritative account of the arguments for rationalization.[41]

The movement had its advocates among Modernist architects and designers in Europe. Ironically, as some feminist critics pointed out at the time, ideals of efficiency helped raise the standard of what was considered acceptable housekeeping. Instead of helping women at home save time, the new standards created more work for them to do. One important difference in the adaptation of these ideas to Weimar Germany was that the focus was principally on the working-class mother, who was envisaged as resident of the new housing estates. In this shift, the management of servants, so often the focus of the earlier American studies, was transferred to the organization of the home by the housewife herself. With more modest means, she nonetheless had as the norm services such as readily available hot water, an inbuilt kitchen and hygienic circumstances for food preparation.

The most important figure for the adaptation of these ideals into practice in Germany was the Viennese-born Grete Schütte-Lihotsky, the only woman in the Frankfurt architects' department. Lihotsky specialized in the design of domestic and institutional kitchens. Her most famous became known as the 'Frankfurt kitchen', of which at least 10,000 were built. The room in its most typical format was 1.9 by 3.4 metres in dimension and provided a well-lit 'laboratory' with storage for equipment and dry goods, a drop-down ironing board and units measured to suit the height of the average woman. Each room was given an adjustable-height stool for use while seated at the sink.[42] Such rationalization of the kitchen was supported by socialist planning authorities in the belief that it would free the housewife from burdensome domestic chores to allow her more time either to undertake paid employment, as more women entered the job market, or to organize her domestic and leisure time effectively. Modernizers such as Lihotsky favoured the planned small kitchen, totally dedicated to cooking and related activities, known as the *Kochküche*. She believed it gave the woman in particular a specialized space, professionalizing her activity and acknowledging its importance for the family. Opponents spoke out in favour of the more traditional *Wohnküche*, or living kitchen, a larger room where cooking could be combined with other activities, most importantly child-minding.[43]

Illustrations of 'before and after' room arrangements were a typical publishing strategy throughout the period. For instance, in Bruno Taut's previously mentioned *Die neue Wohnung*, interior schemes were juxtaposed to show the improvements that modernization could bring, with emphasis on plain surfaces and arrangements according to formal design principles.

The architect eradicated a crucial element, the private life of individual occupants of the house, and the possibility of attaching memory or sentiment to objects and decoration, something that Walter Benjamin had identified as the province of the bourgeois interior.

Taut's drawings offer several important clues about the prescribed way of life. The 'good room', the *Gute Stube*, what in Britain would have been called the parlour, was transformed into a space for middle-class, educated pursuits. The original was an arrangement based on comfort, with upholstered chairs and a conversation group and other occasional chairs.[44] This was turned into a room with an irregular seating arrangement that implied activity rather than conventional sociability. Taut gave the room a piano, a chaise longue, a small table and a desk. In spite of this, the dwelling was intended to be for a maximum of five people, in most cases a couple with children, and possibly even three generations. Was this an instance of a modern architect imposing a preferred 'cultured' life based on authentic pursuits – reading, writing, making music – constructive pastimes that predict the intellectual discomfort with leisure characteristic of the Frankfurt School of Social Theory and more generally the radical left? Neither comfort nor homeliness, nor warmth nor individuality, encapsulated in the German term *Gemütlichkeit*, nor the entertaining pleasures of the radio, Hollywood cinema and the increasing commodity culture were accommodated in this vision.

The New Typography

Variously called *die neue Typographie*, *die neue Werbegestaltung* (publicity design), *die neue Reklame* (advertising), *die neue Graphik*, with adjuncts *die neue Fotografie* and *die Fotomontage* (to be noticed here was the use of the

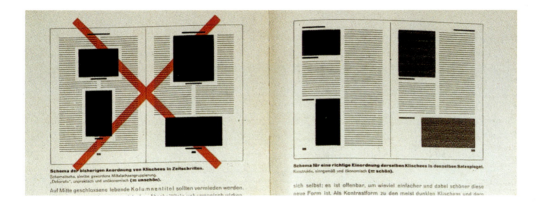

A spread from Jan Tschichold, *Die neue Typographie* of 1928, recommending the principles of asymmetric layout as applied to book design.

modern 'ᴦ'), as their modernized or newly invented names suggested, there can be no doubt that the Weimar period heralded a change in the visual culture of graphic reproduction. We have already seen examples in the form of *die neue linie* magazine at the start of this chapter, as well as the publications produced at the Bauhaus. The new typography deserves further consideration, because possibly, alongside architectural design, it was the most visibly immediate way in which the period became associated with radical, avant-garde design.[45]

As we have seen, the stress on the 'new' was an essential element in conceptualizing design in the 1920s and this was primarily through rejection: of historicism, decoration and unnecessary form. The term 'new typography' entered design language from 1923, but was most extensively commented on in *The New Typography: A Handbook for Modern Designers* (1928) by the eloquent practitioner Jan Tschichold, who at that stage taught in the Meisterschule für Deutschlands Buchdrucker in Munich.[46] Like Modernism itself, the new typography made claims to be an international phenomenon. Significantly, in the case of Tschichold, avant-garde form was associated with socialist, politically progressive content. As a serious book designer and occasional poster artist, he worked, for instance, for socialist book clubs aimed to encourage progressive literature among the working classes: international political ideals were expressed in internationalizing form. Many of the design features and technical choices made by the exponents of the new design were in favour of making communication that might cross borders and which would be technically and visually 'transparent', to use the rhetoric of the day.

As an initial definition for the new typography, Jan Tschichold's comments are instructive:

The new typography distinguishes itself from the earlier in attempting foremost to develop its appearance from the function of the text. Clean and direct expression must be rendered to the contents of the printed material. The 'form' must be brought out from the function, just as in the workings of technology and nature.

In such writing Tschichold claimed a direct relationship between technology and form that some would seek to qualify for its unquestioned determinism. In a later essay in 1937, Tschichold succinctly characterized the design elements of the new typography as incorporating:

Disappearance of ornament
Composition with asymmetric layout
Use of single case and contrasting sans-serif typeforms
Photography as a medium for illustration
Preference for primary coloured inks
Contrast by use of **bold** inks.[47]

In its early stages, the new graphic design clustered in certain countries more than others. At this early stage, along with Germany, other centres for the new graphic design included the Netherlands, Czechoslovakia, the Soviet Union, Hungary and Poland. It was in the 1930s that a broader diffusion of the new typographic design took place, partly through publication and exhibition, and partly through the emigration of some of its protagonists to other parts of the world, making it an approach that could be seen in design circles from New York to Tokyo and Buenos Aires to Zurich. As an example of this, the Werkbund exhibition of 1929, *Film und Foto*, was shown in several German cities before travelling to Osaka and Tokyo.[48]

The cause of the new graphic design was further promoted by the association Ring neuer werbegestalter (Circle of New Advertising Designers). The association echoed by name a group of modern architects based in Berlin. It was announced in the magazine *Das Kunstblatt* in 1928: 'A group of nine artists active as advertising designers has formed under the presidency of Kurt Schwitters. Baumeister, Burchartz, Dexel, Domela, Michel, Schwitters, Trump, Tschichold and Vordemberge-Gildewart belong to the association.'[49]

The affiliation of the Ring appears to have been loose, its activities consisting mainly of exhibitions, either promoting the group on its own or contributing to larger events. Most of the original members came from backgrounds in the visual arts and were self-taught in typography. An initial exhibition travelled to Wiesbaden, Barmen, Bochum, Hamburg,

Rotterdam, Halle, Dresden, Hanover, Bremen and Magdeburg during 1928 and 1929. As symptom of the escalation of interest in the new design, the Ring made group contributions to the important Werkbund exhibition *Film und Foto* and the Berlin *Neue Typographie* of 1930, where they showed alongside Bayer, Moholy-Nagy, Karel Teige, Van Doesburg and Johannes Molzahn. The members later participated in the exhibitions *Fotomontage* in Berlin in 1931, *Neue Werbegraphik* in the Kunstgewerbe (Arts and Crafts Museum) in Basel in 1930, the international exhibition *Kunst der Werbung* (Art of Publicity) in Essen in 1931 and the exhibition *Internationaal Reklamedrukwerk* (International Advertising Design) in the Stedelijk Museum, Amsterdam, in 1931.

Their point of view was most succinctly defined by the Dutch designer Paul Schuitema in their joint publication, *Gefesselter Blick* (The Captured Glance) in 1930: 'The designer is not a draughtsman, but rather an organizer of optical and technical factors. His work should not be limited to making notes, placing in groups and organizing things technically.'[50] In this, Schuitema acknowledged that modern design involved the separation of hand and machine that previous generations had so strongly fought against.

There are many ways that the origins of the new typography can be explained – several starting points. In the German-language case, the main incentive to think typography afresh in Modernism came in the immediate post-1918 years, within an educational and design context aimed towards industry and business. On a broad cultural front, to turn to Roman fonts and to use only lower-case typefaces was all the more shocking for a country used to *Fraktur* and the capitalizing of nouns. The graphic arts were taught at a number of specialist schools, most famously Leipzig, Frankfurt am Main and Munich. Until the mid-1920s, despite the eagerness to employ them in the modern compositions, no new sans-serif typefaces had been actually designed. Instead, existing nineteenth-century forms were generally available at major foundries and reworked in modern layout. The most successful variant of a new typeface was achieved in 'Futura' for the Bauer foundry (1926–8) by the designer Paul Renner. Renner, who taught at the Frankfurt Kunstschule then the Meisterschule für Deutschlands Buchdrucker in Munich, alongside Georg Trump and Jan Tschichold, was among the less doctrinaire of the new typographers, and he continued to design Roman seriffed typefaces and modest Gothic forms, not perceiving this as a conflict, since he was of the opinion that the new typography was not suited to all jobs.[51]

The new typography was crucial in the promotion of the new architecture, furniture and industrial design, as well as avant-garde film. The tendency was for the new design in this respect to be self-referential, and often the first Modernist designs showed a visual awkwardness or tension, no doubt adding to the sense of aesthetic novelty. Designs could be abrupt, possibly difficult for the viewer not used to such ideas, although often praised as 'matter of fact' and 'objective' by proponents. The design certainly did not allow for the comforts of consumer culture. Reflecting on this as early as 1927, Elsa Taterka, who taught graphic design at the Reimannschule in Berlin, suggested that: 'Clean objective form is not enough for modern consumers, whose speed of life and emotions need something akin to the fantasy of film or novels to capture their attention.'[52] It is tempting to read Taterka's comments as an example of a highly perceptive, early gendered critique of the potentially restrictive nature of the new typography.

Another pull for graphic designers in the 1920s naturally came from the USA. There, a contrasting modernity existed, sometimes intersecting with the avant-garde interests of the new typographers. In the range of commentaries, whether critical, as in the early writings of the Frankfurt school, or celebratory, as in advertising journalism, publicity culture became synonymous with 'Americanization'. In the 1920s, for example, many international advertising agencies were established and texts published in German depending on some of the early studies of advertising, such as Walter Dill Scott's analysis of advertising and marketing *The Psychology of Advertising*, originally published in 1909.

Trips to the US were made in order to understand new models of business organization. The successful poster and interior designer Lucian Bernhard established a design studio in New York in the early 1920s and operated the Bernhard-Rosen partnership between America and Berlin during the decade, developing clients in both countries.[53] And in 1924 the gifted young designer Hans Schleger left Berlin where he had been a student at the Kunstgewerbeschule to establish his studio in Madison Avenue under the pseudonym Zéro, proving particularly successful in applying a modern approach to publicity design for fashion and perfume companies.[54] To what extent could Americanization be considered a challenge to Modernism, even a contradiction? And to what extent could capitalism be accommodated beyond the more obvious cultural projects that Modernists preferred? Admittedly, they admired the stress on organization of Taylorism and Fordism and these were frequently invoked as metaphors for design in designers' writings. Scientific management, whether the application of rational organization to the home, the simplification of typefaces to a group of sans-serif alphabets which every printer could hold, or the use of photography as a mechanical, exactly repeatable

Designing Modern Germany

internationale ausstellung
kunst der werbung
essen 1931 30.mai – 5.juli ausstellungshallen

Max Burchartz, poster for the international exhibition, *Kunst der Werbung* (Art of Advertising), held in Essen in 1931.

illustrative technique, were offered as justifications on the grounds of economic efficiency. When designers left the security of an educational context, attempts were made to adjust the principles of Modernism to the pragmatic concerns of everyday publicity. As a piece of clever commentary on the role of graphic design, Max Burchartz adapted Constructivist visual language to produce a poster to announce the exhibition *Die Werbung*, in which a hand 'pulls the strings', suggesting the manipulation at work in much graphic design and advertising.

Conservative Taste in the Weimar Period

Without doubt, Weimar Modernism produced some of the most compelling definitions of the role of modern design, ideas for the application of design for contemporary industry, and a profound interrogation into the language of design that had a lasting impact on design education. Nevertheless, if we consider design in the Weimar period through a different lens, the emphasis on the avant-garde and new that so dominates design history comes into question. A review of many of the design periodicals aimed at a broader readership reveals that while certainly the subject of a great deal of promotion from certain sectors, Modernism was far from the mainstream or most commonplace choice for the everyday German household. As is now well understood, despite what appeared as the dominant presence of Modernism, alternatives also existed. Indeed, it is clear that stylistic pluralism continued, even if the persuasive force of Weimar as both myth and reality tends to have overshadowed this. An area that adds to a more complex understanding of design during the interwar years is the tradition of skilled craftsmanship associated with the decorative arts that had been such a hallmark of the pre-1914 years. In this respect we might ask, whatever happened to *dekorative Kunst*, decorative art aimed towards mainstream middle-class taste?

Walter Riezler, *Die Form ohne Ornament (Form without Ornament)* of 1924 was the first in the series of the Werkbund Bücher der Form.

The history of design provides one answer: that of its exclusion. Ever since the publication of the essay *Ornament und Verbrechen* (Ornament and Crime) in 1908 by the radically polemical early Modernist architect Adolf Loos, and Loos's lecture tours to promote his cause, ornament was conceived by many designers to be a problem.[55] As we have seen, Modernists frequently argued that only inherent ornament that was derived from the properties of the material itself could be justified. It comes as no surprise, therefore, that the German Werkbund put on the exhibition *Form ohne Ornament* (Form without Ornament) in 1924, which traced tendencies of the 'undecorated' object across time and cultures.[56] Modernist historiography, however, should not entirely colour our perceptions of the period. Histories of design in other countries in the 1920s immediately show continued lively traditions of decoration. An obvious case was the Paris *Exposition des arts décoratifs et industriels modernes* of 1925 (the exhibition that in the 1960s belatedly gave rise to the term Art Deco), when the élan of the French *artiste-décorateur* was internationally celebrated. Many other countries also offered enduring versions of decorative traditions at this exhibition, some steeped in folk art, such as the central and east European countries, others, like Sweden, a neo-Classicism that could also be modern and which earned the title 'Swedish Grace'.[57] All showed serious interest and continuity in the decorative arts. So where did Germany stand in all this?

By 1925 Franco–German diplomatic relations were at their lowest following the First World War, when Germany, in economic crisis, was charged with meeting significant war reparations. Therefore, although invited to contribute to the Paris exhibition, Germany declined and the nation's designers were denied the opportunity of this exposure. This does not mean that designs that could be classified as Deco or *moderne* did not exist, as in the other countries mentioned. Reviewing ranges of ceramics

Designing Modern Germany

and glass or textiles and furniture available from specialist retailers and the department stores, it becomes clear that lines included modern items that were more decorative than allowed for by Modernist theory. Indeed, as the pages of the magazines *Dekorative Kunst* and *Innendekoration* or the annual compendium *Farbige Raumkunst* suggest, it was possible to equip the home throughout the 1920s in a number of styles, from the historical and eclectic, the neo-Biedermeier, the folk-inspired vernacular, southern neo-Rococo, to the luxury of *moderne*. In particular, historicism continued as a viable approach in both elite and non-elite domestic and public spaces, despite the overt identification of the Weimar Republic with the progressive force of modernity and rejection of the past.[58]

This seemed to be particularly apparent in South Germany. Having established its reputation largely through the *Werkstätte*, Munich reasserted its significance as an important centre for the production and display of the decorative arts in 1922 when the city held the exhibition *Deutsche Gewerbeschau* (German Trade Show).[59] Funded in part by the German Werkbund, the exhibition took as its emblem three heads, the inventor's, the artist's and the worker's, in a conscious revival of pre-1914 visual rhetoric.

Photograph of the installation of the 'bazaar' for arts and crafts, designed by architect K. J. Mossner for the Munich Deutsche Gewerbeschau, 1922. The display showed the range of ceramics, from decorative figures to everyday tableware.

Work ranged from what might be referred to as light Expressionism to neo-Rococo, a style particularly identified with the mountainous south. Too soon after the war for complete interiors to be installed, the Munich displays were rich in what Bruno Paul, with the benefit of hindsight, described as 'expositions of modest size and modest contents – embroideries, hand-woven articles and rugs, bowls and vases, objects of glass and individual pieces of furniture'.[60]

Commentators have gone so far as to suggest that for Germany and its arts and crafts, the Munich exhibition of 1922 was as important as the Paris one of 1925.[61] Historically, Munich was cast as an 'art city' associated with the modern artistic movement of Der Blaue Reiter, but also with the Bavarian dukes, electors and kings, who had ceased to hold power only in 1918, at the end of the war. For centuries, the Wittelsbach family had commissioned artisans to build and enhance their palaces. The Residenz Hofburg and various prominent buildings in the city were opened to the public in 1920, following the abdication of Kaiser Wilhelm and the foundation of the Weimar Republic. This appeared to provide a reason for the revival of popular interest in specialist, elite decorative traditions that could then be diverted from aristocratic to middle-class interests. In the

D. J. Heymann, ornamental frame for the first-class salon of the liner Alfred Ballin, HAPAG Hamburg, 1922.

Designing Modern Germany

years of aftermath following the First World War it is therefore perhaps not surprising that one reaction among artists and designers was to return to history and tradition.

Writing about the contemporary situation in France, art historian Kenneth Silver applied the poet Jean Cocteau's phrase 'le rappel à l'ordre' (call to order) to characterize such recourse to the past.[62] Munich experienced a similar shift, even if it was manifest in reference to different styles, a 'return', in this case, into the safe hands of decoration and evocations of the styles of the Baroque and Rococo. Although usually Weimar Germany is understood to have followed the more radical route of functionalism and Bauhaus experiment, with their iconoclasm or extreme abstraction, Munich, a conservative city, presents a significant contrast. For instance, reports on the Munich exhibition of 1922 commented on a return to quiet, well-mannered pursuits, such as hand-engraved visiting cards and traditional book arts. Another eighteenth-century accomplishment in the form of paper-cuts and silhouettes was revived and interestingly adapted to a suit more modern subjects. The technique would subsequently be adapted for use in animated films.

Among the designers who were responsible for this revival of decorative tradition, referred to as *Stilkunst*, were Fritz August Breuhaus de Groot, Oskar Kaufmann, Richard Ermisch, Josef Wackerle and Max Wiederanders. One of the most remarkable decorative schemes from 1922 was by the Munich-based Josef Wackerle, an accomplished decorative artist who combined the lightness of touch associated with Bavarian plasterwork and wood carving with the contemporary fashion for Chinoiserie felt in many parts of Europe at the time. He exhibited panels depicting the four continents, destined for the salon of the ocean liner *Columbus*, completed in 1922 for Norddeutscher Lloyd of Bremen, where they would draw the attention of transatlantic passengers to the continued distinctiveness of German design.[63]

Decorative Porcelain and Germany at Monza

Another area in which the curious twist of modernity and tradition was manifest was at the high end of ceramic and glass manufacture for the long-established companies such as Meissen, Dresden and KPM. These were internationally renowned and equal to their French, Czech and Scandinavian counterparts. In the 1920s they proved themselves able to offer important historical continuity while also introducing new styles. The commission of designers at the former Königliche Porzellan-Manufaktur

(Royal Porcelain Manufacture) of Berlin revealed this. Before the war, KPM's reputation was in excelling in historical models, and it was awarded prizes at many of the international exhibitions. When the German Empire ceased to exist on the formation of the Republic, the prestigious art manufacture changed its name to the Staatliche Porzellan-Manufactur (State Porcelain Manufacture), although KPM continued to be used as its marque.[64]

In the 1920s a succession of different art directors followed their personal stylistic preferences to introduce a more open attitude towards modern design and decoration. For example, tradition and modernity were combined, and Chinoiserie, Expressionist and *moderne* decorative elements introduced. In Ernst Böhm's design for large-scale lamp bases, for example, strong geometric and graphic decoration was applied to forms reminiscent of Prussian classicism. These works were commissioned by Dr Nicola Moufang as part of the studio ceramics tradition in which eminent figures were invited to contribute their designs. She favoured what became known as 'Art Deco' styles. By contrast, the next art director, Günther Freiherr von Pechmann, made a more self-conscious attempt to embrace modernity and *Neue Sachlichkeit* (New Objectivity) in designs for ceramics for everyday use, as well as one-off sculptural pieces, such as Ernst Ludwig Gies's 'Jazz Band' of 1929. Constructed in white porcelain, this depicted a modern subject in an experimental, post-Cubist manner. A final example, Gerhard Marcks, who had taught at the Bauhaus and subsequently led the ceramics department at the Arts and Crafts school Burg Giebichenstein, introduced 'Bagdad', a white porcelain coffee service based on geometric shapes in 1930. As was often the case with Modernist services, it was possible to choose an undecorated, plain white version or a luxury range with the addition of an elegant stripe in gold glaze.

Denied the opportunity to exhibit in Paris, German designers were encouraged to contribute to the biennial exhibitions of decorative arts at Monza in northern Italy in 1923, 1925 and 1927, and, through these, they started to gather international acclaim. A leading force for promoting the German contributions was Bruno Paul, who from his position as director of the Berlin United State School for Applied Art was on the organizing committee. Its director-general, Guido Marangoni, announced of the *Third International Exposition of Decorative Arts* at Monza:

> We expect our artists, artisans and manufacturers, to make a strenuous effort to contribute to our exposition not only 'exposition' pieces, but also typical normal and average products – samples of mass production, objects for everyday use that are noble and dig-

nified withal. Our aim is to assemble at Monza the best of current, everyday production; to show the most useful and most beautiful necessities of life.[65]

Monza also provided the opportunity for the designers of the Deutsche Werkstätte to exhibit lines that could not be seen in Paris. The range of work covered all media of the applied arts, ceramics, metalwork, textiles and glass, while both stylistically and technically the work revealed an interest in historical continuity of craftsmanship.

As we have seen in chapter One, Bruno Paul contributed to the major exhibitions of Paris (1900), Turin (1902) and St Louis (1904). It has been suggested that, by the 1910s, on the decline of *Jugendstil*, Paul was Germany's most prominent architect-interior designer.[66] The second half of his career from the 1920s is less well documented. It was then that, characteristically for his generation, as an established designer he continued to produce interior schemes that showed a solid, bourgeois restraint that proved popular on both sides of the Atlantic. Forced to leave his post as director at the Berlin United State Schools for Free and Applied Arts as a Jew, he passed the position to Hans Poelzig in 1933.

In his introductory essay to the Monza exhibition of 1925, Walter Riezler, a founder member of the Werkbund since 1907 and editor of its magazine *Die Form*, highlighted the issues surrounding the applied arts in the 1920s. He commented that the term *Kunstgewerbe*, the applied arts, was by then a much derided and abused term. Although its significance for the state and society had been shown by the fact that the French had devoted an entire world exhibition to them, *Kunstgewerbe* had become a form of swear word associated with the superficial and seen only as a way to give modern products falsely artistic qualities. Riezler suggested, somewhat prophetically:

> Whoever tries, perhaps intentionally, to emphasize the attributes of national character and to allocate these a weightier role than it deserves on the part of artistic temperament and the task as such, may very well momentarily cause confusion. He will not be granted a victory, a decisive influence on the development. Even the mightiest dictator will not be able to create the new national style.[67]

Two years later, in 1927, Bruno Paul took responsibility for the organization of the third German contribution at Monza. Interestingly, the catalogue produced to accompany the exhibition immediately signalled an

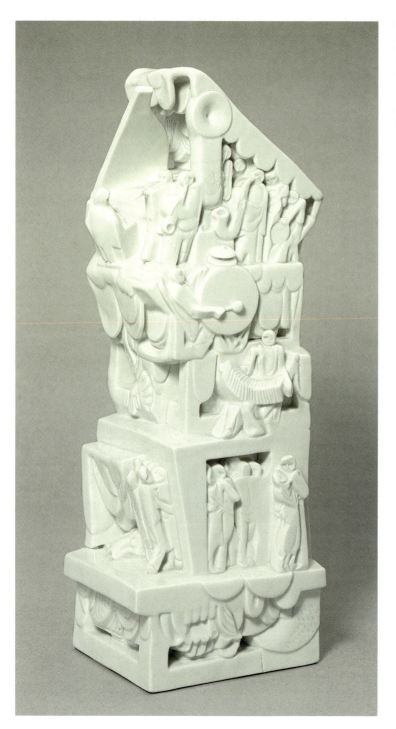

Ernst Ludwig Gies, 'Jazz Band' ceramic sculpture, made by the State Porcelain Manufactory, 1929. The white glaze accentuates the play of forms in the composition, while the subject engages with a modern theme.

For the Art Lover, *Christmas 1930*, the leaflet for the State Porcelain Manufactory, while modern in layout, advertises a decorative figurine of a Christmas angel by Ruth Schaumann, a Munich-based sculptor and silhouette artist.

FÜR DEN KUNSTFREUND

RUTH SCHAUMANN. »KLEINPLASTIK« STAATLICHE PORZELLAN-MANUFAKTUR—BERLIN.

WEIHNACHTEN 1930

assured traditionalism. Paul contributed a short essay, *Das Neue*, 'The New'. In this he began by stressing the importance of international exhibitions to encourage understanding and trade between nations. The essay then became a more pragmatic statement about the requirements for the applied arts to flourish and was less controversial or polemical than Riezler's earlier writings.

Through his reputation and sales of his furniture in America, Paul was chosen as the German representative for *An International Exposition of Art in*

Display of designs by the
United State Schools of
Berlin at the 1927 Monza
exhibition.

Industry, held at Macy's department store in New York from 14 to 26 May 1928. Altogether there were Swedish, Italian, German, American and French contributions and strong connections with Monza. Paul's short essay, 'Prospects and Retrospects', offered a summary of the *Kunstgewerbe* movement. He wrote:

> When the 'Exposition des Arts Décoratifs Modernes 1925' at Paris pre-
> sented the idea of the modern artcraft to the entire world, German
> achievement was not represented. Germany would have been well pre-
> pared to take a front place in this peaceful competition of the peoples.
> Her participation in the International Exposition at Monza, Italy, in
> 1927, demonstrated the great success of modern German artcrafts and
> furnished the inducement to participate at Macy's in New York.[68]

After what he called a 'cult of handicraft' Paul welcomed the bringing together of the handmade and machine-made. From the vantage point in Berlin, he announced to his New York readers his wish for the new design to traverse cultural borders and national boundaries, continuing:

> Clearly discernible in all this is the goal of the whole movement, in which today all civilized countries are united . . . a new style is rising which will not be limited to countries or continents. It is the style of the modern man who masters the distances between the countries and continents with the airplane; of the man of today whose clear voice resounds all over the globe, and whose feeling and thinking transcend the confines of countries and continents.[69]

Such pragmatic thinking, based on an awareness of the international market for desirable furniture of high quality, was a recipe for Paul's success at Macy's in New York and separated him from the younger generation of modern designers. His rooms showed him to be a progressive traditionalist, someone who knew his own business inside out and was prepared to adapt designs rooted in tradition, style and elegance to more modern tastes.

Taking into account the opportunities offered to German designers by exhibitions such as Monza, it is clear that it would misrepresent the Weimar years if attention were exclusively focused on Modernism. Instead, as in other European countries in the 1920s, modernity brought with it a plurality of styles. Germany's situation, in the face of increasing political polarization, took on a particular poignancy that marked the end of the Weimar Republic. The continued presence of conservative political forces escalated when, following world economic crisis after the Wall Street crash of October 1929, votes for National Socialist party representatives increased in local government elections. This suggested that the heady days of Weimar 'surface culture', their associations with bohemianism and the embrace of radical artistic and design experiment, were numbered.

3

Politics and Design: Reaction and Consolidation, 1933–45

The degree to which the Third Reich can be interpreted as a distinct period of German cultural, political and social history between 1933 and 1945 has become an important point of debate among historians in recent years. Organized as an autocratic regime and intended to last one thousand years through sustained state intervention in all areas of artistic and design culture, trade and industry, public and private life – at least at the level of propaganda – the official National Socialist message was that the totalitarian regime would achieve a complete break with the past. Recent historical writing, however, has indicated that Nazi policies were often open to ambiguity, being more contradictory than was professed. Most importantly, for the area of design, it would appear that the regime depended on a selective anti-Modernism rather than its complete prohibition. For design history, this means assessing the implication that, as well as rupture, continuities were evident across political change. Research into various forms of cultural manifestation suggests that it is necessary to distinguish between propaganda and practice. With this in mind, this chapter will explore the level of effectiveness of the National Socialist regime in proposing new design values; it will consider official designs and the degree to which alternatives were permitted, as well as its impact on a variety of designers.

Change in Cultural Policy

A craftsman from the Berlin Handwerkerschule executing a design of the German eagle and swastika, 1937.

In her important study of the German Werkbund, historian Joan Campbell indicated that a period of transition took place when organizations went through what was known as *Gleichschaltung*, a form of cultural alignment introduced to effect political change. It was a gradual process, beginning before 1933 and continuing into the first years of the regime. Through this, leadership positions were taken over by Party members and policies adapted to suit the National Socialists' broader aims. Campbell suggests:

> As far as the Werkbund is concerned, closer examination reveals that National Socialist elements had infiltrated the association well before 1933, that the National Socialist *Weltanschauung* incorporated features compatible with Werkbund principles, and that Werkbund ideas – and Werkbund men – continued to influence cultural policy in the Third Reich after the association as such ceased to exist.[1]

When in 1933 the National Socialist party came to power, it attempted to re-direct many of the advances in design made during the Weimar years, often disguising more overt use of modern techniques with messages that confirmed a return to tradition and archaic values. Adolf Hitler was appointed as Chancellor of Germany on 30 January 1933. The following elections on 5 March 1933 allowed an alliance between the National Socialist Workers' Party (NSDAP, Nationalsozialistische Deutsche Arbeiterpartei) and other nationalist parties to gain a majority in the Reichstag, marking the start of the Third Reich. On their accession to power, the National Socialists introduced a comprehensive range of reforms in most areas of cultural and political life, among which they appointed artists, architects and designers who were expected to be loyal to the German tradition. Design came under the control of Joseph Goebbels, the Reich Minister for People's Enlightenment and Propaganda, and a series of cultural chambers was formed. On 22 September 1933 the Reichskulturkammer Gesetz (Reich's Cultural Chamber Law) established the Reichsminister's right to organize those active in the areas under his jurisdiction into corporate bodies, *Körperschaften*. The six divisions comprised: 1) Literature, 2) Press, 3) Broadcasting, 4) Theatre, 5) Music and 6) Visual Arts. Within the office for visual arts, individual sections covered specialist groups, such as Department III: Architecture, Landscape Architecture and Interior Decoration; Department IV: Painting and Graphic Arts; Department V: Illustration and Graphic Design; Department VI: Art Promotion, Artists' Associations and Craft Associations; and Department VIII: Art Publishing, Art Sales and Art Auctioning.[2]

Architects and designers could only practice, for example, if they held membership of the Reichskulturkammer (RKK). As a consequence, when such bureaucratic, centralized control of cultural production took effect, many designers were forced to emigrate, cease practice or undergo an inner

Designing Modern Germany

migration that involved removal from public life. In the first months of the regime, the Nazis implemented 'a systematic purge of government-controlled art schools, universities, and museums in the course of which many Werkbund people lost their positions'.[3] In many respects, the German Werkbund could be taken as a barometer of the national design culture in 1933. Yet, as historian Paul Betts has pointed out, the situation was far from clear-cut. He has questioned the effectiveness of Nazi policy to implement a coherent line and, indeed, drew attention to the continuation of modern industrial design, suggesting: 'For was it not the case that modern industrial designers remained virtually untouched by the Nazi policy of Gleichschaltung? Were not Bauhaus graphic designers actively recruited by the new regime to lend Nazi exhibitions a more Modernist spirit?'[4]

It is impossible to offer a comprehensive account of all the reactions of designers and the individual dilemmas facing them in this critical political situation. Designers' positions varied from total support of the new government to active resistance. And designers, like the remainder of the German population, could be open to self-contradiction and compromise, often through force of familial or material circumstance, as well as political beliefs. For example, Richard Riemerschmid, the prominent furniture designer whose career spanned forty years, managed to maintain his position. Despite his opposition to the National Socialists, he stayed on as head of the Munich branch of the Werkbund after 1933. By contrast, also in Munich, the radical typographer and book designer Jan Tschichold was taken into 'protective custody' in March 1933 and forced to leave his teaching post at the Munich Meisterschule, accused of 'cultural bolshevism'.[5] An important figure for the continuation of enlightened modern design ideals, Tschichold was able to leave for Basel in Switzerland, where he taught at the Gewerbeschule and worked for the printer-publisher Benno Schwabe. In another case, Joost Schmidt, a designer who had taken over as head of the Bauhaus graphics workshop in 1928 and had worked for a short while on exhibition designs in the new regime, including collaboration, for example, with Walter Gropius on a display of non-ferrous metals at the *Deutsches Volk Deutsche Arbeit* installation of 1934 in Berlin, chose to relinquish his practice in his dismay at the political direction his country was taking. He nonetheless remained in residence in Germany.[6] Conversely, Peter Behrens, whose name connected him by association with the prominent Jewish businessman Walther Rathenau, former owner of AEG, chose to transfer his architectural practice from Vienna, returning to Germany in 1936, when he took on official National Socialist commissions and adapted to their favoured architectural style for public buildings, overblown neo-Classicism.[7] Finally, in the case of Herbert Bayer, his graphic design approach, combining photomontage with the novelties of Constructivism and Surrealism, proved effective for a series of official exhibitions, explicitly National Socialist in their message, which were held at Berlin's most prominent venue at least up to 1936.[8]

To make manifest the change in cultural outlook, Joseph Goebbels introduced a policy to ridicule styles associated with the liberal Weimar years, and in turn, advocated designs loyal to a native 'Germanic' tradition. What art historian Berthold Hinz described as a 'battle for art' took place between 1933 and 1937 in the area of the fine arts. On one side of the conflict were promoters of Expressionism, who advocated it as the appropriate national style on account of its recourse to craft, the Gothic and an assumed 'northern' expressiveness.[9] By the time of the official *Grosse Deutsche Ausstellung* (Great German Art Exhibition), which opened in Munich in 1937, it was clear in the fine arts that a form of idealized, academic figuration was the victor. While architecture was also much debated and the National Socialists invested significant cultural value and resources in it,

In the poster for the *Entartete Kunst* (Degenerate Art) exhibition in Munich of 1936, the designer Vierthaler made a deliberate attempt to ridicule Suprematist art. Part of the text reads 'what we see in this interesting show was once taken seriously!'

design was not subject to the same level of discourse, possibly because within the traditional hierarchy of the arts, which the National Socialists were eager to reassert, it carried less cultural value. Nonetheless, the broader aesthetic climate set the tone for design. The year 1937 was also that of the notorious *Entartete Kunst* (Degenerate Art) and *Entartete Musik* (Degenerate Music) exhibitions, versions of which were shown in Munich, Berlin, Leipzig, Düsseldorf and Frankfurt am Main, announcing the formal end of modern artistic and design experiment in Germany while denouncing and ridiculing it.[10]

Underlying National Socialist aesthetic policy was the concept of 'degeneration' or *Entartung*, which was felt across the hierarchy of fine and applied arts, design and architecture. The term was first applied to culture by the Austro-Hungarian physician and social critic Max Nordau, who was also an important Zionist, in the book entitled *Entartung* of 1893. Degeneration was a significant ingredient of the

Designing Modern Germany

wider movement of national conservatism and cultural pessimism that gathered strong interest in Germany at the time.[11] In the face of what they perceived to be cultural decline resulting from the incursions of international modernity, this generation of theoreticians took it upon themselves to proscribe tendencies that were alien to the 'national' spirit. At its most explicit, fear of 'degeneracy' was articulated through the concept of Aryanization and linked directly to race and the goal of cultivating a pure nation, or *Volk*, through eugenics and control of the population. In light of this, the National Socialists enforced membership of official bodies to eradicate 'undesirable' elements in the workforce and professions, as in the case of the Jewish and homosexual populations, and Communist Party members. Only designers approved by the appropriate government chamber were allowed to continue their work.

In the German case, Aryanization most explicitly depended on anti-Semitism. Indeed, design was to feel this impact early on: 'The Werkbund, under pressure from the Kampfbund für deutsche Kultur, became one of the first cultural organizations in Germany formally to exclude non-Aryans.'[12] The official boycott of Jewish shops, lawyers, bankers and doctors began in April 1933. By November 1936 the Reichskulturkammer declared itself 'free of Jews'. Symptomatic of the escalating campaign, *Der Ewige Jude* (The Eternal Jew), an anti-Semitic exhibition organized by the Munich National Socialist leadership and the Ministry of Reichspropaganda, also opened in 1937. It was largely composed of works confiscated from public collections. Visited by more than 400,000 people in eight weeks, it falsely attacked Jews for 'contaminating German culture'. Versions of the exhibition travelled to other German cities accompanied by the propaganda film *Jud Süss*, which traced the origins of German Jewry to the ghettos of Poland and tendentiously accused prominent Jews of corrupting Germany through their associations with international capital. The following year synagogues in many German cities were destroyed, culminating in Kristallnacht, the smashing of windows and looting of Jewish business concerns in the pogrom on 9 and 10 November 1938.[13]

Design and Industry under National Socialism

At its core, the issue of standards and functional requirements in design for industry remained a priority for the National Socialist government. In his work of the late 1970s, design historian John Heskett was among the first to identify significant structural points of continuity between Weimar and the Third Reich in terms of the administration of design. This view has been extended in research into the continuing legacy of the Bauhaus and designers in Werkbund circles after 1933.[14] Overall, historical opinion has questioned the previously held view that Modernism survived despite National Socialism, an interpretation that gave an unwarranted autonomy to design to determine its own fate.[15] Instead, a more nuanced relationship between Modernism and political ideology suggests that central tenets of Modernism were compatible with National Socialism. Even if Party ideologues did not personally subscribe to it as a style, it was in their interest not to stand in the way of the underlying appeals to rationalization and standardization, which they recognized were essential for certain branches of German industrial manufacture.

Accordingly, the National Socialists found that the movement to standardize industry led by the Deutsche Normenausschuss (German Standards Commission) through DIN (Deutsche Industrie Normen) standards, which they introduced in 1926, paved the way to efficient, rational organization of manufacture, and they sustained it. With attention turned to shaping a new German nation through road construction, extension of railways and heavy industrial production, National Socialist policy adapted such technological and economic functionalism towards rebuilding Germany's industrial power under the changed labour relations of the German Labour Front (Deutsche Arbeiter Front, DAF). In 1936 the results were displayed in the propaganda exhibition announcing the government's Four Year Plan, *Gebt mir vier Jahre Zeit*, with its declared intention of putting Germany on a war footing by 1940.[16]

The idea of an unproblematic relationship between aesthetic avant-gardism and politically progressive or left-wing thinking has been challenged on many fronts in interpretations of Modernism in and beyond the Third Reich. In German history, Jeffrey Herf coined the term 'reactionary modernism' to explain how conservative forces found it possible to embrace modernity at the level of technical innovation and increased productivity, without subscribing to the more general assumption that these would lead to a democratic realization of a new society based on a modern, urbanized state. In this case, among elite engineers and philosophers of technology, conservative advocates of a national technological drive offered an important reconciliation between modern technology and an aggressively national vision.[17] For such a programme to be realized, Germany's heavy industries were crucial, as witnessed in an iconography found on posters, pamphlets and industrial photographs that asserted their strength as a core part of Nazi identity. Paradoxically, this hard-line vision of a masculine national state was not the only one to be sustained. If

A newly-built Autobahn with service station and views of countryside, c. 1936–9. The rhetoric of the image connected motoring with the experience of the expansive German landscape.

Party ideologues were to promote Germany as a modern technocracy, challenges presented themselves from other quarters. For instance, new materials such as plastics and light metals were also needed for Germany to become less dependent on imports and to reach its goal of self-sufficiency. The skilled *Handwerker*, or craftsmen, also formed a vocal and significant section of the population, whose interests needed to be met. And by contrast, the burgeoning consumer culture that had developed during the Weimar Republic, in part taking its inspiration from the United States of America, with dreams propelled by advertising, fashion and style, was also something that needed careful attention during the Third Reich, not least by the Party elite themselves, who were all too aware of their near-'star' status.

The Case of Wilhelm Wagenfeld

Wilhelm Wagenfeld was a specialist designer of silverware and glass who had studied at drawing schools before undertaking an apprenticeship in the specialist silverware manufacture Koch and Bergfeld in Bremen between 1914 and 1919. Wide-scale recognition came with his move to the Bauhaus, where he joined the metal workshop and was strongly impressed by the teachings of Moholy-Nagy, especially of exploring innovative ways of combining glass and metal. The lamp 'WG 24', designed together with K. J. Juncker in 1924, would become one of the most famous Bauhaus designs.

Wilhelm Wagenfeld, 'Kubus Geschirr', manufactured by VLG Weisswasser, 1938.

On leaving the Bauhaus, Wagenfeld went to teach at the Staatliche Kunsthochschule in Berlin between 1931 and 1935.[18]

A prominent member of the Deutsche Werkbund, he was one of only a few to stand against its *Gleichschaltung* during the political change of 1933. The paradox of Wagenfeld's situation continued, since his work for important factories such as Jenaer Glaswerke and Vereinigte Lausitzer Glaswerke in Weisswasser was selected to represent Germany throughout the 1930s. The 'Kubus' line of stacking cuboid containers, for instance, designed for production by Lausitzer works in 1938, for use from the refrigerator to the table, was entirely in sympathy with Modernist principles in material, form and function. Wagenfeld nonetheless was chosen to represent Germany and awarded prizes at national exhibitions, such as *Schaffendes Volk* (A Nation at Work) in Düsseldorf in 1937, as well as internationally in Paris in 1937 at the *Exposition internationale des arts et techniques*, and again at the Milan Triennale. It could be said that Wagenfeld's reputation was marred by the acclaimed profile of his work during the Third Reich, yet the designer remained adamant in his political convictions, and during the Second World War he was sent to a prisoners' camp on the Russian front for his refusal to serve the National Socialist regime.[19]

Two Gothic typefaces, Offenbach – 'a surprisingly great success' for Gebr. Klingspor and Brahms – Gotisch for Gensch and Heyse of Hamburg. The first was designed by Rudolf Koch, an established letter artist prior to 1933, while Heinz Beck's Brahms, a later design, was intended to have specifically national associations. (Reproduced in *Gebrauchsgraphik*, May 1937.)

Propaganda for the New German Reich: A National Script?

Even with such complications taken into account, it was clear that design could be used directly to manifest political change in many fundamental ways. One highly visible sphere, which had a general impact on the entire population, was typeface design. For instance, in the printing industry and related design fields of typography and commercial graphics, the change in regime was indicated through legislation around typefaces. In many respects, this was to be expected. German book arts and printing were considered a national strength and source of cultural pride, with historic centres such as Leipzig, Mainz and Offenbach am Main and associations going back as far as Johannes Gutenberg and the invention of moveable type in the mid-fifteenth century. Moreover, in Gothic script, German-speaking lands had a distinctive printing tradition to which to return. As an embodiment of Germanic, *völkisch* values, the National Socialists favoured the use of Blackletter Fraktur and Gothic typefaces, and in 1933 they demanded that all school textbooks, official printed matter and news-papers return to setting in Fraktur.[20]

In keeping with their reactive policies, the message was that the Weimar Republic had seen the growth in use of Roman typefaces, in many cases sans-serif, as a symptom of modern international communication; therefore, during the first years of National Socialism several new Black-letter founts were commissioned from the same type foundries. The names

Europa Haus in Berlin
illuminated by advertising,
as it appeared in an issue
of the magazine
Gebrauchsgraphik in 1937.

of the designs carried national connotations, among them Tannenberg, National, Deutschland and Gotenburg. Described ironically by their detractors as 'Jackboot grotesques' (*Schaftstiefelgrotesken*), they were dismissed and unfavourably compared with their more refined, historical counterparts.[21]

A further indication of the vagaries of National Socialist policy in regulating the German script came in 1941, in the case of a decree by Martin Bormann, by then head of the Party Chancellery. In the middle of the Second World War, the policy of recommending Fraktur as the official type was revoked when Gothic types were denounced as 'Jewish Schwabacher'. In occupied lands, the German script had proved illegible to many, and this, as well as the further spurious suggestion that Gutenberg was in fact Jewish, was used to justify a return to Roman script. Such contradictions abound. Even at the height of its strictest legislation, not all areas of print conformed to official rules, as a review of poster design, advertising and street signage in 1930s Germany reveals. It would appear that Party dogma could not stand in the way of commerce. As opportunities for coloured neon-light architecture for modern office buildings developed through technical advances, Germany's modern cities became sites of international advertising, at the same time as they were to be venues for important national political events.

As a further complication, Hitler's preferred lettering for inscription on official buildings and design for publication tended to be classical Roman forms. This was the case, for instance, for the highly prestigious art magazine *Die Kunst im Dritten Reich*, published between 1937 and 1939 and intended to impress an international readership. Its cover design, by Richard Klein, featured a relief of a helmeted, Graeco-Roman soldier above the German eagle and Party emblem with flaming torch, accompanied by elegant but authoritative neo-Classical typography.[22]

Mechanized Messages

Beyond the specific instances of type design, the National Socialists were extremely aware of the power of the mediated message. It was no coincidence that their rise to power took place at the time of the rapid proliferation of mass communication in the form of magazines and advertising, the rise of radio broadcasting and cinemagoing and a general increase in the psychological persuasiveness of these media to mould public opinion in Western Europe and the United States of America. The most famous essay on the predicament of such new visual communication undergoing political change, 'The Work of

Art in the Age of Mechanical Reproduction', was written by Walter Benjamin and delivered in Paris at a conference for the study of Fascism in 1935.[23] It amounted to a serious and enlightening reflection on the late Weimar years and their transition to totalitarianism. Benjamin, primarily a literary scholar and cultural philosopher, was concerned with considering the impact of film and photography as reproductive media and their possibilities for revolutionary visual communication. Elsewhere, he analysed Brechtian theatre and Surrealism as alternative strategies for critique, but in the 1935 essay in particular, he contrasted the experience of art in a museum to that of viewing photographic reproduction on a page or as film. Benjamin initially identified what he saw as the progressive potential of photography to avoid ritual or 'aura', and through the absence of an original that would prompt a more engaged, active response in the audience. Observing the mass propaganda of Hitler's Third Reich during its first years, how-

Leonid, 'All Germany listens to the Führer with the People's Radio', 1935. The poster showed an enlarged version of the apparatus designed by Walter Maria Kersting and familiar to many households.

ever, Benjamin also realized that many of the novel effects of the new typographers and photographers of the 1920s had been appropriated and transformed by the far right: he concluded that the democratic utopia of the new vision was not to be realized. Appalled by the appropriation of modish techniques by the National Socialists, he wrote: 'The logical result of Fascism is the introduction of aesthetics into political life ... All efforts to render politics aesthetic culminate in one thing: war.'[24] A case in point was one of the first major propaganda initiatives orchestrated by Hitler, *The Triumph of the Will*, a record of the official Party convention in Nuremberg in 1934, which was filmed by Leni Riefenstahl. It was subsequently recognized to have been an 'historic event serving as the set of a film'.[25] In particular, *The Triumph of the Will* has been analysed for its adaptation of montage techniques, associated with experimental avant-garde film of the Soviet Union and Weimar Republic, to construct a seamless-narrative Führer worship, depicted through the assembly of troops, the arrival of Hitler, the presentation of speeches and the greetings of the crowds. Countering the idea that the political persuasion of the National Socialists should necessarily mean reactionary design, the American critic and writer Susan Sontag, in the provocatively titled essay 'Fascinating Fascism',

Designing Modern Germany

confronted the idea that the Nazi uniform, and specifically that of the ss (Schutzstaffel), such a central part of the Riefenstahl film, could have aesthetic and sexual appeal. Comparing it with other uniforms, Sontag wrote:

> ss uniforms were stylish, well-cut, with a touch (but not too much) of eccentricity. Compare the rather boring and not very well cut American army uniform: jacket, shirt, tie, pants, socks, and lace-up shoes – essentially civilian clothes no matter how bedecked with medals and badges. ss uniforms were tight, heavy, stiff and included gloves to confine the hands and boots that made legs and feet feel heavy, encased, obliging their wearer to stand up straight.[26]

This awareness of the power of design carried over into other areas of National Socialist propaganda.

A portrait photograph of a soldier in the ss service uniform of the Oberschurführer, 1938.

The Swastika

It is instructive to extend Benjamin's commentary to areas that he had been witness to, but did not address in detail in this essay, including strategies central to National Socialism, such as the swastika as a Party brand identity. For along with the cult of the Führer and idolization of Adolf Hitler, sustained through the official photographs of Heinrich Hoffmann and the films of Leni Riefenstahl, the larger Party was most convincingly signified through the symbol of the swastika. As a form of state design, the symbol was effective for the world's press, as well as when published in numerous illustrated magazines and photo-books aimed at the domestic market. Commentators have suggested that, in the public's mind, the swastika was so powerful that it could act as a symbol for the Party and as a metaphor for Adolf Hitler himself, even at events when he was not personally present.[27]

Before its appropriation in the writings and political campaigns of Hitler, the swastika had been a recognized ancient symbol used across many cultures. The justification for adoption by the National Socialists was that it was thought to be the oldest Aryan symbol. Possibly representing the course of the sun in the heavens, it was widely used in Asian religious and spiritual cultures and as an occult symbol in late nineteenth-century Germany, by, among others, the Theosophists. The swastika entered German military use when adopted by the Reichshammer Bund in 1912. Despite its archaic associations, the swastika as developed by the National Socialists had all the requisite elements of a modern trademark, much in the way of the Italian Fascist Party's adaptation of the *fasci* as its symbol, and in line with modern marketing and design thinking. In the way it took the form of a simplified motif composed of regular geometrical black lines, set on a white circle against a red background, it worked as both an individual sign set against a uniform or on a flag, and also gathered most impact when seen in mass rallies, as an exactly repeatable, standardized element that conveyed a collective presence. Symptomatic of how important the symbol was in the Party's eyes, the 'Law for the Protection of National Symbols' (*Zum Schutz der nationalen Symbole*) was introduced on 19 May 1933 by Joseph Goebbels, to protect the national emblem and prevent unauthorized use, especially in commercial contexts.[28]

Another commentator of the Weimar period, Siegfried Kracauer, drew further light on understanding how the National Socialists adapted existing constructions of mass performance to their particular needs. Writing in the essay *The Mass Ornament* of 1927, the critic and philosopher identified the phenomenon of mass groupings to convey modernity, as in collective sports events, organized by political extremes on both far left and far right. Such public displays of physical achievements were continued under Nazism, but added to them were military performances of marching soldiers and flag-bearing civilians, arranged as collectivized units. As well as sports events, Kracauer was interested in the mass-formation entertainment of groups such as the American dance team The Tiller Girls. He suggested that it was with the introduction of photography and film, mechanized ways of seeing and recording, that the full extent of the shift in ornament could be captured and appreciated on an abstract level. Kracauer attributed the same qualities to these staged choreographed performances as to Fordism and mass production in the factory: 'The mass ornament is the aesthetic reflex of the rationality aspired to by the prevailing economic system', he wrote.[29] Furthermore, Kracauer went on to define the ability of the new media to bring people together across geographical difference, something that was to preoccupy the National Socialists. Prophetically, he wrote:

> The tiniest village, which they have not yet reached, learns about them through the weekly newsreels. One need only glance at the

Designing Modern Germany

For an official visit by Adolf Hitler in 1938, the centre of Naples was re-modelled through dramatic lighting and the installation of columns bearing National Socialist symbols.

screen to learn that ornaments are composed of thousands of bodies, sexless bodies in bathing suits. The regularity of their patterns is cheered by the masses, themselves arranged by the stands in tier upon ordered tier.[30]

To find a means by which to unite rural and urban populations was of central concern to the Party. To this end, they developed ways to reconfigure both city and country through design, to their own ends. If the countryside could be treated as a blank canvas on which to project an expansionist vision of *Lebensraum*, cities in particular presented a problem for the National Socialists. During the Weimar Republic, they had been sites of urban unrest, radical political assembly and working-class uprisings. The challenge of National Socialist propaganda was to turn attention away from these perceived negative elements of the city and to reconnect the sizeable urban populations with the German countryside.

Architectural historians have explored the various tensions in selecting an architectural style to embody National Socialist ideals. They have examined the circumstances for prestigious public monumental buildings, to which great attention was given at the time, as well as building projects that fell into the realm of a more pared-down functionalism to serve industrial and technological requirements.[31] At the most explicit level of built form as propaganda, Hitler's first official architect was the Munich-based Paul Ludwig Troost. On his death in March 1934, he was succeeded by Albert Speer, who was to become 'general inspector of buildings' for Berlin at a time when Hitler published his wider directives for the planning of German cities. In these architects' hands, Munich was cast as 'art city', Nuremberg 'congress city' and Berlin, the most difficult, as 'political city'. It was also to be renamed 'Germania', as capital of 'greater Germany'.[32]

The contribution of design in this urban redefinition was through what was termed *Inszenierung*, the inscription on to the cityscape of more ephemeral designed elements that would assist in mobilizing the permanent built structures as settings for political events. The National Socialists used temporary structures, for instance, on which to display street decorations in the form of flags, banners and other Party regalia. As we have seen, the filmic analogy was totally in keeping with the aim of recording and broadcasting the message. To take an example, the Lustgarten, the large rectangular square facing Karl Friedrich Schinkel's Altes Museum in Berlin, was used as the setting for a series of events, including the celebrations of 1 May 1936, as a prelude to the Olympic Games later that year. Iain Boyd Whyte has written:

> The stage management of this event offers clear insights into the con-
> scription of architecture, urban form, scenographic decorations, and
> painting as essential tools in the construction of the myths on which
> National Socialist ideology was based . . . Every possible medium was
> exploited, from medievalizing frescos in Luftwaffe messes to the
> instant reportage of the newsreel.[33]

To aid this politicization of the public sphere, special-effect lighting was used to create night scenes, the overwhelming scale of events encouraging a heightened level of expectation, excitement and emotional response in the assembled crowds.

Volkswagen: The People's Car

The National Socialists realized that the propagandistic potential of design need not be restricted to areas of communication, or to designs with representational messages. Instead, all kinds of design and material culture were identified as possible carriers of values, a most prominent case being the Volkswagen.[34]

Ferdinand Porsche was a renowned Austrian automotive engineer with a record of working for Austro-Daimler when he established his own design consultancy in Stuttgart, already a centre for car manufacture, in 1931. Once settled in Germany, Porsche became interested in the development of a small car and, with a team of up to twelve specialists, began working on several prototypes. The distinctive styling of the first cars he developed in this vein, Porsche Typ 12 and 32, resulted from his collaboration with his chief designer Erwin Komenda, who was interested in aerodynamics and the streamlining being applied in vehicle design more generally at this time, especially in the USA. In 1933 Hitler approached Ferdinand Porsche with his urgent desire to place the motorization of Germany centrally in his policies. His idea was to develop a people's car, intended to suit two adults and three children. The Führer further stipulated that he would like the car to have a top speed of 100 kilometres per hour. The Kraft durch Freude (Strength through Joy) car, or people's car, 'Volkswagen', as eventually it would be called, became a case study of a complicated and contradictory project to produce a car that could compete with American models of consumption and mobility, and especially the Model T Ford.

To accompany the car-building programme, the National Socialists introduced an extensive Autobahn network across Germany, a result of the Deutsche Arbeitsfront (DAF), German Labour Front projects. The Autobahn was promoted as a symptom of modernity. Even if the everyday experience of driving was not a reality for many Germans and the roads were used more by military than domestic vehicles, in the early years the open stretches of road also served to promote the concept of *Lebensraum*.

Porsche developed the first models of the car in collaboration with Zündapp of Nuremberg, a motorcycle engineering company. The Volkswagen was introduced as a promise for every German worker, through the Kraft durch Freude movement in 1936. A car intended for everyday consumption among the German population, it was important in Hitler's

Werner von Axster-Heudtlass, publicity brochure *Dein kdf-Wagen*, part of the promotional campaign for the 'strength through joy' car, 1939.

propaganda campaign in presenting the consumer benefits of the regime. The car was promoted through diverse marketing techniques, in which politics and consumption were directly related. One kdf (Kraft durch Freude) propaganda poster read:

> The Führer promised the motorization of Germany
> The Führer gave 250,000 unemployed national comrades work
>   and bread
> The Führer achieved the People's car
> Therefore German people – thank the Führer on 29 March 1936
> Give him your vote![35]

The price of the car was set at 990 Reichsmark (the average income monthly at this time was 32 Marks). The car was available only through instalments of 5 Marks per week, which changed to 5 Marks per month at the start of the war, and was delivered only after the final payment. Its production was in fact redirected towards preparation for military and war use before private models were available, and instead the 200 cars produced were allocated to senior Party members.

In 1939 the plant, which was intended to manufacture between 400,000 and 500,000 cars a year, opened in a new purpose-built town with workers' housing and other services along with the factories. It was close to Schloss Wolfsburg, initially named kdf Stadt (Strength through Joy town)

Designing Modern Germany

Adolf Hitler inspecting a model of the Volkswagen on his 49th birthday on 20 April 1938. *Die Strasse*, 1938.

near the strategic Autobahn route between Berlin and the industrial Ruhr district, and only later became Wolfsburg, the name associated with the centre for Volkswagen automobile production in post-war Germany. By 1940 there were 300,000 potential purchasers, but no cars were manufactured for civilians until after the Second World War.[36]

National Socialist Interiors

Every hand that really works creatively is part of the great power.[37]

To mark the contribution of the League of German Handworkers to the celebration of three years of Adolf Hitler's rule in 1936, the statement 'Jede Hand die Wirkend Schafft ist ein Teil der Grossen Kraft' was mounted on the House of German Crafts. The other decorations on the building included a metalwork grille with the swastika motif, depictions of working craftsmen, oak leaves and acorns. At the same time, the Führer sent the *Reichshandwerkmeister* W. G. Schmidt the following telegram message: 'It is my wish and will that German handcraft, deeply rooted in venerable tradition, in conjunction with the people (*Volk*) and state, will look forward to a new blossoming.'[38]

Through the Kampfbund für deutsche Kultur (Combat League for German Culture), craft guilds that had disbanded in the earlier part of the twentieth century were re-established within a broader change of policy

Photograph by Heinz Adrian celebrating the craftsmanship of glass-blowing, 1937. F. Matthies-Masuren, *Das Atelier des Fotografen*, Halle, 1937.

towards 'rural settlement and the crafts'.[39] The German skilled craftsmen (*Handwerker*) formed an important and influential section of the workforce, with an estimated total of 4.5 million employed in various craft occupations officially overseen by the guild. It should be stressed that with Germany's relatively late industrialization, the term *Handwerker* was more extended and encompassed a greater number of skills than the use of the English word 'craft' would denote at this point. As in the case of heavy industry, the tendency was to employ German materials, reducing dependence on imports. This was more easily realized in areas such as ceramics and glass, woodworking, metalwork, textiles and leatherwork than larger-scale manufacture. It was vital for this element in the German workforce not to be excluded at the level

Designing Modern Germany

of political rhetoric, and in popular imagery and wider dissemination of their ideals the National Socialist commitment to the value of hand labour, skill and materials was stressed. Indeed, depictions of men in skilled occupations, forging metal, blowing glass, turning wood or cutting letterforms, occurred as popular images in amateur and professional photography, often accompanied by visions of non-industrialized agriculture in the form of hay-making, lake fishing or apple harvesting.[40] If the crafts and hand skills were not to be challenged by potential subordination to rationalization and technocracy, the regime needed to offer reassurance to this sector, even if in many cases this was in fact the reality. A possible tension also existed between the needs of a mass market for inexpensive industrially produced goods and more expensive craft items that resulted from such hand processes. It is difficult to ascertain the extent to which the various crafts were subsidized or maintained for their ideological, as opposed to their actual, value. Certainly, many exhibitions and national events reflected the desire to project Germany as a nation of craftsmanship, with intact regional folk arts.

Hand work came under the legislation of the office Schönheit der Arbeit (Beauty in Work), which was responsible for promoting appropriate exemplary objects through selections of lighting, ceramics and glass, wallpapers, textiles and furniture for the home, along with administering funds and support, and controlling the ranges made. The office of Schönheit der Arbeit, led by architect Albert Speer, was placed within a division of the larger Deutsche Arbeitsfront (German Labour Front), which covered all industry, under the leadership of Robert Ley. In turn, this was a subsidiary of the KdF movement. The broadest aim of the latter was to instil work with a renewed beauty and dignity, for the creation of a greater sense of community or *Gemeinschaft*. The result of these activities culminated in the first international handcrafts exhibition in Berlin in 1938, and this was followed in 1940 when the ceramic designer Hermann Gretsch edited the publication *Gestaltendes Handwerk* (Designed Crafts) of 1940.[41] As in other design fields, structural continuities meant that even with a change in personnel, such organizations as the renowned furniture workshops of Deutsche Werkstätten in Dresden-Hellerau remained important. Indeed, it was feasible for Werkbund principles such as 'simplicity, honesty, clarity and unornamented form' to be sustained within furniture manufacture, even when first appearing to be values of a previous era.[42]

In the areas of furniture and interior design, three main prevailing styles served distinct purposes. For large-scale public commissions that received major press attention, often as backdrops to Party events, splendid luxury was employed with no expense spared. This was a tradition

already established in the historicist interiors that Paul Ludwig Troost, the Munich architect, had developed for the Amerika-Line ocean liners in the 1920s and adapted to other use. The style included massive-scale upholstered furniture, with marble and highly polished wood-panelled fittings and surfaces; together with these, heraldry, chandeliers, monumental ceramics and ironwork were all suggestive of the feudal lifestyle that Party elites wished to invoke. The proportions of the rooms, the vastness of the halls and the overall grandeur of the decorative schemes reinforced the message that it was the Party leadership, rather than royalty or aristocracy, that would contribute a sense of permanence to the regime.

A second broad tendency, aimed towards everyday public consumption among the middle classes, took the form of a people's design (*Volk*), expressed in simple, clear forms, in ways compatible with earlier Design Reform ideals. Their characteristics included good craftsmanship and 'honesty' of construction, with materials chosen that had national associations with Germany, such as oak for furniture, stoneware for ceramics, and regional textile traditions; all were by implication now Aryan qualities. Although standardized, the designs consciously avoided the modernity of the Weimar years, and wherever possible made reference to the rural rather than the urban. The pages of the magazine *Innendekoration* promoted these designs, for example, often arranged as ensembles. Even if they would prove unaffordable to many, and it would be more usual to purchase a single item of furniture, a typical arrangement

Designing Modern Germany

was the full dining-room suite. As a setting for this combination of table, hardback chairs and buffet, the last the most important item of furniture, the rooms tended to be dressed with light curtains to stress fresh air, a woven rug and a vase of flowers or houseplants. In the absence of any specific reference to political iconography or direct Party symbolism, such interiors might have been also found in similar contemporary design displays in Britain or Scandinavia, aimed towards a modest, and possibly conservative, taste.

The third major category of interior to receive attention in the design and architectural press showed furniture produced in mass form for the new collective building types introduced by the National Socialists, such as barracks, youth hostels, village and town meeting halls, and other large public buildings built to hold Party events and ceremonies. Important to these was the sense that, although on a large scale and often industrial in scope, their associative values would evoke a reassuring feeling of *Heimat*. This could be realized through murals and inscriptions on the exterior of buildings, or in the detailing, however anachronistic in scale, of vernacular references such as half-timbering. In terms of equipping these spaces with appropriate furniture and fittings, the message was similar: vernacular models for chairs and small touches in minor decorative elements were sometimes all that was needed to take the interior away from appearing too rationally driven. Since the interiors were composite designs, it was also possible to include lines that appeared to come from the Weimar period. A

'The Lower-Saxon Room' designed by Ludwig Reiniking of Hildesheim, displayed at the Internationale Handwerksausstellung in Berlin in 1938. (Reproduced in *Innendekoration*, October 1938.)

»NIEDERSACHSEN-RAUM« DEUTSCHE SCHAU DER INTERNATIONALEN HANDWERKS-AUSSTELLUNG case in point was the '1382' ceramic service by Hermann Gretsch, a plain white set that fulfilled the criteria of a Modernist design originally produced in 1931, but which continued to be featured throughout the Third Reich and promoted through official channels as a good design choice.[43]

Not all members of the German population could afford to act as private consumers of interior design. Beyond the experience of these privileged spaces, nevertheless, the home was targeted by the National Socialists as a place where practices in everyday life could instil Party virtues. A geographical sense of place, as the specific domestic environment and village, town or city, was extended in the concept of *Heimat* to associate

A *völkisch* approach was taken to the design of the interiors of restaurants and other public spaces where vernacular furniture types, painted wall decorations and references to regional customs were often included. *Innendekoration*, March 1941.

Designing Modern Germany

home with an ideological and spiritual space. Official Nazi rhetoric linked home and family life directly to the community, and through these beyond to the state and nation. One indication of this was the intervention of the Party into well-established religious activities. As one concerned National Socialist wrote in 1939, in an article 'One Recognizes a National Socialist by his Home!':

> In these things, too, National Socialism wants to reach the entire people, and lead it to what is consistent with its deepest nature. Family festivals, too, are not what they should be, which leaves a gap and dissatisfaction. We are not quite sure what to do, and cannot figure it out just by thinking about it; we lack the proper customs.[44]

One of the author's examples was the wedding festival, which he was concerned to inscribe with National Socialist rather than religious meaning. He continued by describing the role of the arrangement of apparently simple everyday objects and their ritual place within a secular ceremony. He continued:

> A wedding is the next important life festival. Two people join their lives, surrounded by their loved ones and friends. The room is appropriately decorated. A candlestick, the light of life that they will preserve and pass on. A family cabinet for documents, jewelry, valuable clothing, a family candelabra, with space above for the name and candles for each of the children, with the man and wife below, with their ancestors to either side.

And, he concluded, 'Little things are often decisive; their simplicity has something compelling about it.'[45]

The emphasis on the family as the foundation of the state put a particularly strong demand on the role of women, who, according to National Socialist ideology, were responsible for running the household in ways that served national interests and upheld German values. The housewife was also the key to the future in her role as mother, nurturing future children of the state. In this respect, the National Socialists needed to confront the social changes that had taken place during the Weimar period, specifically the liberal values associated with the 'New Woman', who at work and in her leisure time, and especially her sexual redefinition, presented many challenges. The National Socialists therefore needed to refashion women to meet their own ideals.

As could be expected from the other manifestations of state involvement in design under the Third Reich so far discussed, a strong message was also conveyed through official photography, propaganda posters, exhibitions, film and educational textbooks about the ideal human types of men, women and children that National Socialism favoured. These ideals, in turn, would influence the discourses surrounding fashion design and dress.[46] The most straightforward and prolific propagandistic image of the National Socialist woman was as mother and housewife. She was blonde-haired, blue-eyed, 'natural' in appearance, physically active, healthy and unselfconsciously happy in demeanour. When compared with the urban archetype of the modern woman of Weimar Germany, such as Louise Brookes in the film *Die Büchse der Pandora* (Pandora's Box, 1928), again the policy seems to be one of reaction. With her shining dark hair in typical geometric bob, attracted to the glamour and fashionability of urban distraction, the New Woman raised complications in gender stereotyping. She was complex to decode, as the preoccupation with androgyny in women's magazines and popular weeklies, often illustrated through hostile caricature, revealed.[47] At a simple level, National

Nazi ideals in fashion were often presented through photojournalism as well as official fashion magazines. In this case, traditional dress was combined with motoring, a symptom of modernity.

Socialism offered a corrective to the perceived corrupted values of Weimar, and the wider policies of encouraging women to be housewives and raise families supported this. For instance, stemming from the last years of the Wilhelmine era, the essentially conservative vision of woman's role as being responsible for the physical and spiritual well-being of the family was encapsulated in the popular phrase 'Kinder, Küche, Kirche' (literally, 'Children, Kitchen, Church'). This was adapted by the National Socialist Women's Organization, when it replaced the values of official religions by 'spiritual' concerns in the interest of the Party.[48]

For the ordinary, non-persecuted German woman, dress was also intended to be a further visible sign of being a member of the German national community (*Volksgemeinschaft*). As seen in the propaganda images as well as the popular press, elements included the wearing of the

Kostüme und Mäntel

S 1609. Aus schwarzer Kunstseide (Sulgacoate), einem stark glänzenden Kostümmaterial, besteht das neuzeitliche **Jackenkleid**. Den Zweibahnenrock ergänzt ein unten zwischengefügter Teil, der oben blendenartig aufgesteppt ist. Neuartige Keulenärmel. Weißes Glasbatistjabot von modischer Neuheit. Stoff (Gr. II) 4,15 m 94 cm breit. Schnitt auf dem Bogen. Gr. Schnitt in den Größen II, III und IV erh.	M 2469. Der sportliche **Frühjahrsmantel** aus beigefarbenem Fischgrätenstoff zeigt eine modisch betonte Schulterpartie, da sich die Rückenpasse bis auf die Oberärmel erstreckt. Die Anbringung der Taschen in hüfthohen Längseinschnitten in diesjährig. Auch der auf acht Knöpfe gestellte Schluß, Ledergürtel. Stoff (Gr. I) 3,35 m 140 cm breit. Schnitt siehe Bogen. Großer Schnitt Größe I, II, III erh.	M 2477. Der hübsche **Nachmittagsmantel** kraußicher Art ist aus schwarzem Wollgeorgette gefertigt. Er weist eine besondere Neuheit der Frühjahrsmode auf: die bauschigen Ärmel mit Soutachebesatz, von einem Bündchen am Handgelenk zusammengefaßt. Ein Hermelinfellchen garniert den Schulterkragen. Stoff (Größe III) 3,50 m 130 cm br. Schnitt auf d. Bg. Großer Schnitt in Gr. I, II, III erh.	S 1616. Sehr modisch in Form und Material ist dieses frühlingsmäßige **Jackenkleid**. Man hat dazu einen fischgrünen Wollfresko verarbeitet, den feine weiße Härchen bedecken. Die Vielteiligkeit des Jäckchens und die stark taillierten Vorderteile bewirken den guten Sitz der Einknopfjacke. Stoff (Gr. I) 2,60 m 140 cm breit. Schnitt auf dem Bogen. Großer Schnitt in den Größen I, II und III erhältl.

Zu allen Modellen gibt es unter den hier angegebenen Nummern Ullstein-Schnittmuster in Kaufhäusern und Modewarengeschäften fast aller Städte. Ferner zu allen Modellen auch Schnitte auf dem Doppel-Bogen, der auf Wunsch beiliegt.
Bestellschein für Ullstein-Schnittmuster und Handarbeitsmuster am Schluß des Heftes

495

Dirndl, a waistcoated dress with a full skirt, and a white blouse, both decorated with regional folk motifs. Hair was worn plaited by the young, or loose and seemingly naturally wavy by older women. No apparent make-up was worn. The references in such dress were to rural or homely occupations, and they studiously avoided urban sophistication or independent, reflective activities. Crucially, this essentially conservative vision of National Socialist womanhood had to be carefully constructed to avoid becoming too similar to the contemporary Soviet heroicized vision of woman as labourer.

In summary, therefore, at the level of propaganda, the Aryanization of women was achievable and given clear visual signs. Historian Irene Guenther, however, has questioned the extent to which this stereotype was actually adhered to by women in 1930s Germany.[49] As in other areas of the consumption of goods, the National Socialists needed to maintain production and markets for fashion design to sustain its textile industries. German women were also aware of international changes in style and fashion through daily reference to newspapers, films, magazines and advertising. Even if not receiving approbation from the Party and risking charges of inappropriate taste, ample evidence suggests that a buoyant fashion system prevailed throughout the Third Reich that paralleled other countries with developed economies, most obviously France and the USA.

At least three levels of fashion consumption can be identified to have survived throughout the Third Reich. The first was the official, propagandistic model mentioned above. Secondly, for those belonging to high society, German couture houses continued to produce exclusive lines, based on Paris fashions. The wives of the Party elite, for example, enjoyed the cycle of the constantly new, and defined themselves through a fashion system that compared them with other European society figures. They were profiled for their participation in events of the season in the popular illustrated press. Then, for women of more modest means, the department stores continued to supply dresses, skirts, blouses, coats, suits and accessories that kept up with fashion internationally. Women's magazines such as *Die Dame* and *Das Blatt für die Frau* continued to provide articles on how to source new items from the stores, and also, how, for those with more slender means, the housewife could emulate goods for sale through home dress-making, embroidery and hand-knitting. Finally, in the sphere of manufacture rather than of consumption, an overlooked activity was the work of Jewish prisoner seamstresses. As recent work has shown, the couture garments that appeared on the fashion catwalks of the Third Reich were available as a result of the labour of those too often hidden from history.[50]

'German' Design in Migration

The closure of the Bauhaus in Berlin on 20 July 1933 has been understood as a sign of the broader attitude of the National Socialists towards experimental culture. The school's reputation for leading its students towards industrial design, its aim to unite 'art and technology', which signalled a rejection of craft values, and the internationalism of its staff and students were all clearly antithetical to National Socialist policies. In easier times, the school had established good relations largely with local governments of a social democratic kind. While the Bauhaus was dismissed as another instance of 'cultural bolshevism', apart from the period under Hannes Meyer's directorship, charges of extreme direct political engagement could not be proven.

The ambiguities of the broader political situation were echoed at the school. Some Bauhaus staff sought to compromise with the new government, suggesting professional openings for modern designers, among them Walter Gropius, Herbert Bayer and Mies van der Rohe. Yet records also show 24 arrests or internments of Bauhaus staff and students in the early years of the regime, and that at least eight Bauhaus people were murdered in concentration camps.[51]

The more significant story for the reputation and lasting impact of the Bauhaus, and by implication the promotion of 'German' design values to a wider world, was the transfer of many of its staff to new countries and situations. While members of the older generation such as Paul Klee and Wassily Kandinsky migrated within Europe, it was Gropius, Anni and Josef Albers, Bayer, Breuer, Mies and Moholy-Nagy who at different stages turned to the United States as their final destination. Significantly, they did not return to re-establish themselves in Germany after 1945.

Peter Hahn has pointed out that among the most prominent former Bauhaus members, it is most fitting to see their destinations as a result of professional negotiation towards new employment and career enhancement as 'exponents and the ambassadors of a cultural movement: Modernism', rather than as more vulnerable émigrés.[52] For instance, Walter Gropius initially left Germany for England in 1934, seeking permission to do so from the Reichskulturkammer. After unsuccessful attempts to establish himself in the British architectural establishment, with only a few buildings realized through collaboration with other architects, Gropius took up a professorship in architecture at Harvard University in 1937. Marcel Breuer also made moves to develop his furniture design and career as an architect in partnership with F.R.S. Yorke in England, before following Gropius to the Harvard School of Architecture in 1937. Josef Albers continued his investigation into colour theory and Anni Albers her textile design and painting, both as professors at the Black Mountain College in North Carolina between 1933 and 1949. In 1938, following a period of exhibition and graphic design in Berlin, Bayer used the opportunity of the *Bauhaus, 1919–28* exhibition at the Museum of Modern Art in New York to take up residency in the United States before establishing himself, first as consultant art director in New York, then in Aspen, Colorado.

The MOMA exhibition was extremely important for the reputation of the school. The idea was developed in 1937, through discussion between John McAndrew, curator at the museum, and Ise and Walter Gropius, Marcel Breuer and Moholy-Nagy. The plan was for Herbert Bayer, still in Germany, to assemble the work and help in its realization both as an exhibition and a catalogue. The chosen framing dates for the exhibition of 1919 to 1928 could be explained as marking the period when the figures involved in its curation were most active. It would therefore focus on two contrasting stages of the school's history, the emphasis on craft and experiment at Weimar in the years 1919–25 and the turn towards industrial-design prototypes and realized architectural projects at Dessau between 1925 and 1928. In this way, neither the political difficulty of Hannes Meyer's move towards Communist housing solutions nor the subsequent closure of the school by the Nazis were discussed in detail.[53]

Most of the career destinations of the established Bauhaus staff indicate a move into established art or architectural educational contexts. It was only Moholy-Nagy who, having attempted to establish himself first in Amsterdam in 1934, then in London, before travelling to the United States in 1937, ventured to continue the original Bauhaus experiment of interdis-

An impromptu meeting held at the Chicago Institute of Design on 14 August 1945, V-J Day, between Moholy-Nagy and Walter Gropius (first and second rear right) and students, to discuss the implications of the end of the Second World War.

Designing Modern Germany

ciplinary design education. The New Bauhaus in Chicago that the Hungarian designer led, sponsored by the Association of Art and Industries, existed for only one year, between 1937 and 1938.[54] Through lack of wider support, the institution closed, but in 1939 Moholy-Nagy founded the Chicago School of Design, which, with a change in name to the Institute of Design in 1944, two years before his death, became a central force in preparing students for the future world of communication and industrial design.

dwb

neues wohnen

werkbundausstellung

KÖLN 1949 vom 14. Mai
bis 3. JULI

messehallen KÖLN DEUTZ

KÖLN. VERLAGSDRUCKEREI G-M-B-H-KÖLN KÖW 2/P O 2/350 1860U8000 449-KI-8

4

Reconstruction and the Tale of Two Germanys, 1945–75

Reconstruction does not only mean to build anew again, but rather the design of a new form and will for life.

Wera Meyer-Waldeck and Hans Schwippert[1]

As a defeated country in August 1945, at the end of the Second World War, Germany faced the enormous task of reconstruction. The term *Stunde Null* or 'zero hour' has been used to characterize the point that the country had reached by this stage.[2] With 10 per cent of the nation's population killed and much of the infrastructure of towns and cities destroyed, a period of mass exodus and migration followed, while between 1945 and 1948 the priority was to retrieve what could be found among the ruins. The image of the *Trümmerfrauen* (rubble women) standing in line passing buckets of rubble and remnants of goods across Europe's cities survives as one of the most evocative from this period. Indeed, some of the first examples of post-war handwork from this time took the form of startling but essential adaptations of military goods for domestic use. These included handmade textile goods to be worn, adapted from military camouflage, and metal kitchenware improvised from soldiers' helmets. All were made according to what might be called an improvisatory principle that would inform a significant proportion of the population of post-war societies in their attitude towards material possessions in Germany and many other European countries for the years before and even after economic revival.

At a political level, if the end of the war implied starting again, as the above quote suggests, reconstruction was by no means straightforward or unproblematic. It immediately raised questions and choices that in the aftermath of such devastation were on occasion unbearable. In such a situation, design could not be at the top of the agenda. Instead, priority was given to restoring existing industries and resuming production by whatever means. The dilemma of exactly how to re-start life was the subject of the

Jupp (Joseph Caspar) Ernst, poster for the 'Neues Wohnen' exhibition, organized by the German Werkbund in Cologne in 1949.

German philosopher Theodor Adorno's *Minima Moralia: Reflections from Damaged Life*, a set of essays written in 1944 and 1945. In these Adorno was pessimistic about the possibilities of re-establishing house and home:

> The house is past. The bombing of European cities, as well as the labour and concentration camps, merely proceed as executors, with what immanent development of technology had long decided was to be the fate of houses.

And he continued by reflecting on the range of artistic choices available and the implications for his own situation:

> The best mode of conduct, in face of all this, still seems an uncommitted, suspended one: to lead a private life, as far as the social order and one's own needs will tolerate nothing else, but not to attach weight to it as something still socially substantial and individually appropriate. 'It is even part of my good fortune not to be a house-owner', Nietzsche already wrote in the *Gay Science*. Today we should have to add: it is part of morality not to be at home in one's home.[3]

We will return to Adorno's dilemma. Significantly, at the level of Realpolitik, in the London Agreements of 12 September and 14 November 1944, it was decided to divide Germany into three zones with occupying armed forces of the USA, Britain and the Soviet Union. This agreement was extended at the Yalta conference to include France.[4] Ostensibly to prevent

Designing Modern Germany

the re-Nazification of Germany, the country was subdivided into occupied zones and sectors with a military presence of the Allied forces, which oversaw political, economic and administrative affairs. Accordingly, the British took control of the north and the north-west, France the central parts, and the USA the south. Crucially, for what was to follow, the Soviet Union held responsibility for the north-east and eastern zones, which incorporated Berlin. As the capital city, Berlin was therefore in an extremely sensitive location, and the Allies subdivided it by sector, in the hope of guaranteeing stability in ways that mirrored the larger division of the country as a whole. As became all the more significant once relations between the Soviet Union and the Western Allies turned from suspicion to hostility through the period of the Cold War, under these circumstances the western sectors of Berlin became a virtual island, surrounded by the Soviet sector.

From June 1948 to May 1949, the sense of isolation and tension in Berlin came to a head when Soviet forces prevented goods coming into the western part of the city. This blockade action in turn prompted the Berlin Airlift, as Allied aircraft were used to drop supplies into the city. Symbolically, this marked the breakdown of cooperation between the sectors. A further momentous stage of the city's history was the later building of the Berlin Wall, in September 1961, understood by the GDR authorities to be the anti-fascist protection wall, *anti-faschistische Schutzwall*, and the division of the entire East German sector from its immediate neighbours.[5] A subject of contentious debate ever since, the wall was thought necessary, on the one hand to curb the migration from the eastern sector of members of the skilled and educated labour force, on the other to remedy the extreme disparity between the two currency systems. Through its erection, Berlin became the city above all others that encapsulated the condition of the Cold War, a war of ideologies, between the two extreme world powers of the Soviet Union and the USA. At a cultural level, once the immediate demands of survival and restitution had been addressed, the issue of how the country would reconstruct arose, and with it, the extent to which the process could involve invoking well-tested examples from the past, and how 'the new' would be embraced. Where would the balance lie between tradition and modernity? From the point of view of designers, the conditions of the political economy of Germany would confront them on a daily basis and present fundamental challenges about the role of design and material culture in everyday life and the ideological and social implications of their activity.

In relation to design, both Germanys, East and West, witnessed a re-engagement with the intellectual debates from the Weimar years among prominent figures from design education and designers about the appropriateness of Modernism as a way forward for reconstruction. In addition, at a broader cultural and political level, central to post-war modernity was the question of the role of consumption of material goods for a reconstructed society. At its simplest, the western zones were aligned to US patterns of a continuing and increasing consumer society, while the East negotiated a more complex position, with a tension between the Soviet-style command economy and expectations from sectors of the population to be rewarded in consumer goods, just as in the West. At a more fundamental level, issues of freedom of movement and speech in the GDR were to become tested to the extreme during the period.

Design Developments in the Federal Republic

As in other Western democracies, in West Germany the first Christian Democratic Union government under Konrad Adenauer, chancellor from 1949 to 1963, saw its task as stabilizing the country through the adoption of a consumer society, modelled in many respects on the USA. To guarantee this, the American government oversaw the funding of a significant economic aid programme in Europe, under the Marshall Plan, named after Secretary of State George Marshall and introduced on 12 July 1947. Along with economic investment, this programme incorporated cultural projects, intended to stabilize the political situation and further democracy in the name of de-Nazification.[6]

For instance, by 1952, 1.5 billion US dollars had been invested in the industrial infrastructure of West Germany. As well as the area of manufacture, broader cultural initiatives were also introduced, such as exhibitions promoting the American way of life, including its design and architecture. The Fulbright Scholarship and other academic exchanges were focused on the next generations of young scholars who had not directly experienced the traumas of Nazism and world war, their education recognized as another conduit for the process of Americanization, under the guise of democracy. The first institution, founded in 1948, principally through

Women employees assembling ballpoint pens at the factory of Günther-Wagner Pelikan-Werke in Hanover, c. 1960.

Designing Modern Germany

American money, was the Freie Universität (Free University) in Berlin. Established in the western sector of the city, it was planned to offer an alternative to the Humboldt, Berlin's historic university on Unter den Linden, where the curriculum became oriented towards Marxist-Leninism.[7] Significantly for the future of German design, in Ulm in Baden-Württemberg plans for a new form of high school, the second major project to be assisted by substantial US support, were developed by Inge Scholl. The school eventually opened in 1953 as the Hochschule für Gestaltung, as will be discussed below.

Through such investment, West German reconstruction was accelerated and, when compared with its neighbours, its rewards were so noticeable that it was coined an 'economic miracle' (*Wirtschaftswunder*) in the press and subsequent historical commentary. In the realm of household goods, for example, the Federal Republic produced more refrigerators and washing machines than France and Italy together, four times the number of vacuum cleaners and nine times the number of cookers.[8] Soon it was realized at what expense these material goods had been won. By 1955 plans for rearmament in support of the NATO (North Atlantic Treaty Organization) alliance were in place, raising protests and the beginnings of a peace movement that would feed into popular anti-Establishment tendencies, as well as terrorism in the next decades of the Federal Republic.

Despite Adorno's cultural pessimism, a focus on domestic life and home-making could be seen as an inevitable consequence of having to start again, to equip afresh. The message was that the new democratic Germany would not only house its people, but it would also provide shopping precincts, churches, art centres, theatres and opera houses.[9] While car ownership was encouraged, public services played an important part in this welfare society; transport systems, schools, hospitals, parks and recreation facilities were all integrated into this new vision of a civil society. In this sense, home was not just a domestic domain but also a newly constituted physical and spiritual setting for life.

Brigitte Hausmann has commented specifically on the situation of design for the home at this time in West Germany. The impulse to improve or reform taste, which in some respects represented a revival of the pre-war Werkbund model, discussed in chapter One, was understandable in the face of the challenge to find forms of continuity, first in domestic situations rather than in public life. She wrote:

> In the 1950s, the greatest demand came from the private sector. The above-average expenditures for home furnishings in the first half of

the decade are explainable mainly as the result of the war; the later 1950s saw an increased interest in acquiring a new generation of technology. In the area of dwelling and home furnishings, after the currency reform of 1948 and the creation of the Federal Republic of Germany in 1949, a series of 'sample' exhibitions ('Muster' Ausstellungen) were presented, some of them organized in the United States and often intended to mould public taste.[10]

As the above quotation suggests, the West German government's involvement in design took the form of the promotion of design ideals through exhibitions as a case of cultural education and persuasion. Parallel initiatives in the formation of various design councils were advanced, for instance, in Britain, the Netherlands and the Scandinavian countries, where similar approved design selections were made. Among the first of the West German exhibitions were *Neues Wohnen* (New Living/Dwelling) of 1948, organized by the Cologne division of the newly reconstituted Werkbund; *Wie Wohnen?* (How to Dwell/Live) of 1949, which was held at the Landesgewerbemuseum in Stuttgart; and the Swiss travelling exhibition *Gute Form* (Good Design), organized by Max Bill and installed in the town of Ulm in 1949.

As their names suggested, these exhibitions offered prescriptive visions of design ideals. Their emphasis lay in the promotion of domestic design, primarily focused on the small family unit and private life. The design solutions suited urban living since an increasing proportion of Germans now lived in towns and cities. They were strongly influenced by developments in Scandinavia, Switzerland and the United States since 1933, when it had become difficult to practise as a modern designer in Germany. Consequently, in the design selections, emphasis was given to planned rooms, along with fitted furniture. While abstraction was still favoured as the organizing principle for objects in space, it was less severe than in the 1920s. The impact of organic and biomorphic abstraction, rather than pure geometry, could be noticed, lending the designs an air of real or imagined luxury.

These events were followed in the early 1950s by the formation or revival of important public bodies for the encouragement of debate about design. In 1951 the Rat für Formgebung (Council for Design) was established by the Bundestag as the organization responsible for awarding the annual prize and aimed to promote examples of good West German industrial form worldwide.[11] In the following year, the revived German Werkbund launched its new monthly publication *Werk und Zeit* (Work and Time), which promoted design in industry and resumed its advisory role in encouraging relations between the design profession, retailers, industrialists and the public.[12] Also in 1952, the Darmstadt Institut für neue Technische Form was founded. Linked to the nearby Frankfurt Trade Fair (*Messe*), this stressed links between design and technology. Parallel design institutions were reformed in many West German cities. To signal the significance of design as a cultural phenomenon, architect and designer Hans Schwippert, himself a prominent Modernist, was invited to give the third lecture in the series of Darmstädter Gespräche on 'Mensch und Technik' (People and Technology).

Indeed, one of the most significant ways in which the Federal Government aligned itself to Modernism was in the commission of the new

The Federal Republic government buildings in Bonn were designed by architect Hans Schwippert and interior designer Wera Meyer-Waldeck in 1948. The main chamber showed the careful balance between contemporary and traditional references in its political symbolism and use of materials. *Architektur und Wohnform*, 1950.

parliament buildings in Bonn, which opened in September 1949, replacing the Reichstag, which had become impossible to sustain in divided Berlin. The scheme was led by Hans Schwippert as architect and Wera Meyer-Waldeck as interior designer, authors of the opening quotation of this chapter. Their commentary on its interiors stressed how the hall connected to the Rhineland landscape through a 360-square-metre glass wall, in greens and golds, the surfaces intended to make reference to the sun and landscape. Four hundred seats in green leather were provided for press and audiences.[13] The Plenarsaal or main chamber held a stage with black leather seats for the Chancellor and other members of the cabinet, while green leather was chosen for the representatives. The twelve coats of arms of the participating Länder were printed in gold on a curtain. In contrast with the official rooms, in the Bundestag restaurant Thonet tubular-steel canti-levered chairs and upholstered oak seats were well crafted but unostentatious, distinctly non-elite yet modern in character. The designs were some of the first manifestations of themes that would recur in the

Designing Modern Germany

years of reconstruction: a concern for transparency, flow between the interior and exterior of the building, a quiet restraint and understatement of design, and wariness of too overt messages, with high-quality materials in the finishings and discreet references to German regionalism in their choices. In a profile of the new buildings in the periodical *Architektur und Wohnform*, the architect Schwippert commented: 'Politics is a dark affair, we see to it that we bring in some light.'[14]

International Modern

At the high end of designer-led furniture, another form of Modernist initiative arrived with the import of licensed designs in the commercial sector. Most famously, this was apparent in the success of the company Knoll Associates. Hans Knoll, son of a Swabian furniture manufacturer, had emigrated to the United States in 1937. There he met and married Florence Schust, a trained designer whose experiences included a brief period at Cranbrook Academy of Design and work in the architectural offices of Walter Gropius and Marcel Breuer in Cambridge, Massachusetts. Knoll Associates established its initial market for architect-designed furniture from its New York offices, winning, among other prominent commissions, the design of the offices of the Rockefeller brothers.[15]

During the war years, through personal association, the Knolls were aware of the design ideals of the Weimar Republic and provided continuity across political difficulty and geographical distance by connecting with the next generations of American designers. Among these were Harry Bertoia, Charles and Ray Eames, Isamu Noguchi and Eero Saarinen. A further indication of their Modernist credentials came in their graphic design and advertising in the US, which was overseen by Herbert Matter, a Swiss designer by origin who was associated with experimental photography and by then was teaching at Yale.[16]

The Knoll showroom constantly attracted the European design press, and their advertisements were strategically placed in high-quality magazines in Europe and the USA. Re-establishing their European connections, in 1951 the Knolls founded the 'daughter' company Knoll International GmbH in Stuttgart. The characteristic Knoll ensemble was an arrangement of furnishings for office contracts as well as domestic situations, and the formula would be repeated and emulated in more popular and reasonably priced variations by other manufacturers. Constituent parts included a low couch or sofa, occasional armchairs introduced for sculptural effect in contrasting colours, sideboards with strongly horizontal lines, and

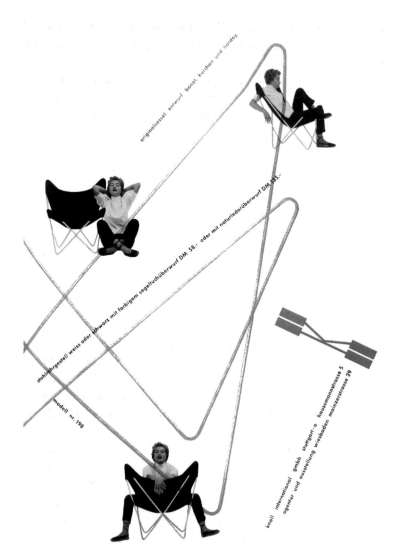

Hans Conrad's advertisement for the Knoll furniture company revealed an awareness of the latest marketing techniques. *Architektur und Wohnform*, 1955.

feature lighting either in pendant or standard form. In contrast with the stark geometry of Weimar Modernist interiors, and following the significant exhibition *Organic Design in Home Furnishings* at the Museum of Modern Art, New York, in 1942, mid-twentieth-century American modern design combined a tendency towards abstraction with biomorphic shapes on surface pattern or smaller items of furniture, ceramics and glass. Strong areas of plain, dark tones were combined with bright, lively colours; the overall effect was to create an informal, sophisticated lifestyle,

Designing Modern Germany

rather than a stringent design philosophy. At this level, an internationally sophisticated design language travelled in the reverse direction, to its original source in Europe.[17]

One indication that the values promoted by such furniture companies and its related advertising had infiltrated middle-class society can be seen in a satirical short story by Heinz Huber, 'The New Apartment', published in 1958. It opened:

> The other evening we were invited round to the Messemers. Marx [sic] Messemer is a colleague of mine at the works, and a most gratifying friendship has grown up in course of time between our two families . . .[18]

The crux of Huber's story was a comedy of manners in which interior decoration played a significant part.

> What I admire above all is the reliability of his judgment, his taste, his modernity. With him everything is exactly right, while with me there's always something just short of perfection. In our home the new tea service always has two cups broken and the tea table is still one of the old kidney-shaped kind. Somehow we just don't manage to replace it with a more modern piece, though we know perfectly well what we want – long and narrow, in reddish-brown wood. It would go so well with our sand-colored chair covers . . .
> The Messemers on the other hand – as we walked in at their door, from our feet to the horizon of the far-distant baseboard there stretched a fine pile surface in graphite gray. At the vanishing point of the perspective lines, in front of a bare wall, a strange looking branch projected from a large glass vase, standing on the ground. Echoes of surrealism, I thought to myself, early De Chirico . . .

The author offered a wry commentary on the concern for tasteful 'gute Form' and makes an amusing parody of the prescription prominent in design journalism at the time:

> There was a slight *contretemps* as we were all arranging ourselves up at the sitting end. Fräulein Kliesing lowered herself into the Messemers' new armchair but immediately shot up again as if she had sat on a pin; her salmon-pink dress, she said, clashed horribly with the raspberry pink of the chair cover, and she was right, too. What made it worse

was that this 'shocking pink' of the cover was chosen with great finesse to contrast with the equally shocking emerald green of the wallpaper behind it. I should never have dared anything like that, but Messemer does dare and, you see, he brings it off.

At one end of the design spectrum, therefore, a fully resolved interior aesthetic was a possibility or aspiration for private middle-class life, stemming partly from across the Atlantic.

Brussels Exposition, 1958

> And if I knew that the world would end tomorrow, today I would plant an apple tree.
>
> Quotation from Martin Luther displayed at the entrance to the
> German pavilion at the Brussels exposition, 1958

The most important international exhibition since the war was held in the Belgian capital in 1958. Following years of rationing and hardship, the recent growth in prosperity led to the Brussels exhibition becoming associated with the economic miracle that was being felt across Western Europe as a whole by this time. Major international companies, manufacturers of cars, consumer goods and the general accoutrements of a consumer society, used it as an opportunity to advertise, display and sell their goods. The exhibition symbol of the Atomium reflected the commonplace and optimistic assumption that science and commerce could work together to the benefits of progress. The West German contribution to Brussels had particular significance for the reputation of the Federal Republic. The last time Germany had contributed to an international exposition was in 1937, in Paris, when the German and Soviet pavilions faced each other, representing a direct ideological expression of their respective political regimes, which in its aggressive monumentality was intended to be unambiguous. In contrast, Brussels gave West Germany an opportunity to correct any lingering doubts about the country's transformation into a living democracy. In addition, it was important for many of those in the organizing committee that the pavilion represented more than a sum of its industrial achievements; moreover, the pavilion was considered to be the chance to display modern design at its best. In this respect, its approach was strongly cultural, and commercial interests, a feature of much of the Brussels exhibition elsewhere, were discretely interpreted and even disguised in the German instance.

Designing Modern Germany

Egon Eiermann and Sepp Ruf, entrance to the German Pavilion at the 1958 Brussels exposition with an inscription from the writings of Martin Luther.

Hans Schwippert, member of the exhibition committee, commented on its purpose with the extended metaphor of 'home':

> The concept of the exhibition 'Living and Working in Germany' avoids the direct, assertive, selective or exclusive emphasis on particular, great German achievements. In which way these may exist, and in whichever areas they might lie, they are known and renowned worldwide. However, if one illustrates that Germans are not only efficient, but are right now in the process of furnishing their life and work in a human way, of designing their country's 'house' homely and beautiful, that they are not only exceeding in their effort, but through this effort are on the verge of making their own home and work worth living – then this

effort can be seen indirectly within a new context: in its orientation towards a practical side of human life, exemplified by one's own existence. To show how our progress, amongst us Germans at home, points at man would be our special contribution to 'le progrès et l'homme'.[19]

As mentioned, the overarching theme of the exhibition, which all participating countries were expected to address, was 'Progress and Man'. The German organizing committee (Ständige Vertreter des Generalkommissars der BRD), led by Dr G. B. von Hartmann, a senior representative of the government, interpreted this as 'Life and Work in Germany' (Leben und Arbeiten in Deutschland). In his introduction, Theodor Heuss, President of the Federal Republic, referred to earlier plans to hold *Die Neue Zeit* (The New Age), which had been cancelled in 1932 because of the economic crisis and changed political circumstances. He warned that it was no longer possible to trust the naive belief in the future that had been strongly adhered to in the Weimar period. He also stressed that West Germany's contribution was not a commercial undertaking, but rather a 'Bilanz der Epoche', a balance sheet of the time.[20]

Ernst Johann, design journalist, furthermore commented in the *Werk und Zeit* review of the exposition:

> Initially, the aim was to find a human architecture for man, the main focus of their exhibition: constructions with correct measurements, which at the same time set a benchmark; rooms in which man finds and doesn't lose himself; proportions in which he feels comfortable, instead of dimensions which frighten him. Hereby they should be made a rule for German architecture, not an exception.[21]

The exhibition was arranged as a series of eight themed pavilions in elegant black steel and glass by its chief architect, Egon Eiermann, who was recognized as one of West Germany's leading furniture designers. By day, the exhibition largely functioned with natural light, and visitors could experience the buildings' transparency and garden setting. By night, the exhibits appeared as silhouettes. The wish to appear 'light, friendly and free' was also expressed in the catalogue. Entering along a raised footbridge, the visitor encountered the pavilions, which covered agriculture, craftwork (*Handwerk*), industrial goods, towns and dwellings, consumer goods, social projects and spare time, health and security, and, finally, education and instruction. There was also a library with 2,200 books, a lecture theatre, a wine bar and a restaurant.

Designing Modern Germany

Egon Eiermann's arrangement of the Korbsessel E10 in the German pavilion at Brussels 1958, originally designed in 1949, was strikingly silhouetted at night.

Reference to recent German history, and specifically the Hitler period, was made at the entrance to the pavilion dealing with education and upbringing:

'The heartbeat of the nation passes through a divided country.' In pavilion 8, these words and the German borders of 1937 are burnt into a big wooden plate; next to it, a mighty, half-burnt beam from an old, destroyed farmer's house looms. Thus, visitors from all over the world are insistently shown Germany's division and the indestructible bonds amongst its people.[22]

The three pavilions with direct relevance to an understanding of how design was treated were respectively devoted to industrial work, craftwork, and towns and dwellings. In the last, under the title 'Living and the Home', the displays included a model apartment, intended as social housing for a six-person family. All the furniture and fittings conformed to Modernist ideals, with emphasis on clean, straight lines, incorporating built-in cupboards and storage; modern light features; and undecorated stacking ceramics and glassware, arranged according to functionalist principles of order and system. Formal stress was on horizontal planes. The children's bedroom followed similar principles, with an emphasis on constructive play. Where colour and pattern featured, these were in the form of textiles, checked or striped hangings for curtains, cut flowers or an occasional tasteful ceramic or metalwork ornament. The clear message was that the Federal Republic could provide a measured, healthy environment for the

education and well-being of its future populations and in this modern design had a definite role.

Responses from some of the popular and more conservative German press, however, took issue with the reserved nature of the displays and the relative 'coolness' of their execution. The reviewer in the *Frankfurter Nachausgabe*, for example, wrote: 'If only one had called to mind our countries and their regional arts (*Heimatkunst*) and, confound it, for all I care, had bound a wreath for German beer and sauerkraut. That would have been better and more appropriate.'[23] The Berlin financial paper *Berliner Wirtschaftsblatt* complained: 'Damned be whoever concocted these German cabinets of rarities', and the popular magazine *Quick* wrote: 'Nothing here seems ostentatious, nothing is "economically miraculous". Germany is not pounding the kettledrum [painting the town red], but playing the violin in Brussels.'[24]

International press responses were considerably more positive. The pavilion was praised for not just displaying industrial achievements but also for offering a wider cultural understanding of society. The building, too, was admired for its plainness, simplicity and clarity. In Britain, *The Times* called the black frame of the pavilions 'a wonder work of elegance and precision' and architectural critic J. M. Richards in *The Listener* wrote:

In addition to the pavilions themselves, the model modern interior exhibited at Brussels 1958 suggested that Germany could be home to Modernism and Modernism in turn could contribute to making an ideal home for West Germans.

Designing Modern Germany

The German pavilion is without doubt the best . . . the German pavilion shows a well-conceived structure, with careful handling of detail
and with unerring taste a 'glass case' – or rather an arrangement of
glass cases which are placed together and penetrate one another very
skilfully – they can surpass the poetics of the circle.[25]

Another prominent British figure, Hugh Casson, wrote in *The Observer* newspaper: 'Behind Great Britain lies West Germany: beautiful as if painted and
precise as a machine part.' And the *Elseviers Weekblad* from The Hague commented: 'The most beautiful section of the entire world exhibition is the
German one. Nothing is made for false effect. The ingenious simplicity of
architectural means and the linked composition of its eight pavilions create
a sense of refinement and tranquillity amidst this clamorous world funfair.'[26]
Finally, Elisabeth Plünnecke of the *Stuttgarter Nachrichten* appreciated the
intentions of the West German committee:

Upon hearing certain garish, critical voices, one cannot help suspect-
ing them of being irritated at the fact that Germany has given such a
muted performance here, that it doesn't want to be special, that one
will find none of the 'German nature, through which the world will
recuperate.' It was criticized that inside, the calm walls with objectively
placed photographs and the plain vitrines with devices and objects are
dull. I have to admit that I enjoyed being, for once, not attacked by the
colourful flickering of innumerable, changing pictures, films, lighting.
Moreover, the fact that one does not step out of the bright sunshine of
the streets into a darkroom, but can instead view everything in natural
daylight, strikes me as pleasant.

And with reference to the quote from Luther, she concluded: 'An apple tree
was planted in Brussels, no African baobab and no orchids. What is there to
be criticized in this?'[27]

Design in the German Democratic Republic

At the end of the Second World War in the eastern sector between October
1945 and April 1946, a political alliance was formed between the KPD
(Communist Party of Germany) under the leadership of Wilhelm Pieck and
the SPD (Socialist Party of Germany) under Otto Grotewohl. This led to the
signing on 22 April 1946 of the agreement to unite the parties, to form the
Sozialistische Einheitspartei Deutschlands (Socialist Unity Party of

Germany). The SED merged Communist and Socialist parties and introduced Soviet-style Socialist Realism in its cultural policies.[28]

The signing of the 1946 agreement also marked the first time that an expression of design under SED was necessary, for immediately the political regime needed to signal in its outward appearance that its new policies would lead to a socialist state. To use the terminology of the regime, under the slogan of becoming a socialist fatherland (*sozialistische Vaterland*), an alternative political model intended to establish 'real existing socialism' (*real existierende Sozialismus*) was developed in contrast to what was termed the capitalist vassal state (*kapitalistische Vasallenstadt*) of the western sector. This sentiment found further expression in the 1950s, when the Federal Republic was accused by its critics, not only in the GDR, for giving way to 'Coca-colonisation'.[29]

The SED was interpreted as the avant-garde of the working classes, striving for a progressive interpretation of Marxist-Leninism. The agenda for the party leader, Wilhelm Pieck, was to instil a different political culture from the one with which the Germans in the eastern sector were familiar, while the task facing architects, designers, artists and all involved in the physical reconstruction of the destroyed towns and cities was to materialize this change in regime through artistic and cultural production. As in the West, design of everyday life could not be an immediate priority in the face of such infrastructural necessity. Nonetheless, design in the form of the creation of a new identity for new state organizations, and the material artefacts of a political culture, took place immediately. In this respect, design *of* the state came before design *for* the state. On 7 October 1949 the German Democratic Republic (Deutsche Demokratische Republik) was founded and Wilhelm Pieck became its first president.

For its overt political culture, the GDR had available several references from the past, most controversially its need to distance itself from the National Socialist system. As we have seen in chapter Three, under Nazism official life had imposed itself on private individuals through consistent display, ritual and the broadcasting media. The contemporary Soviet Union, which was not a fixed reference point but was itself undergoing constant revision and development as it responded to the last years of Stalinism, was the source of political directives to the newly formed state and the GDR's most powerful influence. As Dieter Vorsteher has shown, the immediate and overt manifestation of the political regime came in a familiar form of a parading culture of flag bearers, marching columns, trains of torch-bearers, speaking choirs and the occupation of public space by the state and the Party.[30]

Designing Modern Germany

To achieve this, the role of uniforms became incisive. Their design depended not just on military or functional requirements but also on the political and economic circumstances, which influenced the cut, colour and emblems used. For instance, while the Bundeswehr of the Federal Republic followed US models of uniform, in the GDR the uniforms of the Nationale Volksarmee (NVA, National People's Army) followed Soviet lines, and the uniform of the Freie Deutsche Jugend children's organization (after 1952 called Ernst Thälmann pioneers) was based on the Lenin Pioneers.[31]

Organized around 1 May and other Party days, series of events were planned to coincide with the goals and achievements of the SED production targets; special industry days and anniversaries contributed to a new socialist calendar that replaced the religious and traditional historical landmarks of the year, each intended to instil a new identity among the people. Such messages were not only apparent in the political sphere but shop window displays, for instance, were also arranged to coincide with these major state days.[32] On what may appear to be a more mundane level, paper shopping bags were printed with political messages. In this way, consumption and production became consistently linked in the mind of the consumer through display and marketing strategies. Indeed, all areas of life were open to revision. Banknotes and coins of the Ostmark, the East German currency

The choice of subjects for GDR currency design conveyed a sense of both historical and contemporary priorities and identities. The 50 Ost Mark note, introduced in 1964, carried a portrait of Friedrich Engels and a scene of industrial farming on its reverse.

introduced from 1949, for example, changed appearance through the currency reform. Along with the official emblem of the hammer and sickle, on the reverse of all coins between 1956 and 1990 the portraits of the poets Schiller and Goethe, along with the political figures Engels and Marx, helped the claim that the German Enlightenment tradition was the natural antecedent to humanist socialism.[33]

Building the New City: Stalinallee

For both East and West Germany, built form was one obvious and highly visible medium through which a changed way of life could be inculcated for citizens and announced to outside observers. In 1952 *Neues Deutschland* (*ND*), one of the main official Party newspapers, announced the building of Stalinallee at the start of the Nationalen Aufbauprogramms Berlin (NAP, National Construction Programme), an important part of the first Soviet-style, five-year plan. The new processional boulevard of Stalinallee was designed to be part of an axis from the Brandenburg Gate, along Unter den

Designing Modern Germany

A model of the monumental Stalinallee project was exhibited in the Sports Hall of the district in 1952 under the slogan, 'Look at it Today – Live in it Tomorrow'.

Linden, past the destroyed royal palace, to Alexanderplatz and Frankfurterallee in the direction of Lichtenberg. On 21 December 1949, the 70th birthday of Josef Stalin, the street was renamed in his honour. Its use for political events gained greater *gravitas* because it marked the route of the Red Army in capturing Berlin from the National Socialists, when they had entered from the direction of Frankfurt an der Oder on 21 April 1945. Combined with this political significance, it was suggested that Berliners would spend their Sundays, Easter and Christmas excursions there, promenading along the boulevard, visiting the cafés and window-shopping, rather than in the countryside, as previously. As such, consumer desire was channelled into a form of public political life and given a collective purpose away from individualism.[34]

The architects who worked on the scheme, which extended from Proskauer to Strausberger streets, between 1952 and 1958 included Egon Hartmann, Hanns Hopp, Richard Paulick, Kurt-W. Leucht, Karl Souradny and, later, Hermann Henselmann. Direct precedents for such modernization of the cityscape on a heroic scale could be found in Warsaw and Stalingrad. The National Committee was established by the Minister for

Reconstruction (Aufbau). In one year, between 3 February 1952 and 1953, 1,000 apartments were built. Under the heading 'Ein Volk baut sein Hauptstadt' (A Nation Builds its Capital), it was as much an important propagandistic initiative as it was an urgent housing solution.[35]

The design of the apartments warranted the title *Arbeiter Wohnpalasten*, or workers' palaces, among their proponents. By contrast, detractors referred disparagingly to the 'wedding-cake style' amidst predictions that the level of provision could not be sustained. For their time, the apartments represented unprecedented luxury for such housing. They all came with their own baths, rubbish chutes and central heating. The overall architectural formulation was based on the Soviet urban model – neo-Classical, grand in scale, with sequences of terraces and colonnades and ground-floor shops or offices with apartments above. The street was punctuated by a wide boulevard, in which squares, circuses and domed towers marked important traffic junctions. As proposed

Frankfurter Tor, by architect Hermann Henselmann, formed one of the key landmarks towards the end of Stalinallee. (Photographed in 2006.)

solutions for mass housing, these buildings were distinguished on the one hand from the Weimar modern *Wohnmaschine* (machine for living), and on the other from their immediate contemporary *Schlichtwohnung* (frugal dwelling) of the emergency prefabricated housing programme in the West. While the monumental Stalinallee was being completed, new developments for mass housing introduced the more functional system of Plattenbau, the prefabricated system-built blocks of flats to house workers in more reduced and regularized conditions. These were to become the more general pattern for future housing in estates on the edges of all GDR towns and cities.

The first idealistic stage of the GDR came to a head in a crisis: a premonition of other uprisings that would subsequently occur throughout the Eastern Bloc. Following the introduction of increased food costs on already rationed goods in April 1953, new work norms were introduced by the GDR leader Walter Ulbricht in an attempt to increase productivity and, in June, an unpopular New Course was introduced, in response to Soviet directives. In the context of the threat of a third world war and the added instability of Stalin's death on 5 March 1953, East German workers took to the streets in demonstrations, demanding better living conditions.[36]

Designing Modern Germany

The heads of state remained intent on their policies, and the demonstrations and strikes were quelled by calling in Soviet tanks. As testimony to his will to offer an alternative vision, in the newly established magazine *Neue Werbung* (New Publicity), Ulbricht maintained: 'We possess all necessary requirements to deliver industrial products of high quality under profitable conditions into capitalist countries – and especially colonial and half-colonial countries – and to receive products made in those countries.' He continued:

> Workers in companies of the German Democratic Republic have the task of contributing to worldwide recognition of our republic's goods and respect in all countries of the world through a high quality of export goods. Germany has always . . . to resume foreign trade business and fortify foreign trade with people's democratic countries.[37]

There followed a period of relative relaxation that historians have called the political and cultural Thaw. This was prompted from Moscow when new directives were introduced by the new leader, Nikita Khrushchev. Among other things, Khrushchev revealed the enormity of crimes made on behalf of the previous Stalinist regime, including mass executions, and he went on to discredit his predecessor Stalin's cult of the individual.[38] In cultural terms, this thaw was manifest in a renewed commitment to relative freedom of expression in the arts, to allow a distinctive form of representation that still offered socialist content while engaging with the international artistic language of Modernism.

For example, the East German Verband bildender Künstler (Association of Visual Artists) formed in 1950 to commission public art works. These were intended to show how applied art could synthesize with architecture in the development of 'the social system of socialism and its higher aims'.[39] With headquarters in Berlin, the association was divided under the leadership of the central executive committee into fifteen district federations, in which disciplines were placed in eight sections: painting and graphics, sculpture, industrial design, arts and crafts, architecture, history of art, publication design and caricature, and a group for conservators and restorers. Its president represented the arts on the central executive committee of the SED.

Through an intense period of activity in the late 1950s and '60s, existing government buildings were given new decorative schemes in which sculptures and fountains were installed, new garden designs applied and

The House of the Teachers
in Berlin Alexanderplatz
carried Walter Womacka's
decorative mosaic frieze
in enamel and aluminium,
1963–4.

stained-glass windows, murals and ceramic friezes added, with strong symbolic content combined with a tendency towards abstraction and the School of Paris. Many new buildings also had applied decorations. A strong interest in public art forms such as the Mexican mural traditions proved influential on these artistic programmes, which were intended to escape charges of individualism, while giving artistic innovation an important presence in the new street landscape. At the level of rhetoric, the applied decoration with socialist content prevented these new buildings from appearing as just another instance of international modern architecture, too similar in kind to the Federal Republic.

Through these efforts, the ordinary GDR worker might have lunch in a canteen decorated with depictions of the industrial benefits of his or her labour; meanwhile, their children would pass similar visual displays in their school entrance halls, and in their playgrounds experimental art forms transformed play equipment. For the weekend, parks were remodelled. At the high end of the scale, customers at the exclusive Moskau restaurant on Karl Marx Allee in Berlin would pass a grand mosaic by Bernd Heller, entitled *From the Life of the Soviet Union* and completed in 1964.

Moves to Marketing: Consumers in the GDR

One response to the civil unrest of 1953 and the subsequent liberalization that continued until the Party's Eleventh Plenum in 1965 was to offer a greater sense of economic well-being and prospects to workers who were loyal to the new state. Several initiatives were introduced that appeared to offer a compromise between the extremes of individualistic consumer society and the hard-line Marxist-Leninism of the early political policies of the Party.

In this movement, the concept of *Geschenkpolitik*, literally the politics of gifts, was used to distinguish the two republics.[40] The message from the GDR was that, in the West, 'nothing is given free' (*nichts wird geschenkt*). By contrast, the socialist state could provide a cycle of annual and longer-term anniversaries. Closely related to production targets for its industries, major political feast days were organized and other newly invented festivities introduced, often to mark alliances between other Eastern Bloc states. 'Gifts' in the form of lines of consumer goods or the production of commemorative souvenirs were aligned to this calendar. Underlying this was a need to justify consumption and its place in a socialist state by confirming its political and propagandistic purpose alongside those of the economic and social.

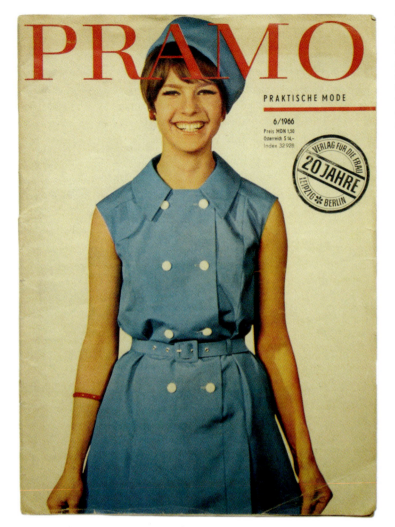

PRAMO

PRAKTISCHE MODE

6/1966
Preis MDN 1,50
Österreich S 14,–
Index 32 928

VERLAG FÜR DIE FRAU
20 JAHRE
LEIPZIG ✶ BERLIN

The popular East German fashion magazine *Pramo* (Praktische Mode) offered fashion advice along with patterns for home dressmaking. The June 1966 issue celebrated twenty years of the publishing house Verlag der Frau.

A case in point was the Präsent 20 series of clothing, announced in 1969 as a new fashion line to mark the twentieth anniversary of the foundation of the Republic.[41] While it was clearly not affordable or attainable for all, its synthetic fabrics in bright colours, convenient for care, signalled a fashionable modernity important for the regime. In the same year, the city of Leipzig celebrated that it had a total of twelve state-run department stores.[42]

A paradox lay at the centre of GDR economic policy. On the one hand, it was necessary to protect its economy through the building of the Berlin Wall and wider division of the Eastern Bloc, while on the other, it was clear that the standard of living in the Federal Republic remained the gauge by

Designing Modern Germany

which to measure the economy in terms of ownership of consumer goods and the semblance of a modern market economy. The GDR system indicated that autarky was not sufficient; a more discursive relationship between East and West needed to exist. Therefore, in the area of individual ownership of washing machines, fridges, cars and telephones, the GDR strove to keep abreast of Western economies, keen to present statistics to this effect, while in the shopping streets self-service supermarkets modelled on Western patterns were introduced. This depended on a basic consensus between the state and the citizens. Everyone was expected to contribute to the same message of well-being, happiness and contentment. If this creates a picture of homogenous or controlled consumption, Ine Merkel has suggested that, despite the strict regulations for state-run manufacturing companies, shops and organizations, alternative ways of provisioning the home also existed.[43] Evidence indicates that people found ways to 'hunt and gather', and that if the state did not or could not provide for everything that made life possible or pleasurable, various forms of exchange networks developed that allowed for more nuanced forms of consumption to take place, including the bartering or selling of home-grown produce, second-hand or handmade goods.

If the attainment of an adequate standard of living was the expressed goal of the Party, luxury goods, often those associated with more overt styling and design, presented a further paradox. It is clear that class-defined consumption persisted, formed according to Party privilege rather than the capitalist system of loans and benefits. This came to the fore with the introduction of GENEX and Intershop, retail outlets that until 1974 were officially only for foreign visitors to the GDR and that were prohibitively expensive for most of the population. Their counterparts, the elite Exquisit and Deliktläden outlets, stocked highly priced Western goods and hard-to-attain luxuries.[44]

The packaging and advertising of goods also presented possible difficulties for the Party position. The opinion that products did not require much attention because there was little competition was a commonplace point of view officially expressed in the GDR. Certainly when compared with Western societies, the streets appeared relatively blank and the signs of a consumer culture muted. Nonetheless, in an industrial society dependent on mass production and distribution to both home and foreign markets, modern systems of communication and their safeguard in transit were necessary to maintain levels of sales. The literature on graphic design suggests that in fact considerable attention was given to packaging design. The 1950s and '60s in particular saw innovations in technologies for paper and cardboard manufacture, glass and tin metal, along with chemicals for paints, inks and other forms of colouring. In 1960 a dedicated journal, *Die Verpackung*, was launched. This showed the GDR to be at the crossroads between capitalist advertising and what was termed *Gesellschaft Werbung*, literally, 'society publicity'.[45] In West Germany, the market was driven by fashion, whereas under a planned economy, such a corrective was officially missing. In the East German design press, advertising and publicity campaigns were praised for showing 'clarity, solidity and lack of ambiguity' rather than the full persuasive or suggestive promises of Western-style advertising. Beyond official sources, it was clear that fashion systems still operated on many levels.[46]

Another symptom of the GDR's modernity was in how science was employed. Priority was on industrial production but, within this, there was a willingness to embrace new materials. Plastics, for example, products of a highly developed chemical industry, could compensate for loss of other raw materials due to the Republic's relative isolation or dependence on imports from a decreased range of supplier countries. To ease the situation the Chemieprogramm (Chemical Programme) was announced in 1958.[47] By 1959 the GDR was ninth in the list of industrial nations, yet as a leading productive world economy it faced significant environmental damage. A major cause was that its industries depended on brown coal (lignite) as a major fuel source, which was mined in the region but caused substantial air pollution.

To be able to satisfy the expectations of the modern consumer, the state developed its motor industry through the production of small automobiles for the private market. More than anything else, in the 1950s and '60s car ownership was heralded as the major visible material sign of success in the developed world. If not necessarily always on the same scale as American conspicuous consumption, then at least most Western governments were determined to support their car industries, in some cases through nationalization. Because the West Germans had the Volkswagen, the GDR needed to follow suit, and in this two names dominated in East German streets: Trabant and Wartburg.[48]

The case of the Trabant highlights how the reception and meaning of industrial design can change dramatically over time. The car was produced from 1957 by the VEB Sachsenring Automobilwerke Zwickau in Saxony, an adapted motorcycle plant. The Trabant was designed to accommodate a driver and three passengers with limited luggage. The name, chosen through a competition in 1957, the year of the launch of the Sputnik Soviet space programme, was synonymous with satellite in the German language.

The car came in two principal models: Trabant 500, or P50 as it became known, was produced between 1957 and 1963, to be succeeded by the Trabant P60 series, which ran from 1963 to 1991. The second model incorporated the synthetic material Duroplast for its body, made of recycled cotton waste from the Soviet Union and phenol resins from the home dye industry, to compensate for difficulties in procuring steel through foreign imports. The cars' bright colours of pale blue and cream along with sharply angled lines stressed their modernity. The engine was small, two-stroke with two cylinders, but as ecological awareness grew through the period of the Trabant's manufacture, the significant amount of exhaust emissions was criticized.[49] The strict control and priorities of GDR production meant that people might have to wait for several years before owning their vehicle, and once this was achieved, they tended to keep their model, repairing and updating it through the circulation of mechanical knowledge by magazines and word of mouth. Ironically, while the car became unwanted by many of its original owners after the fall of the Wall in 1989, it also subsequently became subject to a wave of popular nostalgic affection and a cult object.

If the Trabant found difficulty sustaining an international reputation when faced with comparison with the achievements of other small car manufacturers, the Wartburg had greater success, and it was exported to other Eastern Bloc countries as well as further afield. The Wartburg saloon 353 was designed by Clauss Dietel and Lutz Rudolph between 1962 and 1964 and had characteristic modern clean lines associated with much of the industrial design of those years. A 5-door estate 'Tourist' version by Rudolph appeared from the manufacturer, VEB Karosseriewerke Halle, in 1967.[50] The designers were among the most prominent industrial designers of the time, combining work for important industrial engineering sectors with teaching, while advising on design committees and maintaining their own studios.

Beyond the question of consumer goods, the liberal years of the Thaw meant that by the mid-1960s it was possible to speak of a developed counter-culture, along the lines of those in other European countries. One focus for this was the nineteenth-century district close to the centre of East Berlin, Prenzlauer Berg. At this time, leading cultural and intellectual figures, designers and architects among them, believed that, following the building of the Wall, opportunities for life might develop without interference from the West. The renowned author Christa Wolf retrospectively commented about this time:

Clauss Dietel, a set of models for the design of a private car described as being intended for the 'lower working classes', 1960.

We, most members of the one generation, who lived in this land in an engaged way . . . had the feeling that this was one of the last moments in which to steer the development of the GDR in the direction to be able to make this state into an alternative to the capitalist Federal Republic. We wanted to strengthen the socialist mouthpiece as much as possible so that the GDR could also be spiritually 'marketable'. And we saw ourselves connected with people in business, in science, who thought and worked in the right direction. There were personal contacts; we spoke with one another. We were even able to speak to a few individuals in the Central Committee.[51]

Significantly, the areas that Wolf particularly identified were journalism, literature, film, music and lyrics, possibly because of the difficult paradoxes presented by material culture. Even so, Wolf's own writings from this time often describe characters' experience of daily life, including close detail of everyday objects and environments, and the tensions these caused.[52]

Designing Modern Germany

Professional Design in the GDR: The Formalism Debate

The nature of the political and economic system of the GDR and its consumer provision helps us to understand the difficulties faced by the design profession. At the highest level, the place of the designer received approval, as was attested in the words of Walter Ulbricht, which were used to introduce an exhibition in 1961 at the Grassi Museum, the arts and crafts museum of Leipzig. They ran: 'Artistic achievement is not only a means of helping to fulfil a task, but also an integrating element of the complete plan, leading to the victory of socialism.'[53]

The particular understanding of 'artistic achievement', however, was not without controversy. To start with, one might expect the premise of a socialist design policy to be design for all. The legacy of debates from the earlier periods of German design was revived in the changed climate of the early GDR years. The origins of thinking about design in series went back at least to the 1920s at the Bauhaus and earlier to the Werkbund. Design awards offered one way to understand the continuity between Weimar Modernism and the new conditions in the GDR. For the first significant non-domestic building after the war, the Parteihochschule Karl Marx in Kleinmachnow of 1947, a new chair, the 'Seminar Stuhl', was designed and

Selman Selmanagić, Seminar Stuhl, 1947 was produced by the Deutsche Werkstätten Hellerau. The chair was an early example of 'good design' approved by the East German authorities.

manufactured by the reorganized Handwerksbetriebe SAG-Betriebe.[54] This fulfilled the promise that designers could concentrate on products for social use, with mass production in mind, supported by the government. At this time, the designer Horst Michel introduced the White Lily and Hammer, an award to be given for the best work in the field of the applied arts (Gütezeichen für Kunsthandwerk und Gewerbe). Originally for the region of Thuringia, it was subsequently applied to the whole of East Germany as administered by the Grassi Museum from 1949. A sign of continuity with pre-1933 also came when the first furniture series of the Deutsche Werkstätten Hellerau appeared at the Leipzig Spring Fair of 1950. The chair Modell 50 642, designed by Franz Ehrlich and Selman Selmanagić, was awarded the prize, praised for the Modernist principle of realizing its form from minimum material means.[55]

At the same time as these developments, the Centre of Formgestaltung (Design Council) for East Germany was established in Weimar, as part of the Deutsche Zentralverwaltung für Volksbildung (German Central Committee for People's Education). The reopening of the Staatliche Hochschule für Baukunst und Bildende Künste in Weimar with its important legacy as the site of the first Bauhaus was another significant step. It was here that Horst Michel led the Arbeitsgemeinschaft Formgestaltung (literally, Work Association for Design), which at first concentrated on toys and small domestic goods. Michel, along with Gustav Hassenpflug and Peter Keler, both former *Bauhäusler*, taught a version of a foundation course (*Vorkurs*) modelled on the school's ideas. In the difficult years of reconstruction, emphasis initially fell on textiles and ceramics to be promoted at the Leipzig fairs. On 1 May 1950 a further sign of continuity between the Weimar period and the GDR was the appointment of the Dutch functionalist designer and architect Mart Stam as Rektor of the Hochschule für angewandte Kunst (High School for Applied Arts) in Berlin Weissensee, who was reportedly received 'with his cool rationalism like a cold shower'.[56]

Taking into account the constraints of the time, teaching in craft and industrial production reflected what was practicable. To begin with design for toys, textiles, wallpapers, glass and ceramics and other small-scale household goods was possible. Plastics, together with what would become known as 'industrial design', came later in the 1950s. The first exhibition to show the fruits of the revived design education, *Industriewaren von heute* (Industrial Goods of Today), was held in Berlin in 1952 and attracted a significant 45,000 visitors. Already criticism was voiced that what was displayed would reach only the industrial fairs at Leipzig, aimed at export trade, rather than the domestic shop window or the real home of the consumer.[57]

Recourse to Modernist principles soon proved controversial. The issue of pure form versus decoration came to the fore in two exhibitions, *Schöne Industriewaren* (Beautiful Industrial Wares) and *Deutsche Angewandte Kunst* (German Applied Art), both held in 1954. These exhibitions prompted a discussion on the meaning of decoration under the new political circumstances. Some viewed any recourse to decoration as kitsch, reviving the long-standing question originally articulated by Adolf Loos in the famous essay *Ornament and Crime* of 1908. Surprisingly, rather than meeting approval for the Modernist argument of economic functionalism, undecorated objects in a socialist context were accused by some of showing symptoms of 'bourgeois formalism' and an over-reliance on aesthetic principles associated with the West. This was neatly encompassed in the opinion of Walter Heisig, director of the Institute of Applied Arts, who claimed in 1957 that 'a piece of cutlery without ornament is formalism'.[58]

Instead, a strong sense prevailed that a socialist object, even if industrial and mass-produced, should be imbued with other, more associative qualities. As one critic, Ernst R. Vogenauer, who took over industrial design on Stam's departure, commenting on the *Schöne Industriewaren* exhibition, wrote, 'The rigidity of former shapes has been loosened, the puritanical austerity transcended. The "new" appears more lively, more likeable and warm. This is not least due to the remembrance of values inherent in "Heimatkunst".'[59]

It was not without paradox that a member of the socialist administration invoked a concept usually associated with conservative, patriotic, if not always nationalist, rhetoric. The situation was far from resolved, and, as we shall see, individual designers stayed the course of good modern design. Through the official channels, lip service, at least, was paid to values that would meet the approval of international designers and juries. Increasingly, the goal was for objects to be 'socialist in content and national in form'.[60]

Margaret Jahny

It is clear that even in the face of charges of bourgeois formalism, functional designs were nonetheless often the norm, possibly, at times, for the reason that they were exactly those that could meet economic targets. There are many examples of East German design fulfilling the requirements for a standardized, modern design with the clean lines, simple forms and geometrical decoration associated with Modernism. To take just one, Margaret Jahny is considered by many to be the *grande dame* of GDR design. As a student of the former Bauhaus designer Marianne Brandt, she graduated from

The 'Rationell' ceramic service by Margaret Jahny and Erich Müller for the Zentral Institut für Gestaltung 1973, was used in numerous public contexts in the GDR as well as in the home.

the Dresden Hochschule für bildende Kunst in 1952. Jahny's diploma work consisted of an all-white porcelain service that successfully went into production with the VEB Porzellanwerk Reichenbach (Oberlausitz). In this, softened, organic forms paralleled mid-twentieth-century modern and contemporary design elsewhere in the field of international ceramic design.

Jahny's later career was directed towards providing functional designs for mainstream use. For instance, she worked together with Erich Müller to develop a ceramic service called 'Gastronomie-Geschirr, rationell' (rational), its title in modern lower-case type. This became omnipresent in areas of GDR public life, in many respects an industry standard. Produced by the VEB Porzellankombinat Colditz in Saxony (VEB Volkseigenen Betrieb), it was a stacking service used in public spaces, including the dining cars of Mitropa, the East German international railway network.[61]

Design Democracy in the West: Ulm Hochschule für Gestaltung

To return to West Germany and parallel interests to establish purposeful modern design, the case study of the Ulm Hochschule für Gestaltung (HfG) is instructive. The school began its teaching programme in 1953 and was inaugurated in purpose-built premises designed by its first rector, Max Bill, on the outskirts of the city in October 1955. The school was one of several initiatives of Inge Scholl, a member of a prominent family from Ulm, who wished to commemorate her brother Hans and sister Sophie, who, as

Designing Modern Germany

members of the White Rose Resistance movement, had been murdered by the Nazis during the Second World War.[62] As well as establishing the Geschwister Scholl Foundation and encouraging the work of the Volkshochschule, an adult community college in Ulm, which introduced cultural, political and social educational programmes intended to aid in the reconstruction of German society, Inge Scholl collaborated with the writer and founder of Gruppe 47, Hans Werner Richter, and the self-taught graphic designer Otl Aicher on the formation of HfG. Aicher, who married Scholl, would become rector of the school between 1962 and 1964. The idea, which had a long gestation period until its final opening, was to establish a new kind of educational institution that could provide a model for other German universities. Original plans changed from a school addressing politics and the social sciences to one at which the materialization of policies could be realized through design.

The project was made possible with the funding of the Geschwister Scholl foundation, but also the support of, among others, the regional government of Baden-Württemberg and the American High Commissioner, General McCloy. The appointment of Max Bill as rector meant that associations with the Bauhaus were inevitable. Bill had been a student at the Bauhaus in Dessau from 1927 to 1929, before returning to his native Switzerland to become a leading artist, designer and architect, with particular emphasis in the 1930s on graphic and exhibition design.[63] In many respects, there were

Exhibition of work by staff and students in the refectory and lecture hall of Ulm Hochschule für Gestaltung, 1958.

similarities between the two institutions. Both were internationally oriented and defied normal definitions by not fitting neatly within educational schema – they were neither art academies nor arts and crafts schools. Instead, as specialist institutions with their own internally devised pedagogy, fluctuating with the rise and fall of the staff, they expected their students to take on a shared worldview and cultural outlook. At times at Ulm, this could be parodied as taking the form of a design monastery, where students with cropped hair wearing black polo-necks listened to the Modern Jazz Quartet.[64]

Before taking up his position as rector, Bill's exhibition *Gute Form* had travelled from Basel to be shown in Ulm in 1949, as part of the Volkshochschule programme, no doubt providing a forum for discussions with Inge Scholl and Otl Aicher about the project's directions. Unlike the Bauhaus, where Gropius saw architecture as the highest goal of the curriculum, Inge Aicher-Scholl conceived the HfG as 'eine Forschungsinstitut für Produktform' – a research institute for product form (design). Furthermore, the aim was to combine the teachings of a design school with a general humanist education, giving design a moral authority in defining the character of post-war life.

At one level, therefore, Ulm can be deemed a success. Indeed, many of the most famous icons of Ulm design are products – electrical goods for Braun and Kodak, transport systems and vehicle designs, systems design for Lufthansa and international signage systems. Its lasting contribution to design history, however, is as much to do with the larger debate about the education of the designer in modern society, and the tension between different and sometimes conflicting design ideals, as it is the realized designs. On its opening, the choice facing the school was discussed. Walter Gropius's inaugural lecture, 'Die Notwendigkeit des Künstlers in der demokratischen

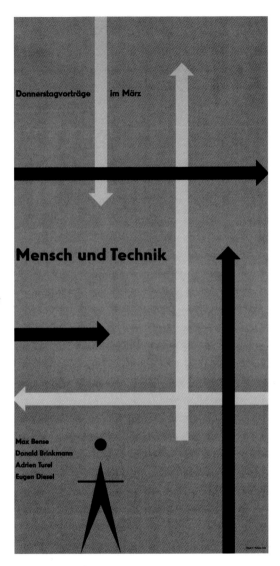

Otl Aicher, poster 'Mensch und Technik' (People and Technology) for a lecture held at Ulm HfG in 1952.

Designing Modern Germany

Gesellschaft' (The Necessity of the Artist in Democratic Society), raised the long-standing issue of the relationship between art and design, one that would prove to be contentious throughout the life of the school. In a change of position from his years as director of the Bauhaus, when fine art was excluded from the curriculum, Gropius stood in favour of seeing design as a cultural, artistic endeavour. Bill's own understanding of his mission was expressed in the essay 'Die Aufgaben der Hochschule für Gestaltung' (The Tasks of the HfG), in which he wrote: 'The task of the HfG, in our technical age, is to help to create a consensual and unanimous philosophy of life.'[65]

The curriculum introduced by Max Bill took the form of four years of study, beginning with a preliminary course that was reminiscent of the *Vorkurs* at the Bauhaus. It was intended that this course would allow students to experience all workshops, through which they made the decision for their future study. The departments were organized into building, significantly not called architecture, product design and visual communication; film design came later. The 150 students, 40 per cent of whom were from beyond Germany, were all expected to pursue studies in photography, typography, free and technical drawing and the understanding of materials, since these were intended as a set of tools for future study. Lectures and seminars were given in the history of art, philosophy and psychology, and semiology. Product design was taught in conjunction with the workshops for wood, metal, plaster, plastics and modelling with the goal of developing the form of useful goods from a basis in experiment.

The curriculum was oriented to address the future directions of industry. In the case of visual communication, the results of theoretical experiments were applied to the design of printed goods, photography, film and television. Significantly, the applications of design went beyond the earlier definition of graphic design's association with print media alone.

Max Bill appointed staff who represented current as well as future generations. Among them were Otl Aicher, Hans Gugelot, Tomás Maldonado and Fritz Pfeil. Through guest lecturers such as Josef Albers, Johannes Itten and Helen Nonné Schmidt, Bill also established a direct lineage with the Bauhaus, while the artist Friedrich Vordemberge-Gildewart, tutor for abstract painting, represented the previous generation, versed in Constructivism.[66]

The underlying principle of Scholl and Aicher was to develop designs that would not be consumer-driven or led by style and fashion, but rather developed with an emphasis on the rational and systematic. Within this, the notion of timelessness was invoked as an important criterion, defined against the phenomenon of conspicuous consumption and in-built obsolescence of the American system of industrial styling. In contrast with the latter, Ulm goods were neutral in colour; publications employed sans-serif typeface and objective photography; and the overall rhetoric was of a serious and scientific world based on analysis, synthesis and the testing of design alternatives as if in the laboratory.

Dieter Rams

While never a member of staff at Ulm, one of Germany's most prominent designers has had close associations with the school, sharing its major principles, which he has realized in a long career as a product designer and as an important spokesperson for design. Indeed, Rams is a figure who could be considered to have changed the professional and international face and reputation of German industrial design more than any other designer during the second half of the twentieth century. He originally embarked on his architectural studies at the Werkkunstschule in Wiesbaden in 1947, changing to training as a cabinet-maker up to 1953. Rams found employment in the small Frankfurt am Main company Radio Braun, by chance, two years later. Originally appointed as an interior designer and architect, he soon gravitated towards design, taking on product design for Braun and furniture design for Otto Zapf, which became Vitsoe Zapf after 1959. By 1961

Hans Gugelot and Dieter Rams, Radio – Phono-kombination sk 4/6, 1956, manufactured by Max Braun of Frankfurt am Main. The design was remarkable at the time for the combination of white plastic and blond wood surfaces. With its transparent lid, it became known colloquially as 'Snow White's Coffin'.

Designing Modern Germany

Ram was head of the design department at Braun, where he led the company into a period when its distinctive design approach was internationally recognized. Between 1981 and his retirement in 1997 Rams was Professor of Industrial Design at the Hamburg Hochschule für Bildende Künste and an important ambassador for West German design.[67]

Critical Reception of Ulm

To return to Ulm, by and large the language of instruction mirrored the intended objectivity of the results. A brief for the visual communication students developed by Anthony Frøshaug and Horst Rittel from 1959, for example, was all presented in lower-case typewriter Courier and indicated the level of abstraction expected of the students. It read:

> given is a population of white beans. to be determined (measured) is the distribution of their length. the results of the measurement are to be suitably recorded. the relative incidence of the results of the measurement is to be graphically represented.[68]

Commentators on Ulm have pointed to the tensions in the relationship between the school's ideals and wider societal trends. It has been suggested that these mounted in the face of the federal government's desire to build a society of consumers and the educational principles of Ulm. Its original formation had been a product of an age of austerity, in part prompted by shock. Brigitte Hausmann has suggested:

> The consumerism propagated by the Minister for the Economy Ludwig Erhard conflicted with the urge to save and the continual 'shortage consciousness' (*Knappheit Bewusstsein*) of the general population. This so-called 'mentality of the frugal household' (*Mentalität des sparsamen Haushaltens*) likewise shaped the aesthetic of the Ulm School of Design.[69]

Furthermore, increasingly the relationship between Ulm designs and the wider tendencies of industrial design in Western countries was one of tension. In hindsight, another former member of teaching staff, Tomás Maldonado, wrote:

> In Ulm we believed that there was 'the design', an absolutization of product design. That was not correct. There are different types of

product design, which correspond to different levels of production or kinds of production.[70]

Interestingly, while acknowledging design plurality, even in this measured re-evaluation of Ulm thinking Maldonado did not take the step to acknowledge consumption as a possible driving force. In 1975, in a period of decay and disinterest in the Ulm school and its former building, Claude Schnaidt, himself a student of Maldonado, suggested: 'There came a point when industry no longer found the innovations of Ulm important.'[71]

This question came to the forefront of debate on the occasion when Reyner Banham, the British architectural and design historian and critic, gave two lectures at the school in March 1959 on 'The Influence of Expendability on Product Design' and 'Democratic Taste'. This introduced to Ulm ideas that had circulated within the Independent Group in Britain, who collectively examined the character of mass culture and its artistic implications, particularly in relation to America, as an early stage of an emergent Pop sensibility.[72] Banham's interests were always defined by a fascination with the popular, and he proposed that designers and commentators should take seriously the American preoccupation with styling as a form of democratic taste. His argument presented a significant challenge to both *Gute Form* and the problem-solving model of design research at Ulm. Also conscious of the gulf between principle and reality, and how West German prosperity and materialism were forming strong distractions to the apparent moral austerity of Ulm, the German philosopher Hans Magnus Enzensberger commented: 'The Neckermann mail-order catalogues of the time – or "bestsellers" – provide illuminating insights into the contemporary product culture and in particular the electrification of the German household.'[73]

In a further ironic twist, by 1968, when closure of the school was immanent, the students themselves commented: 'Braun appliances, once the most exclusive evidence for the progressive character of the Ulm School of Design, now fill Neckermann and Quelle catalogues.'[74] One could suggest that this was the fulfilment of Ulm. In 1968, in an open letter, the students renounced cooperation with the instructors: 'The HFG concretized the hope for a democratic renaissance of West Germany and died with it'.[75]

The timing of the crisis at Ulm Hochschule für Gestaltung in June 1968, and its eventual closure in November that year, was symptomatic of more than just a localized disaffection with the direction of design pedagogy at a single institution or conflict between its faculty and state legislature. That year also saw a worldwide generational call for change in the political

Designing Modern Germany

Ulm magazine, May 1964. According to its modernist ambitions, the school's publications conformed to what was by then called 'Swiss style' graphic design.

culture that fundamentally affected the USA and East and West Europe, in response to the continuing Vietnam War, the Soviet invasion of Prague, campaigns for civil rights and the Paris student and workers' revolt. Along with the Prague Spring, the peace movement and increasing ecological awareness, these events signalled that the notion of a consensual democratic society, upon which many of the modern design ideals had been based, was challenged to the core. Germany's strong cultural commitment to the benefits of Modernism in design, which had come to the fore in both the Federal Republic and German Democratic Republic in the years of reconstruction, was to become subject to further radical reassessment in the last decades of the twentieth century.

5
Reunification: Design in a Global Context, 1975–2005

Despite German design's traditional wish to have an international outlook, the great differences in the political, cultural, and economic forms of the two German states also resulted in differences in matters of design, and above all, in their practical realization, so that only partial correspondences were possible.[1]

For design in Germany, the years after 1975 were marked by stylistic revivalism and eclecticism on both sides of the political division. In the Federal Republic, this was matched by a boom in museum building and a growing acceptance of design as lifestyle, in common with the situation in other developed economies. At the same time, in the German Democratic Republic, the continuing struggle to satisfy consumer demand remained a priority, while signs of civil dissatisfaction and unrest increased. On both sides of the Wall, Berlin was a site of frenzied building activity. In the West, the *Internationale Bauausstellung* (International Building Exhibition) of 1984 provided an opportunity for international architects to offer housing solutions in areas of the western city, some close to the Wall, in recognition that Berlin was now to be permanently divided. An innovation at this exhibition, which distinguished it from other IBA precedents, *Am Weissenhof* in Stuttgart of 1927 and the *Hansaviertel* building exhibition of 1957, was how by 1984 renovation of existing buildings was combined with commissions to international architects for new works. On the other side of the Wall, in 1988, the urban complex of East Berlin, by then renamed Hauptstadt der DDR, capital of the German Democratic Republic, was inaugurated as an historical as well as a modern city. In acknowledging the potential of modern tourism and leisure, along with the collectivist principles of its earlier urban plan, the schemes for East Berlin and other historic cities such as Dresden, Leipzig and Weimar could be said to have represented a version of state socialist Postmodernism.

Ingo Maurer, 'Bibibibi' lamp in porcelain, metal and plastic, 1982.

Through such shifts, both East and West Germany recognized the importance of identity and history, as well as continuing to offer competing visions of the future. Derived from separate circumstances, the two traditions unexpectedly collided in 1989, when the Berlin Wall fell. For many, this momentous political event was symptomatic of the power of the individual citizen to force political change in the form of the collapse of a monolithic regime through direct action. Designed goods were therefore central to the recognition of this change, as both symptom and agent.

The Legacy of Modernism: The Challenge of Postmodernism

The last 30 years of the twentieth century were marked by fundamental challenges in the cultural and philosophical premises of the Western world that questioned Enlightenment principles stemming from the eighteenth century. This had an inevitable impact on the way that German design was to develop. In many respects, through its position on a major political fault line, the debate about a significant break in tradition took on deepest resonance in Germany. The terms Late Modern and Postmodern became a form of shorthand to characterize the different philosophical positions, although they were by no means all-inclusive. As design styles, the Late Modern and the Postmodern coexisted throughout the 1970s to 1990s and should not necessarily be understood to be sequential in chronology. Rather, reflecting different points of view, the former suggested continuity and gradual transformation, while the latter implied a more radical break with the past.

Philosophers and historians were split in their diagnosis of the implications of changing from a technological to an information-based society. One clear challenge in Europe was how the manufacturing base for industrial and technological goods was moving from a concentration in the 'old' established countries to development in Asia under financially competitive circumstances. In this, Germany was no exception, although certain industrial sectors remained buoyant, most notably the automotive industry, with world-leading companies Audi, BMW, Mercedes, Porsche and Volkswagen, all recognized for their combination of innovation in design and technology. The larger question, however, was whether a category shift was identifiable in the economic and technological base of society from high to late capitalism and, if so, what would be the implications for design.

As an advanced industrial state with a prominent intellectual tradition, West Germany figured strongly in debates about Postmodernism. One of the country's leading philosophers, Jürgen Habermas, became a central figure for his diagnosis of the character of late industrialism. Habermas

Designing Modern Germany

engaged with what he saw as the transformation of the public sphere through the expansion of consumer society, which, he suggested, led to the inevitable privatization of lifestyles. A crucial question was the exact nature of this transformation. Was it more appropriate to characterize it as late modernity or Postmodernism? The former implied possibilities of continuity across the century, while the latter suggested a fundamental break. Habermas was more open than contemporary French post-structuralists to the idea that the Modernist project could be renewed and, as such, rejected a totalizing idea of the Postmodern. Even if few designers would have read Habermas's own words, his position was influential in these circles because it offered an opportunity to extend rather than break with tradition.[2]

In contrast to the late Modernist position, which looked to the machine and took a production-oriented view of design, organized on the principles of Fordism and industrially organized labour based on standardization, Postmodernism became associated with flexible production methods and new technologies, digital and service industries. These could satisfy more niche-oriented consumption, with an emphasis on design for pleasure contributing to personal identity, rather than as previously design for the public good. At a stylistic level, Postmodernism advocated a return to ornament, symbolism, wit and other associative values, already apparent in much Pop-oriented art and design, in particular stemming from the USA.

To understand the situation of German designers at this point means taking account of the wider change in sensibility across the world. Significantly, it was in writing about architecture, rather than design, that the first definitions of Postmodernism were articulated in an increasingly international arena. In 1966 Robert Venturi and Denise Scott-Brown published *Complexity and Contradiction in Architecture*, which they followed in 1972 with *Learning from Las Vegas*, a book co-written with fellow architect Steven Izenour. These texts, crucial in the formulation of an alternative aesthetic position to the still-dominant architectural formalism, became available in German translation, respectively in 1978 and 1979. Their message to designers was to embrace what had previously been dismissed as vulgar, 'mass' and popular. Instead, their authors enjoyed the linguistic possibilities of built form and argued, for instance, that the commercial strip of American cities was replete with an iconography that offered symbols to inspire architects and designers. Rather than disparaging or dismissing these as kitsch, Venturi advocated their rich meaning as a way to enliven architectural and design discourse, treating buildings and their environments as a field of signification. This linguistic analogy opened up many possibilities for varied forms of design.[3]

Stiletto studios (Frank Schreiner), 'Consumer's Rest' chair, 1983. The chair's resonance came from its combination of humour and implicit criticism of consumer society.

Another important text, translated into German in 1980, was Charles Jencks's *The Language of Postmodern Architecture* (1977). This also argued for the significance of the linguistic and symbolic character of architecture and broke with the Modernist past, which it saw as unnecessarily reductive. Postmodernism became a style defined by its playfulness, with elements such as parody, pastiche and quotation from previous historical styles and deliberate eclecticism brought to the fore. Despite the delay in the full dissemination of their ideas, in many respects design and architectural critics set the agenda in the previous decade for what would happen to design in the 1980s.

The linguistic turn in culture, as it has often been termed, made its impact on a number of different levels of German design. For already established designers, brought up on the principles of Modernism in the 1950s and '60s, this often involved inflecting their designs with a new sensibility. Such was the case, for instance, for Germany's most celebrated lighting designer, Ingo Maurer. Already a successful name when Postmodernism spread across Europe, Maurer's lighting design took off in many fruitful new directions.

This was not only at a theoretical level. Technological developments also contributed to these new paths, such as the invention of the halogen light bulb and the growing sophistication of LEDs (light-emitting diodes), which offered greater freedom of experiment in dematerialized form. These were less bound by the ideas of functional necessity of Modernist dogma. Such technology acted as a catalyst for Maurer to create lighting that crossed boundaries between contemporary art and design, with increased metaphorical sophistication and playfulness, as in 'Bibibibi' of 1982, a table lamp with the iconography of a bird made in porcelain, metal, plaster and feathers.[4]

For designers of the next generation, Postmodern critique also opened possibilities for a renewed engagement with the social potential of design, in part prompted by the Punk movement of the late 1970s and early 1980s. The mix offered a more expanded field in which to challenge accepted cultural boundaries. As part of the Neue deutsche Welle (New German Wave), experimental environmental, furniture and industrial design were partners to the music and sound performance of bands such as Einstürzende Neubauten, Abstürzende Brieftauben and Rasende Leichenbestatter. Often happening in a post-industrial setting of disused factories, its imagery was abrasive, embracing the aesthetic properties of demolition and detritus, while flaunting cynicism and introducing a sense of apocalypse. Materials such as corrugated cardboard, steel, glass, concrete and perforated metal had an improvisatory freshness, often visceral, that demanded a response from the viewer. Stiletto studio in West Berlin, led by Frank Schreiner, became famous for a series of chairs made from supermarket trolleys, begun in 1983. The principle of the chair was to convert a ready-made object into an item of furniture through minor adjustments of craftsmanship but a major re-conceptualization. Significantly, the name 'Consumer's Rest' appeared in the English language. In 1985 the ironically named series Neue deutsche Gemütlichkeit (New German Cosiness) included an occasional table, 'TV Dinner' made from a television tube, tubular steel, lamp and sheet glass, and 'Flying Spots', a set of television cabinets filled with living flies. Stiletto's combination of the ready-made with the industrial and electronic was typical of the period.[5]

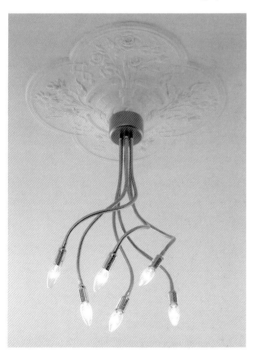

Stiletto studios (Frank Schreiner), 'Calamari and Shrimp', six-armed ceiling light, designed in 1985.

As in the Weimar period, the prefix *neu* appeared to signal a generational change of attitude. What distinguished the periods was that in the 1920s the young subscribed to the belief that the design could lead to a utopian new society, whereas in the 1980s, at its most extreme, the New Wave engaged with a dystopian vision of critical nihilism and energized excess. As another designer, Siegfried Michail Syniuga, wrote at the time, 'Furniture must be political, radiate eroticism, dissolve religion. Furniture must function not just under your arse, but in your head and in your soul.'[6]

The Last Days of 'Good Design'

In the late 1970s, however international the agenda, it was questionable whether the position of East or West Germany could be straightforwardly compared with the USA, where much of the debate originated. Both countries had a more sustained public investment in social housing, and public assumptions about patterns of consumer society differed from the American model. Added to this, the legacy of the design reform movement lingered on, proving influential on how many German designers were to negotiate the challenge of Postmodernism.

For West Germany, the destiny of its Rat für Formgebung (Design Council) epitomized the broader tensions that design experienced in the second half of the twentieth century in changes to design outlook. As was discussed in chapter Four, the Rat für Formgebung had taken on the mantle for design promotion previously held by the German Werkbund. Its history paralleled other official councils that were formed to promote design in the post-war period, for example, in Britain, the Netherlands and the Scandinavian countries. When it was agreed by the Bonn parliament to establish the Rat für Formgebung in 1951, Mia Seeger, its first director, led the programme of exhibitions by announcing her goal to establish for the country 'Wertmassstäbe und Formen einer durch den Krieg veränderten kulturellen Identität' (Standards and Forms of a Cultural Identity Changed by War).[7] Symptomatic of the time, Seeger quoted Max Bill on how design should concern itself with everything 'from the spoon to the city' ('vom Löffel bis zur Stadt reichen'). Established in Messel House in the Mathildenhöhe district of Darmstadt, RfF projects largely took the form of the promotion of German design through international exhibitions, and the proximity to Frankfurt allowed relations between the trade fairs to develop. West Germany was concerned to adopt the role of good citizen of the wider world and, as part of this initiative, sent abroad examples in exhibition of good industrial design, for example, to Pakistan, Iran and India. In

1962 *Design Center, Stuttgart* opened in the capital of Baden-Württemberg, a city surrounded by industry and commerce, and one of the most thriving federal capitals. Here, selections of the 'best' in all fields of design were displayed for retailers, industrialists and discerning consumers alike. By the mid-1960s, the question facing the Rat für Formgebung was how to develop a more extended understanding of *Gute Form*, while also adapting to alternative values and changed lifestyles of youth culture and popular design. Like Design Councils elsewhere in Europe, the institution directed its energies towards developing an extended advisory relationship with industry, becoming an information centre, advising authorities and governments, and building networks with other design institutions. By 1969 the Berlin-based IDZ – Internationales Design Zentrum – opened as a centre to develop thematic, historical and culturally oriented exhibitions and publications. At the same time, RfF introduced the *Bundespreis Gute Form*, an official German design prize intended to promote the 'economic meaning of product design as a competitive factor', clearly signalling the wish to maintain good relations with the government to justify its role. Competitions became thematically oriented, as in 1974, when to address the impact of the worldwide oil crisis, the subject was *Fahrräder und was dazu gehört – umweltfreundliche Individualfahrzeuge* (Bicycles and their Implications – Environmentally Friendly Vehicles), coinciding with a widespread engagement with ecology felt at a popular political level.[8]

Under the director Herbert Ohl, who took on the role from 1973, the RfF became a forum for design and technology to provide a context for the education of industrial designers and subject specialists in other design fields under the title *Design-Dialoge Darmstadt*. By the end of the 1980s the Rat für Formgebung had left Darmstadt to take up offices at the Frankfurt Trade Fair, with the encouragement of *Messe* Frankfurt and the regional government of Hesse. In this new setting, director Michael Erlhoff installed thematic exhibitions such as *Ritual und Gegenstand* (Ritual and Object) and *Unternehmenskultur und Stammeskultur* (Employer Culture and Tribal Culture), which took wider social and cultural perspectives on design.

The altered identities and changing roles of the RfF reflected wider shifts in design discourse itself, from a preoccupation with taste and aesthetic judgement to a broader, inter-disciplinary approach in which the concept of design embraced social, industrial and ecological concerns. The change was signalled when the *Bundespreis Gute Form* ceased to be awarded in 1985, implying that the concept 'good design', primarily based on aesthetic criteria, was no longer applicable. Nevertheless, in 1992 the design prize was reintroduced as *Bundespreis Produktdesign* with the intention of

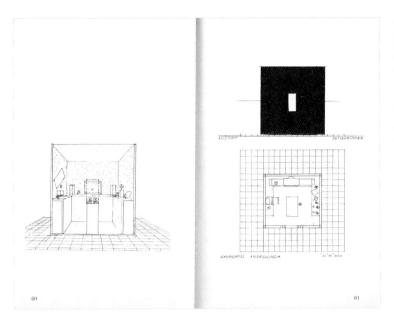

awarding products that had made an international impact. Themes were not totally prescribed but their criteria included *Gebrauchstäglichkeit* (everyday usefulness) and *Umweltverträglichkeit* (environmental compatibility), along with safety in use.

As Gwendolyn Ristant has written of this time, officially approved design in the Federal Republic was generally associated with following the belief in objective criteria for design selection. German style, she suggested, was 'modest in appearance, functional in use, matter-of-fact, with neat right angles, in white, grey or black, without ornamentation, with no more than precise, technically necessary details: such was the look of those mass products that conformed to the ideal of good design'.[9] Evidence of this, for example, was in how the electrical firm Braun, a company associated with all such design values, received an above-average number of awards in the scheme. Prizes were given to companies in other spheres of production that in the eyes of the judges produced high-quality technical products whose 'design combines functionality and aesthetics'. Selected products for the award in 1996, for instance, included Audi and Porsche automobiles, Lamy pens, the NOBLEX 135 U Panorama camera, the Schindler transparent lift for ease of access to buildings, Blanco Med medical equipment and Rodenstock spectacle frames.[10] To commentators beyond its borders, West German design became synonymous with products of this technologically oriented sphere: a world of domestic appliances, machine tools, cameras, radios,

The award-winning Somatom Spirit CT scanner, 2006, designed by the Munich group Designafairs (Klaus Thormann and Sebastian Maier) for Siemens AG, Medical Solutions was praised for its awareness of patient needs, based on ergonomic studies. Many of its characteristics are associated with high-end German industrial design.

modes of transportation, audio equipment, televisions, articles for the office, furniture systems and information design. Such a characterization, based on a strong record of achievement, was something that designers of the following generations sought to negotiate and at times distance themselves from.

Anton Stankowski: Modern Graphic Design

In much the way that Peter Behrens or Bruno Paul could be said to have encapsulated design values closely associated with the official institutions of German design discourse early in the twentieth century, a figure such as Anton Stankowski can be seen as a designer emblematic of official values, a 'hero' of modern design later in the century. Interestingly, Stankowski's career connects 1920s functionalism with 1950s and '60s corporate Modernism, and represents a continuation of these ideas into the late twentieth century.[11]

Stankowski came out of the tradition of the new typography. Originally trained as an interior decorator in Düsseldorf, he moved to the Folkwangschule in Essen, where he studied in 1928 to 1929 with Max

Kreissparkasse
Esslingen–Nürtingen
1984 – zehn Jahre

Burchartz, one of the main protagonists of modern graphic design. Stankowski then joined the small graphic design studio *werbe-bau* run by Johannes Canis in Bochum, another landmark in Constructivist-inspired design. The designer then spent the 1930s in Switzerland, where he taught at the Gewerbeschule in Zurich, developing his theories of an abstract, formal language of visual communication while also working for Max Dalang advertising studio. Stankowski continued to experiment through painting: each series of works examined properties of composition and colour theory

Designing Modern Germany

that ran parallel to their realization as designs. Testing ideas in black and white as well as through colour exercises, Stankowski was especially interested in the theories of Josef Albers, the Bauhaus-trained designer who by then was teaching at Black Mountain College, North Carolina. Returning to Germany, in the 1950s Stankowski established a successful design studio in Stuttgart, where he attracted many industrial and corporate clients. Drawn to the challenge of industrial graphics, he designed brochures and magazine advertisements for many companies on the engineering end of production. It was in the post-war world of growing corporate companies, large-scale communication industries and international banking that Stankowski's deceptively simple approach, giving visual order to complex organizations, came to prominence. Clients extended to include Süddeutscher Rundfunk, Deutsche Bank, Vissmann and Behr-Möbel. He was made a professor of design by the state of Baden-Württemberg in 1976, and as founder of his own Stankowski Stiftung (foundation) in 1983 and through many publications, his influence became widespread.

Unlike American designers who were his contemporaries, such as Paul Rand and Milton Glaser, Stankowski stayed strictly within the remit of graphic design. If images were to be used, they were either professional photographs or abstract motifs. He did not cross over to incorporate the 'softer', more humorous side of graphic illustration, or the visual puns of image making. In this sense, Stankowski was an uncompromising Modernist who believed in the power of the abstract graphic symbol and reductive typography to communicate a message effectively. Among these designs were the corporate identity for IBM in Germany and the entire information design for the city of West Berlin in 1967–8 and which combined various abstract motifs with the single sans-serif typeface Akzidenz Grotesk. Appropriately for his commitment to international communication, Stankowski's contributions as chair of the visual design committee for the Olympic Games of 1972 in Munich won him widespread recognition.

Official Design in the Last Years of East Germany

Official design culture in East Germany tended to be organized along similar lines to the Federal Republic, with a design press, albeit much smaller in its quantity of publications, commenting on government-run associations that oversaw its cultural institutions, museums and education, and selection panels and juries who awarded annual prizes for the 'best' in industrial and furniture design, book and poster design, and equivalents in other areas of the applied arts. The intended sphere of influence, however, was

different. If the Federal Republic sought to be both model state in Western Europe and an effective productive economic force worldwide, the East German ambition was to maintain a reputation as leader within the Eastern Bloc in terms of industrial production. In this, design was recognized to be a vital ingredient. To promote its cultural identity, the GDR held a number of events that drew foreign artists, designers and cultural figures to its many exhibitions and award ceremonies.

In 1978, belatedly when compared with Western developments, the *Gutes Design* prize was introduced in the GDR. According to its regulations, it was awarded to makers of 'outstandingly designed products in GDR manufacturing'. This amounted to recognition by the state of 'achievements of industry in the area of industrial product design' for the following criteria:

> products that are significant in their design, products that are shown in trade shows or exhibitions in the GDR. The award shall simultaneously promote the application of design in the development and advancement of products as well as influence through export.[12]

Emphasis lay on engineering design, vehicles for public and industrial transport, and office and institutional furnishings rather than consumer items. More than in the West, GDR design awards were part of a culture that acknowledged individual products or design systems that made significant

Reinhard Kranz, street furniture in Neubrandenburg, 1981. The GDR design awards often recognized design that fulfilled social needs.

Designing Modern Germany

contributions to the economy or that, at a cultural-political level, symbolized ideals held by the state. This was the case, even when the purchase of selected items was beyond individual consumers' financial means, or, more seriously, unavailable because of material shortages.

Neue Werbung / New Publicity

A further perspective on the changes in official positions towards design can be found in the pages of *Neue Werbung*, the monthly magazine that covered graphic and publication design, illustration, marketing and advertising. In the last years of the GDR, design journalism showed many similarities with the West, but also significant differences.[13] DEWAG, the publishing house that produced *Neue Werbung*, was the largest state-run company and oversaw 'sight agitation and propaganda' in the form of posters, pictures, transparencies, audio tapes and wall-newspapers for transport, factory halls, waiting rooms, stations and political meeting rooms, as well as the press across the entire GDR. The associated design magazine, an internal rather than an external critical voice, covered the fields of publicity for commerce and the state, both in the GDR and countries within the satellite of its political influence. Leipzig, East Berlin and Dresden remained important centres for visitors from the international

Two cover designs for the official GDR graphic and publicity design magazine *Neue Werbung*: April 1970 (left) a cover by Helmut Wengler for the special issue to mark the hundredth birthday of Lenin, and May 1970 (right) a design by Axel Bertram for the 25th anniversary of the 'freeing of Germany from Fascism'.

world of graphic design. Graphic designers, graduates of the Kunsthoch-schule Berlin-Weissensee, Halle, or the Leipzig Academy, were members of the Verband Bildender Künstler (Association of Applied Artists), which guaranteed that fees for services were strictly enforced. DEWAG was a major employer, as the only 'advertising agency', but designers also worked for the state, for firms, the SED and theatres. The cultural end of graphic design offered the most freedom.

On reviewing a magazine such as *Neue Werbung*, it becomes clear that certain themes predominate. Particular attention was given, for example, to the strong tradition of Polish posters and East European book design. Intended as an international publication, articles appeared bilingually, in German and Russian, the preferred second language. Such a policy might be contrasted with the established Swiss graphic journal *Graphis*, which since 1944 had appeared in French, German and English. Crucially, the lan-guages allowed *Neue Werbung* to be read in countries under Soviet influence, including the People's Republic of China and Cuba, as well as those of the more expected Eastern Bloc. Through *Neue Werbung*, the GDR established itself as a leader in style, publicity and marketing, like the neighbouring Federal Republic, where *novum Gebrauchsgraphik* was a recognized refer-ence point for graphic design internationally. The events covered in the magazine stressed close ties between culture and the Party interests that prompted them, because major party congresses were reported.[14]

Reflecting the mainstream press attention given to the achievements of major GDR production plants, emphasis turned to industrial graphics in the form of brochures, leaflets and information design: these combined the techniques of object photography with the subject of heavy industry. For instance, a promotion campaign in 1978 under the slogan 'Plaste und Elaste aus Schkopau' drew attention to more than 900 chemical products by VEB Chemische Werke Buna, an employer of 30,000 workers and one of the GDR's most important industries. The graphic designs were explained as an 'Arbeitsmittel' – a work medium – and 'objective' and 'informative' trade-marks, brochures, posters and advertisements were applauded.[15]

In the less competitive sphere of the graphic arts, including book pub-lishing and poster design for cultural events, greater stylistic flexibility was allowed. Graphic works embraced latter-day versions of Surrealism and Expressionism, as worked through by second- and third-generation artists and designers, particularly in editorial illustration and poster designs for theatre, concerts and exhibitions. In parallel to the lasting importance of Brecht to GDR theatre, photomontage was legitimized in the Party's eyes through the radical Communist associations with Berlin Dada, most par-

Cover design by Jochen Filder for the catalogue *100 Beste Plakate*, Erfurt 1987. Poster design in the GDR was one area that offered a relatively relaxed attitude toward artistic independence.

ticularly John Heartfield, who together with his brother Wieland Herzfelde had returned to the GDR after the war. Posters in the 1970s and '80s, often with small print runs, circulated beyond official channels, and artists used small private galleries as venues for their displays in centres such as Leipzig, Erfurt and Karl Marx Stadt (now Chemnitz).

More controversially for the official line taken on the place of graphic design within a socialist society, occasional articles on the best window displays or the interior design of state-run cafés and restaurants introduced the reader to the more expanded field of environmental graphic design. Indeed, by the mid-1980s the magazine had broadened its emphasis to cover profiles of prominent figures of the first generation of graphic designers, such as Fritz Ehmcke, Julius Gipkens and Edmund Edel, under the heading 'Klassiker deutscher Gebrauchsgraphik' (Classics of German Commercial Graphics). Through this, editorial policy became open to cover the 'heroes' of modern design who were already known to successive generations of Western designers, critics and historians. On one level, this was a further acknowledgement of the broader historicism of the age, yet, importantly, it also signalled in the GDR that 'capitalist age' graphic design could now be considered alongside socialist and Communist designs, since most of the work represented was commercial rather than political graphic design from the *Jugend* and Weimar years.

The Presence of the Past

In most European situations, Postmodern discourse required a realignment with recent and more distant history of a complex kind. For Germany, the issues were more sensitive than most. In many respects, the post-war years had witnessed the fulfilment of modernity and the strongest cultural continuity was with the years of the Weimar Republic rather than deeper history. Broader historical reference risked raising more complex and controversial associations. In the mid-1980s in the Federal Republic, what was termed the *Historikerstreit* took place among historians and philosophers and this was to have resonance in the GDR as well. Jürgen Habermas, a major protagonist, accused some historians of revisionism, for relativizing crimes of National Socialism while stressing those of Stalinism. At the same time, historical research turned attention to the lives of ordinary German citizens during the Third Reich and their degree of suffering. This struck to the core the question of German national identity. As commentators have indicated, 'In contrast to renewed attempts at reconstituting Germany as a community shaped by destiny (*Schicksalsgemeinschaft*) or as an ethnically or culturally unique nation, Habermas proposed a patriotism based on allegiance to the constitution (*Verfassungspatriotismus*).'[16]

To alleviate the burden of their national history, many German designers turned to the more open international context of design exhibitions and debate. An important landmark for Postmodernism was the first exhibition entirely dedicated to architecture held at the Venice Biennale in 1980. While the exhibition and subsequent critical debate may have focused on architecture, many of its protagonists were equally engaged with the field of design, and the issues would inform both fields in the next few years. The implications were as significant for Germany as Italy and other European countries.

The organizers acknowledged that 'Postmodernism' existed, using the term drawn from the important work of the French philosopher Jean-François Lyotard, *The Postmodern Condition: A Report on Knowledge* (1979), which was translated into German in 1982. Their reluctance to use the term 'Postmodern', choosing instead 'The Presence of the Past' for the title, prompted a debate about the 'return' to history. The architect and critic Paolo Portoghesi contributed the introductory essay, 'The End of Prohibitionism'. His premise was not without controversy. In one instance, Kenneth Frampton, the architectural critic and historian, resigned from the committee, withdrawing his essay because he could not agree with the overarching interpretation of the group of critics and architects. These included Hans Hollein, Rem Koolhaas and OMA, Michael Graves, Jeremy Dixon, Arata Isozaki, Robert Venturi, John Rauch and

Denise Scott-Brown. Portoghesi positioned the project on an ambitious scale. He signalled a break, both with the apparent singularity of the Modernist position and the systematic cataloguing of nineteenth-century eclecticism, until then the strongest viable alternative to modern orthodoxy.

Portoghesi wrote:

> The relationship with the history of architecture which the 'postmodern' condition makes possible doesn't need the eclectic method anymore, because it can count on a form of 'disenchantment', on a much greater psychological detachment . . .
>
> History is the 'material' of logical and constructive operations whose only purpose is that of joining the real and the imaginary through the communication mechanisms whose effectiveness can be verified; it is material utilizable for the socialization of aesthetic experience, since it presents sign systems of great conventional value which make it possible to think and make others think through architecture.

And with reference to cultural location and the political implications of his point of view, he went on to suggest: 'In this sense, architecture can once again be returned to the places and regions of the earth without a return to a racial or religious metaphysic.'[17]

Especially important for German architects and designers was the invitation in his last words to draw on history, without the inevitable accusation of invoking a difficult, if not impossible past. For some, including Frampton, Portoghesi's position risked taking architecture beyond the sphere of direct or engaged contexts into a global, nomadic space. This was a point of view echoed more generally in subsequent criticism of Postmodern design. For others, it was liberating. Of all contributors, it was Aldo Rossi, then chair of architectural composition at the Venice University Institute of Architecture, who captured the main tenets of the exhibition and the public imagination with his designs. Rossi exhibited an extension to a cemetery in Modena, a design for a school and an inspiring model and installation, the 'Teatro del mondo', an arrangement of buildings intended to encapsulate history and memory. According to Charles Jencks,

> Aldo Rossi was instrumental in turning architects' attention back to the city morphology and the way the city and its monuments form a collective memory.
>
> Street, arcade, piazza, monument – these traditional elements reappeared in his work.[18]

The boundaries between architecture and design in Italy were traditionally very fluid and it was usual for architects to enter various design fields. At the prompting of Alessandro Mendini, the Alessi company in Crusinallo in northern Italy, established in 1921 and until then a relatively small specialist metalwork company commissioning modern design, turned to many of the architects associated with the Venice Biennale to contribute to its design project 'Tea and Coffee Piazza'. The result was a series of silver services that enacted similar narratives to those rehearsed in the architectural drawings at Venice. They were realized on a domestic scale in the form of tea and coffee services, opening up the possibility for design for objects destined for the interior to work as a 'domestic landscape'. The series was arranged as an exhibition by the Austrian architect Hans Hollein in Milan in 1983.[19]

This commission proved a landmark in the history of design and its impact was felt throughout Germany, just as elsewhere. Not necessarily affordable for the everyday consumer, the series nevertheless struck the imagination of design curators to the extent that a considerable number of collections in arts and crafts museums and the new international design museums felt compelled to acquire them. Their collective presence in museums and in the satellite lifestyle design shops that were proliferating around the time signalled a significant step away from the rational, functionalist tradition of design to a new level of symbolism and poetry in objects. In the 1980s, the years that became identified as the 'designer decade', the

In recent years Alessi stores opened in Hamburg, Munich and Cologne, following the design concept that Hani Rashid initially created for their shops in the USA. In the Cologne store, the horizontal display case provided an imaginative setting for the signature 'Tea and Coffee Piazza' range.

Designing Modern Germany

Aldo Rossi, apartment block, part of a housing complex built for the Berlin Internationale Bauausstellung, 1984.

word design became a prefix extended to many areas of human activity. The term also entered the German language in the form of *Grafik-design*, *Textil-design* and *Möbel-design*.

In the case of Alessi the group of international designers ranged across Italy, Austria, Germany and the USA. Among the German contributors, Joseph-Paul Kleihues, then professor of architectural theory and planning at the University of Dortmund, became a figure of central importance for the development of West Berlin as the director of the *Internationale Bauausstellung* (*IBA*), which culminated in the opening of the building projects in the city in 1984. The *IBA Neubau* scheme brought in international architects to provide model new housing, among them Aldo Rossi, Rob Krier and Hans Hollein, whose designs reflected a consciousness of the debates about history and context, as rehearsed in Venice. References were made to Berlin's building types drawn from across the domestic, commercial and industrial scene. An interesting aspect of the project was the *Altbau* scheme, which incorporated consultation with German-Turkish residents of the city and led to the restoration and remodelling of previously run-down historical quarters of the city, involving local planners, politicians, community groups and residents in the process. Recognition of history, both in the urban typology of the new build, and in the conscious effort to retain buildings from earlier periods, marked a significant change in approach in the history of building exhibitions.[20]

The Alessi project proved an extremely influential model for other companies to follow. While some, like the ceramic company Rosenthal, had well-established traditions of commissioning designers to contribute to its studio lines, others followed suit. In 1986 several designers were invited by WMF (Württembergische Metallwarenfabrik), a leading manufacture of cooking and tableware aiming to re-position itself within the contemporary design sphere. WMF chose to do this with a series of plastic trays that could be immediately identified by their designer. Signalling this Postmodern moment, they incorporated a characteristic mix of designs inspired by William Morris and *Jugendstil*, as well as more contemporary, fashionable lines.[21]

Despite such commercial engagement with style and ornament, perhaps more than any other country, the critique of Postmodernism struck to the core of the national identity of German design. From the Werkbund, the Bauhaus and Ulm, to the late functionalism of large-scale

housing programmes and city transport systems, even when stereotyped as cold, technocratic or too singular in their design idiom, the underlying principles nevertheless represented a strong sense of continuity that appeared to be under attack. As one commentator, hostile to the Postmodern turn, lamented:

The King Collection was an example of WMF commissioning international designers to develop new studio lines.

> Once, at the Bauhaus or the Hochschule für Gestaltung in Ulm, the intention was to develop *the* chair, *the* spoon, *the* radio, *the* design for a terrace house, *the* cell in which to live, but recently the élite of the profession has come to terms with the fact of developing or disguising objects that become out of date in a short time, instead of objects that can be used for a long time. Here a designer follows the directives of management, in whatever form they may come, in order to support the throw-away economy as the form of business most likely to bring turnover and profit in a saturated market.[22]

In the GDR during the 1980s the impact of Postmodernism was most apparent in a changed attitude towards design for the urban environment rather than in the sphere of product design or everyday consumer goods. An indication of this was the attention given to the renovation of the historical quarters of its cities. In place of the consistent emphasis on the new of the previous decades, especially in housing, industrial plants and social

Albrecht von Bodecker, poster for '750 years anniversary Berlin', 1987. Von Bodecker went on to become Professor and Rektor at the Hochschule für Grafik und Buchkunst in Leipzig.

services, what Florian Urban has called 'neo-historical' GDR, constructed from ready-made components, took hold.[23] For instance, attention was given to surviving nineteenth-century quarters close to the centre of East Berlin, which had been previously overlooked. With the historical fabric virtually untouched since 1945, emphasis turned to refashioning these intact areas through the introduction of symbols of heritage and tradition, including historicist street furniture, street signs, pavements and planting. According to a notional concept of 'Altberlin', reconstructions of the Spandauer Vorstadt and Nikolaiviertel were opened in 1987, revealing eighteenth- and early nineteenth-century town houses intermingled with modern infill, often mixing bars, restaurants and gift shops with offices and residential areas along re-cobbled streets. Such development mirrored moves in heritage culture more generally across the world. In a similar way, in another significant historical quarter of Prenz-lauerberg, already a district associated with a cultural milieu, renovations were also undertaken. As an indication of this deeper return to history, the Museum of Berliner Arbeiterleben um 1900, a museum of workers' lives in the city around 1900, opened on 1 May 1987, with an emphasis on telling a Marxist-Leninist history of everyday life (*Alltagsgeschichte*).

Such development in the East was not unique to Berlin; other East German towns and cities with historical quarters were also subject to similar attention. For a regime built on the ideals and principles of workerist production, the re-emphasis on cultural patrimony necessarily implied striking a balance between notions of collective history, educational purpose, privatized consumption and changing class values. The authorities became increasingly sensitized to the potential economic importance of leisure and tourism. Many of the plans were in place for the 750th anniversary of Berlin, celebrated in 1987. The fortieth anniversary of the foundation of the GDR, however, scheduled for November 1989, another important event where the achievements in historical urban reconstruction would be displayed, was never to be fully realized.

The Museum Boom

The shift to Postmodernism in the design profession was accompanied by curatorial initiatives to engage with more open-ended definitions of design and its influence. Among the first was an exhibition *Die gewöhnliche Design* (Ordinary Design) held in Darmstadt in 1976 that marked a move away from the overriding concern with 'good form' or status in design. Coinciding with events to mark the 75th anniversary of *Jugendstil*, by then perceived as 'high' design, the exhibition took everyday objects and exposed them to the scrutiny of museum display, breaking away from the usual model of the art museum in which canonical objects were selected for their stylistic significance. In a darkened space with Plexiglass vitrines, everyday objects included an air pump, a plastic bucket, radio batteries, a rail timetable, nylon tights, a milk carton, pencils, a chain, an ice-cream scoop, a pencil sharpener, an aspirin/pain reliever, plastic cutlery and a toilet-roll holder.[24]

The 1980s witnessed a phenomenal growth in the building of museums across the Western world. For some, this overwhelming interest in the past, the documenting and curating of design from earlier times against the backdrop of a post-industrial climate, was a further symptom of Postmodern anxiety about the future. The museums, prominent venues for this re-evaluation, were built to the designs of international architects appointed through competitions and increasingly seen as central to the cultural and economic revival and the landmark identity of cities. One of the first to gain international acclaim as a self-consciously Postmodern project was the

James Stirling's extension to the Staatsgalerie in Stuttgart of 1978 marked the beginning of a postmodern approach to the museum's central role in the cultural rebranding of a German city.

Designing Modern Germany

extension to the Staatsgalerie in Stuttgart, undertaken between 1977 and 1984 to the design of the British architect James Stirling. The building drew on references to the distant and more recent past, including Hadrian's Wall and the architecture of Karl Friedrich Schinkel, but it was also assertively contemporary in its juxtaposition of colours and materials. Such pluralism was shocking for those more in tune with the singularity of a Modernist vision. Stuttgart's success in using a signature building to change the fortunes of a city paralleled its immediate precedent, the Pompidou Centre, which opened in Paris in 1977. It provided a new environment in which to view art or spend leisure time and became a model for other major cities such as Cologne, Bremen, Düsseldorf, Hamburg, Munich and Nuremberg, which realized similar projects through substantial cultural funding. One of the most remarkable was the city of Frankfurt am Main, where the riverside was modelled into a museum quarter, involving the renovation of existing museums and the addition of the new ones, among them the new Museum für Kunsthandwerk by the American architect Richard Meier and Oswald Matthias Ungers's Deutsches Architekturmuseum.[25]

Of the specialist design museums in the Federal Republic, two warrant particular attention in offering contrasting perspectives on the question of curating modern design, a central plank of the country's design identity. The first, the Bauhaus Archiv, was an important project that contributed to the continuing legacy of the school and future generations of the design-interested public. Although the original buildings of Weimar and Dessau lay in the East, Gropius, Breuer, Moholy-Nagy and Bayer and other prominent

Ott+Stein (Nicolaus Ott and Bernard Stein), poster for an exhibition on the Bauhaus Metalworkshop held at the Kunsthalle in Weimar in 1992. It depicted Marianne Brandt's design for a silver and ebony teapot, originally designed in 1924, which also carried significance for a generation of postmodern designers.

staff who had emigrated to the USA were instrumental in returning the heritage to West Germany through the bequest of parts of their archives. The original Bauhaus Archiv was founded by Hans Maria Wingler in the Ernst-Ludwig-Haus on the Mathildenhöhe in Darmstadt in 1960. The first major travelling exhibition, *50 Jahre Bauhaus*, supported by the Federal government, was held in 1968. It was in the 1980s and '90s that the full impact of the Archiv's exhibition programme was felt. Following a move to Berlin in 1971, the archive was first installed in historical rooms facing Schloss Charlottenburg before the completion of a purpose-built gallery, library, offices and storage, built to Gropius's own design, opened near the cultural forum in West Berlin in 1979. The research and exhibition programme of the Archiv subsequently enriched the historical knowledge of the teaching and design achievements of its staff and the students in the various workshops of the school, as well as addressing its lasting impact on contemporary design issues. In the meantime, at Dessau, following reunification, circumstances improved for a parallel collection-based exhibition and publication plan to develop at the historic site, while the school buildings and master houses underwent major conservation and restoration under their classification as a World Heritage Site. Together, these initiatives asserted Germany's definitive significance for Modernism.[26]

Another notable museological project that encouraged a more open-ended consideration of contemporary design was the Vitra Museum, which pointed to the future as well as the past. The original Vitra furniture company was established by Willi Fehlbaum in Basel in 1934 and became one of Europe's most important centres for furniture design. The company was founded in Weil am Rhein on the extreme south-west border between Germany and Switzerland. In 1957 Vitra gained the licensing rights from Herman Miller to distribute Charles and Ray Eames and George Nelson furniture in Europe, forming a parallel to Knoll Associates, discussed in chapter Four. From this secure base the commission of contemporary designers began, the first being Werner Panton's Panton chair of 1967. The project was a significant force in cultivating a lineage of high design from *Jugendstil* to the Bauhaus and mid-twentieth-century modern to Postmodernism. The company published its aims in 2007:

We are convinced that rooms and interior design have a decisive
influence on people's motivation, performance and health. So we
have made it our mission to develop furniture and furnishing systems
that stimulate, inspire and motivate, while also offering the body
comfort, safety and support. In order to attain this goal, we work

Designing Modern Germany

The permanent collection of Vitra Design Museum, Weil am Rhein, telling the history of international modern chair design and arranged as a stacked, wall-mounted display.

with renowned designers and a specialized Vitra team. We experiment with new ideas, and are continuously tackling the new challenges of the world of work.[27]

Under Willi Fehlbaum's son, Rolf, the company grew in cultural significance and ambition: on the site at Weil am Rhein two factories designed by the British architect Nicholas Grimshaw were built in 1981 and 1986. The year 1993 saw the realization of the fire station, the first completed building by the Iraqi-born British architect Zaha Hadid, and a conference pavilion by the Japanese architect Tadao Ando. Just as Vitra became an important site for contemporary architecture, it also became active as an international think-tank, running workshops on themes in architecture and design, and, most importantly, in 1989 opening the Vitra Design Museum under the direction of Alexander von Wegesack in a Frank O. Gehry building. This housed part of the extensive permanent Fehlbaum collection of furniture design and formed the base from which to originate ambitious curatorial projects and publications. In terms of the encouragement of contemporary design cultures, since 1987 Vitra Editions promoted ways for internationally acclaimed designers to develop projects, in laboratory conditions, without the consideration of normal market circumstances as restrictions. To compensate for its geographical distance from many of the important urban centres for design, travelling exhibitions became an important element of the programme, while in 2001 an annexe of the Vitra Design Museum opened in a converted industrial building in Berlin for a short number of years.

If the curatorial projects of design museums in the Federal Republic predominantly engaged with the history and legacy of Modernism, in the GDR, beyond the traditional fine and decorative arts museums, and in keeping with materialist history, emphasis was on understanding everyday life rather than the profession or form of design. On the fall of the Wall, attention continued to be on understanding the GDR's recent past and the lives of ordinary people through exhibitions of political and everyday life in what might be called an archaeology of a political regime. The material culture of everyday life was propelled by political change and a gradual coming to terms with the past 40 years of the regime. In Eisenhüttenstadt, for example, a Dokumentationszentrum Alltagskultur der DDR, a collection of more than 70,000 everyday objects, was drawn on to make exhibitions that combined social, political and aesthetic topics.[28] One curatorial motivation was to counter the prevailing popular nostalgia for the GDR period, *Ostalgie* as it became known, which risked masking by sentiment a more complete understanding of people's actual relations to the material world during the period of the GDR. Another impulse was to correct the view that the history of East German design was simply one of cheap, poor-quality, mass-produced goods, mere pale imitations of goods available in the West. As the curator wrote in the opening text to an exhibition *Die Deutsche Demokratische Republik, 1949–1990*, 'The GDR belongs in the Museum'. The text continued:

Installation of the exhibition *Die Deutsche Demokratische Republik, 1949–1990*, held at the Deutsches Historisches Museum, Berlin in 2007.

Designing Modern Germany

a call for objects and reminiscences to prevent the history of the GDR from disappearing was made in June 1990 by the curators of the Deutsches Historisches Museum and the material interpreted in subsequent exhibitions on the cultural and political life in the Museum's programme.[29]

'German' Design Responds to the Changed Situation

The fall of the Berlin Wall on 9 November 1989 and the subsequent opening of the border between the entire GDR, the Federal Republic and its East European neighbours were followed by the reunification of Germany on 3 October 1990. For designers in the West, no immediate need to change well-established ways of working were called for, although the expanded geography opened many new opportunities. Life in the design cities of the former Federal Republic offered continuity and also a magnet for new designers to migrate from the eastern zone and beyond. For many Germans, citizens of a configuration of states (*Länder*) within a federal constitution, regional structures were as important as national ones, and the country's membership of the European Union also offered an additional perspective through which to see its 'national' question. Rather than identify oneself as German, one solution was to choose to be defined as a citizen of the new Europe.

The greater initial challenge was therefore in the East, where many of the accepted premises of the earlier design culture were undermined by the introduction of market forces. The choice was whether to adapt totally to Western-style practices or to attempt to retain some of the qualities of a distinctive design culture. A large part of GDR identity was associated with strong political intervention, much discredited through the process of change (*die Wende*) and the exposure of the operations of the Stasi secret police and other forms of censorship. A more positive element, however, was to retain the possibility of design as a cultural activity not solely driven by profit.

The reputation of German design since 1989 and the alternative paths open to its designers will be the focus of the rest of this chapter. As commentaries suggested, since its introduction as a marque, 'Made in Germany' had carried a great deal of significance in the wider world throughout the twentieth century, with expectations of the highest quality of products. Now, in a competitive global market, the country faced a stage of redefinition to embrace two differently evolved design cultures under one heading and to present the unified country in a new light.[30]

Jil Sander and Eva Gronbach

A strong contrast in approaches to these issues from designers of different generations highlights the opportunities, in this case, from the field of fashion design. While German design in many fields was held in great esteem, as far as fashion was concerned, it had never claimed an equivalent status to Paris, Milan or New York. Force of circumstance did not help; in a decentralized Federal Republic the idea of a leading or single fashion city, following the model of the post-war couture industry, did not fall naturally onto the German political and cultural map. Instead, it was through the projection of fashion brands onto a global context, rather than through a fashion 'locus', that German fashion designers made their mark in the 1980s and '90s.

Pre-eminent in the field of German women's fashion design was Jil Sander. Born in 1943 in Wesselburen near Hamburg, Sander studied textile engineering at Krefeld, one centre for the West German textile industry, before a two-year period in Los Angeles exposed her to patterns of American marketing. On returning, Sander set up a boutique in Hamburg and her own label then followed in 1968. Sander's reputation grew as a designer who had uncompromising expectations for the level of quality in her garments: her designs stood for 'luxurious simplicity'. Aware of the relationship between design and publicity, partly from a short period as a fashion editor on *Petra*, one of Germany's leading fashion magazines, Sander notoriously used her own face to market her perfume range in 1978. Her confidence in bringing her company and personal identity together was shared with her contemporary American counterparts, Donna Karan, Ralph Lauren and Calvin Klein, who were also realizing the importance of the diversification of their brand labels from clothes to beauty products and lifestyle. Through this, Sander took German fashion design to the global centre stage.[31]

It was possible to trace characteristics associated with German design in Sander's approach: she became understood to design for the modern, self-confident woman. Her company's advertising and marketing campaigns often employed highly stylized black-and-white photography with plain backgrounds and stark cropping, which carried associations with the New Objectivity of the 1920s, the subject of an intense revival of interest in the 1990s. Jil Sander's international stores operate as choreographed spaces: the installation of the clothes in predominantly white, expansive interiors, often part of historical buildings in which architectural detail contrasted with the clothes and minimalist shop fittings. The strong awareness

The Jil Sander Autumn/Winter 2006/07 collection, at Milan Fashion Week, February 2006. Sander's designs began to gain attention in the 1980s and are known for their luxurious simplicity.

Designing Modern Germany

of the creative boundary between architecture and fashion could be seen as 'German', although there were many parallel resonances between Sander and American and Japanese fashion houses.

In contrast to Jil Sander, whose designs avoided controversial discourse and placed the consumer in an idealized space that suggested a disavowal of materialism that paradoxically only money could buy, was the designer of two generations later, Eva Gronbach, who made her reputation through questioning the relationship between fashion design and identity. The fashion range that established Gronbach's name nationally and internationally in the 2000–1 season was 'Déclaration d'amour à Allemagne' (Declaration of Love for Germany). The campaign hit a nerve with the changed sentiment of optimism for a new Germany and was photographed by Donia Pitsc.[32]

Gronbach took old symbols and put them into a new context. The power of the linguistic sign matched by the integration of icons from German history was given a twist, subtle irony and occasional shock or frisson. This was so in 2003, when 'Mutter, Erde Vater, Land' (Mother, Earth Father, Land), a slogan with inevitably patriotic associations, played with the connotations of words that had strong associations within German history. The clothes continued these references with the emblem of the eagle, the use of the colours yellow, white and red, and black shirts. Other ranges and

Eva Gronbach, 'My New Police Dress Uniform' collection, 2004/5. The energy of Gronbach's designs came from her willingness to embrace street style and to offer diverse cultural meanings for the clothing.

Designing Modern Germany

Espresso Machine, XP 5000 series, KRUPS/Groupe SEB, 2004. Konstantin Grcic, head of the well-known Munich-based industrial design group, was commissioned to design a range of coffee-making equipment for the established company Krups. Although manufactured internationally, the products were nonetheless expected to convey 'German' qualities.

slogans included 'My New Police Dress Uniform' for the 2004–5 season, with inscriptions on clothing of 'Willkommen im deutschen Lande', and 'In Honour of Karl Valentin' – the Bavarian comedian, author and film director – in 2007, a collection that was photographed by Iwo Gospodinow.

At a semiotic level, Gronbach allowed her clothes to play with signification, loosening a too rigid identification of design traits to fixed meanings. Instead, what might be understood as the separation of the signifier from the signified allowed the opportunity for the wearer of the clothes to negotiate a more ironic, confrontational and open-ended identity, a strategy commonly employed in popular culture since the 1980s. Representative of the new, post-unification Germany, Gronbach located herself firmly as working in the north-west of Europe. Originally from Cologne, she studied at La Cambre in Brussels and IFM in Paris, before working with several leading designers, including Yohji Yamamoto and John Galliano. In part, her career of travelling from Germany led to the commission of Eva Gronbach to design the uniforms for the staff on the Thalys, the high-speed trains connecting Germany with Paris, Brussels and Amsterdam. Her label, German Jeans, asserted a connection between Germany and street style: a range that made references to the traditional industrial clothing of coal miners of the Ruhr district in order to suggest that overlooked or underrated areas of German life could be opened to interesting cultural interpretation.

'German' design identities

In the field of industrial design, Konstantin Grcic became one of the most successful of his generation to adapt to the requirements of an increasingly international context. He was born in Munich in 1965, but while taking place in part in Germany, his career cannot simply be attributed to one country alone, but rather illustrated the international tendencies of the modern designer. Grcic trained in furniture design at the John Makepeace School for Craftsmen at Parnham, Dorset, and then in design at the Royal

College of Art in London from 1988 to 1990, before returning to found Konstantin Grcic Industrial Design (KGID) in his home city the following year. As a multi-disciplinary design group, KGID developed solutions for lighting, furniture and product design, working for some of Europe's leading design companies. To take an example, Grcic's 'MAYDAY' lamp, a polypropylene portable cone made by the renowned company Flos from 1998, was selected by the Museum of Modern Art in New York and awarded the *Compasso d'Oro*. In 1997 Achille Castiglioni declared him Young Designer of the Year. Grcic's career was therefore an illustration of how systems of recognition and acknowledgement in design operate through a global network of commissions and manufacture, panels and juries, exhibitions and prizes.

Along with ranges of furniture and lighting designs, Grcic's work for the established company Krups raised interesting challenges of design and national identity. Originally a German company founded in 1846, it became a household name beyond German borders for a range of coffee machines and coffee grinders, first introduced in 1961. Krups products were distinctive in their material of die-cast aluminium, in place of the more characteristic plastic used for domestic appliances by other companies at the time. As equipment manufactured to high specification, they consequently incorporated powerful engines that confirmed their reputation. On the strength of his reputation, Grcic was taken on to update the company image through new designs. He commented on the project: 'Krups used to be German. What does it mean to be German? In terms of colours? Sounds? Touch?'[33] He concluded that it was through 'formal codes' that Krups's identity could be retained.

Another designer who has engaged with issues of identity, in this case for many of the country's major organizations and services, Erik Spiekermann is a typographer, designer and professor at the University of the Arts, Bremen. Spiekermann established Metadesign, an independent design group in Berlin, in 1983. In taking on corporate identity and information design systems, Metadesign aimed to challenge the perception that design schemes for major public functions needed to be conformist or, at worst, uninspiring. Together with his wife, Joan Spiekermann, he had set up Fontshop in 1989, which became the first mail-order distributor for digital fonts. From modest beginnings as a small studio, Metadesign grew into an international design agency with successful branches in San Francisco and London, as well as Berlin, until Spiekermann left in 2001, first to establish UDN, United Designers Networks, then Spiekermann Partners in 2007. Spiekermann was one of the most engaged, literate designers of his generation to contribute to the critical discourse on design in the last decades of

Erik Spiekermann and MetaDesign, Gleisdreieck underground station, Berlin, 1993. Following German re-unification, the design programme for the BVG, Berlin Transport Network system, was thoroughly transformed to integrate the city's bus, tram, underground and overhead railway systems through clear, modern signage.

the twentieth century, offering, among other things, measured criticism of the extreme claims being made at the height of Postmodernism, which he published or delivered in lectures internationally. Interestingly, for a city he knew so well, Spiekermann and Metadesign were chosen to redesign the entire BVG transport network signage, which was developed with Rayan Abdullah for reunified Berlin. The Metadesign hallmarks for projects for, among others, Deutsche Post, Deutsche Bahn, Düsseldorf airport signage, Audi and Volkswagen, are explained as a continuation of undogmatic German functionalism.[34]

While new generations of designers still engage with local issues, the spectrum of design activity at the beginning of the twenty-first century meant that no single designer could offer the definitive answer to German design. For the provocatively titled series of interviews with designers, 'Was heisst hier, deutsches Design'?' (What do you mean by German Design?), Richard Sapper was approached. Born in Germany in 1932, Sapper was most recognized as the creator of the Tizio lamp and the Alessi coffee pot '9090', as well as a further 150 other projects. He started his design career working for Gio Ponti in Milan after studies in Munich in the late 1950s.

Although he was an international figure, Sapper's press coverage continued to suggest that his reputation carried 'national' associations of his country of birth. As an internationally placed designer, Sapper contributed to the profile of German companies from his Italian and Los Angeles studio and office. When asked by *Design Report*, he commented: 'No, for me there is no specific "German" design. Design is global, like the economy.'[35]

Not all designers felt the impulse to enter the international arena. Certainly among younger designers, the challenges of the social situation of Germany suggested new design methods that moved away from the preoccupation with design innovation in an industrial context. Anschlaege.de, a young Berlin-based design group, took a name in the form of an online address. *Anschlaege* is one word for placard or advertisement in German, but it can also mean a touch or stroke of a keyboard. They were characteristic of a generation of designers concerned to define design as critique and as a form of social activity. Although formed after reunification, the designers became engaged with the identity and future of German cities in the aftermath of political change and social migration, when unemployment and depopulation led to loss of a sense of place and hope for the future. In the face of this, Anschlaege.de strongly felt that designing more products was not an appropriate solution, but they were more interested in interventions using design thinking that prompted responses and action from people.

Two examples serve to illustrate their approach. The ironically named *Kraut* project, run in 2004, took the form of a self-printed newspaper and a kiosk that the group suggested acted as a Speaker's Corner. They arranged a mobile editorial office that travelled across Germany to a total of twenty

The *Bau an!* project of 2004 turned an uninhabited apartment block into a mushroom factory. It marked the group's interest in design as a form of critical intervention while also making an ironic comment on the legacy of design for social need.

Designing Modern Germany

The *Bau an!* project of 2004 by the Berlin-based Anschlaege.de.

places. It was made up of writers, artists, architects and a black-and-white photocopier, but, significantly, no journalists. For one week, in each location, the group published a daily edition of *Kraut*. The designers took the editions of the paper that were published between May and October 2004 as a 'German mood barometer, and a small re-conquest of the public sphere by people beyond belly-button piercing and viewer ratings'.[36]

A second project from 2005, *Bau an!* (Build On!), was also symptomatic of an 'ethnographic turn' taking place in design cultures more generally in Europe at the time and was driven by a similar social engagement. It also addressed the lack of prospects for economic recovery in eastern Germany. With *Bau An!* the designers suggested agricultural uses for the empty spaces left by those moving for better prospects, economic migrants of the former GDR. The designers wrote: 'Together with biologists and economists we examined the case of Gera in Thuringia and discovered: growing mushrooms in an empty apartment tower is viable. Approximately twelve people could live from it. Building on *Bau An!* a workshop for local high school students called '14+1 Proposals for Gera' took place in December of 2005.'[37]

The designers went on to present the ideas drawn from the project in the international exhibition *Shrinking Cities No 2: Intervention.* In the case of Anschlaege.de the designers were not responsible for developing products or solving a manufacturer's problem. Instead, the designer's role was interpreted as engaging with the consequences of earlier design. Especially poignant in this was the choice of the Plattenbau, a standard housing type that was an iconic reminder of the design values of the previous system.

Conclusion

Many of the ideas in this book were first thought through at a desk in the Berlin Art Library. Not only was I extremely grateful for the staff attentiveness offered to researchers, but I was also fascinated by the view from the building. Over successive summers, Hans Scharoun's Philharmonie concert hall (1956–63) was prepared for the start of the next season. Looking beyond, the cluster of urban excitement of the rebuilt Potsdamer Platz in all different lights and the coming and going of tourist buses and remodelled Trabants on hire for city tours, while the Sony Center vied with the Mercedes and Deutsche Bahn towers, all paying homage to the visionary urban schemes of the 1910s and '20s. Straining further, one even saw the skyline of the facade architecture of the new Leipzigerstrasse, built on the ruins of the Wertheim department store that Göhre and Stresemann so evocatively captured in the extracts in chapter One. Together they make an intriguing cityscape for the twenty-first century.

In a book on German design of the twentieth century, it is possibly most fitting to leave with a set of images and ideas conjured up by film, the pre-eminent visual medium of the century, which has the striking ability to place design and material culture firmly at its centre. The paradoxes, sensitivities and difficulties of ordinary people of the reunified Germany were captured in *Goodbye Lenin!* of 2003, directed by Wolfgang Becker. The film followed the destiny of a small family from East Berlin between the celebration of 40 years of the GDR in October 1989, the fall of the Wall in November and the eventual removal of SED party leader Erich Honecker and the reunification on 3 October 2000.

Crucially, Becker used consumption practices as a way to define the cultural and political differences between the two Germanys, often with much humour, including wry comments on design values. When Christiane Kerner (Katrin Sass) witnesses the arrest of her son Alex (Daniel Brühl) on

MADE IN GERMANY

Strausbergerplatz, Berlin, 2007.

a protest march to open the Wall, she suffers a heart attack and falls into a coma for the crucial period of political transformation. Her world as a staunch SED (Socialist Unity Party) supporter and enthusiastic adult leader in the Young Pioneers is challenged. In her spare time, Christiane has contributed 'constructive criticism' of women's clothing, and her life has been defined by a moral attitude towards consumer and household goods and the state's inability to serve its citizens. The interior of the apartment, in its unexciting regularity of highly patterned wallpapers in brown and orange, traditionally modest furniture and hard-won television and radio set, acts as a metaphor for the entire GDR.

Come *die Wende* (the political change), beyond the Kerners' apartment, used-car lots, Western banks and street markets selling second-hand goods proliferate, as advertising hoardings and graffiti signal an encroachment of Western values. To prevent his mother from experiencing another heart attack, Alex chooses to convince her that Communism has not been overthrown, by reinstating the former interior and excluding any signs of Westernization. As the mother recuperates in her bedroom, the carefully reconstructed pre-1989 room, with its pictures of political heroes hung alongside reproductions of pastoral landscapes, offers a semblance of continuity. Through the window, a vast *Trink Coca-Cola* banner replaces the earlier red banners of the SED, while Christine is diverted from seeing the barrage balloon drifting across the East Berlin skyline announcing West cigarettes to a potential population of newly converted smokers.

The safely ordered yet claustrophobic atmosphere of a standard state apartment is contrasted with the impromptu squat that Alex and his girl-friend, Lara, take over in a nineteenth-century district of the dilapidated East. Here, the combination of run-down stuccoed interior and makeshift, eclectic furniture forms the backdrop for their new, informal and liberated relationship. Further contrast enters when the family retreats to their sum-mer *dacha*, its rural calm and sense of stasis providing a foil for the difficult human situation confronting them. But director Becker offers the strongest contrast of interiors when Alex traces his father, who has chosen to remain in West Berlin to start a new life following an official visit. He now lives in an opulent villa in Wannsee, with an excess of rooms, equipped with the latest electronic goods, their open-plan spaces leading on to a large private garden. Alex's visit jolts the viewer into recognition of the West's easy materialism as experienced through the eyes of someone for the first time.

The film captured people's varied reactions to all manner of goods and the possibilities they offer in both personal and shared values of consump-tion. Some products may have been by named designers, but most were anonymous. They revealed the poignancy of the material world and our everyday activities within it.

References

1 Introduction: The Culture of Design in Germany

1 Michael Erlhoff, *Designed in Germany since 1949*, exh. cat., Rat für Formgebung, Frankfurt am Main (Munich, 1990), p. 9.

2 Audi advertising campaigns continue to use the strap-line today. It replaced the previous slogan, 'Technik die begeistert' – technology that amazes.

3 For a terminology of design in the German language, see Kai Buchholz and Klaus Mackowiak, 'Was heisst eigentlich Design?', in *Im Designerpark: Leben in künstlichen Welten*, exh. cat., Institut Mathildenhöhe, Darmstadt (2004), pp. 36–40.

4 Judy Attfield, *Wild Things: The Material Culture of Everyday Life* (Oxford and New York, 2000), and Guy Julier, *The Culture of Design* (London, 2000).

5 Nikolaus Pevsner, *Pioneers of Modern Design from William Morris to Gropius* [1960] (Harmondsworth, 1964), p. 39.

6 'Gestalt: Visions of German Design, International Design Conference Aspen, 1996', Introduction to the special issue of *Design Report*, 6 (1996).

7 Joan Campbell, *The German Werkbund: The Politics of Reform in the Applied Arts* (Princeton, NJ, 1978); Frederik J. Schwartz, *The Werkbund: Design Theory and Mass Culture before the First World War* (New Haven, CT, and London, 1996); and Paul Betts, *The Authority of Everyday Objects: A Cultural History of West German Industrial Design* (Berkeley, CA, 2004).

8 Benedict Anderson, *Imagined Communities: Reflections on the Origin and Spread of Nationalism* (London, 1983).

9 John Heskett, *Design in Germany, 1870–1919* (London, 1986), and Schwartz, *The Werkbund*.

10 Anton Kaes, Martin Jay and Edward Dimendberg, eds, *The Weimar Republic Sourcebook* (Berkeley, CA, 1994).

11 Hans M. Wingler, *The Bauhaus: Weimar Dessau Berlin Chicago* [1962] (Cambridge, MA, and London, 1976).

12 Jeffrey Herf, *Reactionary Modernism: Technology, Culture and Politics in Weimar and the Third Reich* (Cambridge, 1984).

13 Steven Heller, *The Swastika: Symbol beyond Redemption?* (New York, 2000), and Malcolm Quinn, *The Swastika: Constructing the Symbol* (London and New York, 1997).

14 Stephanie Barron, ed., *Exiles and Emigrés: The Flight of European Artists from Hitler*, exh. cat., Los Angeles County Museum (New York, 1997).

15 An exception was Gert Selle, *Geschichte des Designs in Deutschland* (Frankfurt am Main and New York, 1997), which considered the industrial design of both the FRG and the GDR.

16 David Childs, *The GDR: Moscow's German Ally* (London, 1988), p. 56.

17 Heinz Hirdina, *Gestalten für die Serie in der DDR, 1949–1985* (Dresden, 1988).

18 Godfrey Carr and Georgina Paul, 'Unification and Aftermath: The Challenge of History', in *German Cultural Studies: An Introduction*, ed. Rob Burns (Oxford, 1995), pp. 325–47.

19 Karin Kirsch, *Die Weissenhofsiedlung: Werkbund-Ausstellung, 'Die Wohnung'–Stuttgart 1927* (Stuttgart, 1987), and Jürgen Joedicke, *Weissenhofsiedlung Stuttgart* (Stuttgart, 1989).

20 Renate Ulmer, *Jugendstil Darmstadt* (Darmstadt, 1997).

21 Michael Fehr and Gerhard Storck, eds, *Das Schöne und der Alltag: Deutsches Museum für Kunst in Handel und Gewerbe, 1909–1919*, exh. cat., Kaiser Wilhelm Museum, Krefeld (1998).

22 A symptom of this disaffection was the writing of Hans Magnus Enzensberger, as in the essay 'Constituents of a

Theory of the Media' in *Dreamers of the Absolute: Essays on Ecology, Media and Power* (London, 1988). For a radical critique of the West German political situation, see also Sylvere Lotringer, 'The German Issue', *Semiotext(e)*, IV/2 (1982).

1 Design Ideals, Design Reform, Design Professions, 1870–1914

1 Hermann Muthesius, 'Die Zukunft der Deutschen Form' [1915], in Julius Posener, *Anfänge des Funktionalismus von Arts and Crafts zum Deutschen Werkbund* (Berlin, 1964), pp. 41–2: 'Es gilt viel mehr als die Welt zu beherrschen . . . Es gilt ihr das Gesicht zu geben. Erst das Volk, das dies Tat vollbringt, steht vorhaft an der Spitze der Welt, und Deutschland muss dies Volk werden.'

2 Immanuel Kant, *The Critique of Judgement* [1790], trans. Meredith James Creed (Oxford, 1980), p. 186. For a commentary, see Michael Podro, *The Critical Historians of Art* (New Haven, CT, and London, 1982).

3 'Hermann Schwabe', *Allgemeine Deutsche Biographie* (Leipzig, 1891), vol. XXXIII, pp. 161–2. Schwabe was also editor of the *Berliner Stadt und Gemeinde Kalendar* (Town and Community Calendar).

4 Hermann Schwabe, *Kunstindustrie Bestrebungen in Deutschland*, in association with the Deutsche Gewerbe Museum [German Trade Museum] (Leipzig, 1871).

5 Anthony Burton, *Vision and Accident: The Story of the Victoria and Albert Museum* (London, 1999).

6 Michael Conforti, 'The Idealist Enterprise and the Applied Arts', in *A Grand Design: A History of the Victoria and Albert Museum*, ed. Malcolm Baker and Brenda Richardson, exh. cat., Victoria and Albert Museum / Baltimore Museum of Art (London and New York, 1997), pp. 23–48.

7 Two German editions of *The Origin of Species*, translated by Heinrich Georg Bronn, were published in 1860 and 1863 by the firm E. Schweizerbart'sche Verlagsbuchhandlung of Stuttgart.

8 Owen Jones, *The Grammar of Ornament* (London, 1856).

9 Schwabe, *Kunstindustrie Bestrebungen in Deutschland*, p. 9: 'Der Unterricht für Frauen ist kein wesentlicher Theil der Zeichenschulen, gleichwohl aber seine Einführung zu wünschen. Wo er eingeführt wird, ist er als seine Ergänzung des übrigen Zeichenunterrichts aufzufassen.' Translated by Sarah Owens.

10 Ibid., pp. 18–19: 'Die selbe füllt jetzt vier Säle, von denen der letzte im Juli v. J. eröffnet werden ist. Er enhält Schnitzwerke in verschiedenem Material, Möbel und die Sammlung der Gypsabgüsse, welche bereits auf ca. 600 Nummern aufgewachsen ist; etwa 130 Nummern, welche sich besonders zu Vorbildern beim Unterricht eignen, werden im Museum gegossen und billig verkauft. In den übrigen drei Sälen sind besonders Geflechte, Gewebe, Spitzen, geblasene und geschliffene Gläser, Porzellan- und Thonwaaren, Mosaiken, Email- und Lakarbeiten, sowie Guss- und Schmiedeeisen in mustergültigen oder geschichtlich interessanten Stücke aus den verschiedensten Ländern und Zeitperioden vertreten.' Translated by Sarah Owens.

11 Mitchell Schwarzer, 'The Design Prototype as Artistic Boundary: The Debate on History and Industry in Central European Applied Arts Museums, 1860–1900', *Design Issues*, IX/1 (Autumn 1992), pp. 30–44, and Mitchell Schwarzer, *German Architectural Theory and the Search for Modern Identity* (Cambridge, 1995).

12 Schwabe, *Kunstindustrie Bestrebungen in Deutschland*, p. 19: 'Die Besuchszeit ist täglich (excl. Montags) von 10 by 2 Uhr, die Zahl der Besucher vom Januar bis Ende d. J. 1869 betrug 11,757, einen Zahl, die sich freilich noch bedeutend steigern muss und mit dem Wachsen der Sammlung wohl noch Steigern wird. Das Wiener Museum wird jährlich von ca. 108,000, das Kensington Museum von 800,000 Menschen besucht. Direkt lassen sich zur Zeit das Wiener und Berliner Museum nicht vergleichen, weil letzeres seine Kräfte fast ausschiesslich der Unterrichtsanstalt, ersteres bisher ausschiesslich beim Museum zugendet hat und ausserdem Staatliche Unterstützung erhält, gegen welche hiesige kaum ins Gewicht fällt.' Translated by Sarah Owens.

13 Ibid., p. 20: 'Aber das deutsche Gewerbemuseum hat noch einen weiteren wichtigen Schritt gethan. Um die von ihm angestrebten Ideen in ihrer fegensreichen Wirkung auf die Industrie zu verallgemeinern, hat es auch ein Wandermuseum gegründet und bereits in einigen Städten ausgestellt. Es bedarf nicht erst eines Beweises, in welchem Masse der Unterricht gefördert, die Bildung von Lokalmuseen angeregt und der Geschmack des Publicums gebildet wird, wenn man die gewonnen mustergültigen Kunstschätze beweglich macht und eine Auswahl von kunstgegenständen bei den Provinzialschulen zirkuliren lässt.' Translated by Sarah Owens.

14 Ibid., p. 24: 'Was wir Deutschen der Welt mit der Reformation geleistet haben, das hat Frankreich der modernen Welt mit der Revolution geleistet.' Translated by Sarah Owens.

15 Ibid., p. 25: 'Wenn er so ist in den Sphären der höheren Kunst – wie wird es nun erst auf dem Gebiet der Kunstindustrie aussehen? – Überall eine Zerfahrenheit des Geschmacks, eine prinziplose Stylmischerei, eine armselige "Imitation" ein kopistenhafter Naturalismus. Mit recht sagt daher Falke, der kompetenste Richter auf diesem Gebiet: der französiche Geschmack sei der Ungeschmack, Putz und Schein seien an die Stelle der Kunst getreten, und der Geschmack sei der Sklave der

s/feilen, von der Schönheit losgetrennten Mode geworden. Wie ich schon an anderer Stelle hervorgehoben habe: das wirklich Bestechende an französischen Artikeln der "industrie de luxe", wie sie sehr bezeichnend sagen, ist nicht die Komposition, sondern das äussere coloristische Element, das "savoir vivre", mit dem jeder Gegenstand auftritt, man möchte sagen seine Toilette. Und Kleider machen ja Leute, wenn auch keine Männer.' Translated by Sarah Owens.

16 'Julius Lessing', *Neue Deutsche Biographie* (Berlin, 1985), vol. xiv, pp. 350–51.

17 Julius Lessing, *Führer durch die Ausstellung älterer kunstgewerblicher Gegenstände*, exh. cat., Berlin (1872), p. 45: 'Die japanische Kunst, bedeutend jünger, beruht auf chinesichen Vorbildern, besitzt aber eine grössere Naturwahrheit und Frische als die chinesichen Werke derjenigen Periode, an welche sie sich anlehnt.'

18 Berliner Gewerbeausstellung, *Officieller Haupt-Katalog, Illustrirte Prachtausgabe*, Rudolf Mosse, Berlin (Druckerei des Berliner Tageblatt), published by the Arbeitsausschusses der Berliner Gewerbe Ausstellung (1896).

19 Julius Lessing, *Die Berliner Gewerbeausstellung*, special publication of the *Berliner Rundschau*, ed. Julius Rodenberg, xxii/11 (August 1896).

20 Georg Simmel, 'The Berlin Trade Exhibition', in David Frisby and Mike Featherstone, *Simmel on Culture* (London, Thousand Oaks, ca, and New Delhi, 2006), pp. 255–8. See also Dorothy Rowe, *Representing Berlin: Sexuality and the City in Imperial and Weimar Germany* (Aldershot, 2003). The term 'the dialectic of the commodity' was developed in Frederik J. Schwartz, *The Werkbund: Design Theory and Mass Culture before the First World War* (New Haven, ct, and London, 1996), pp. 61–73

21 Charles Harvey and Jon Press, *William Morris: Design and Enterprise in Victorian Britain* (Manchester, 1991).

22 The first volume contained the individual essays, 'The Lesser Arts' (1877), 'The Art of the People' (1879), 'The Beauty of Life' (1880), 'Making the Best of It' (c. 1879) and 'The Prospects of Architecture in Civilisation' (1880). A second Morris volume was also published by Hermann Seemann, and was followed by Walter Crane's writings on book illustration, as well as essays by Cobden-Sanderson, Lewis F. Day and Emery Walker. See William Morris, *Die niederen Künste, Die Kunst des Volkes, Die Schönheit des Lebens: Wie wir aus dem Bestehenden das Beste machen können, Die Aussichten der Architekten in der Civilisation* (Leipzig, 1901); Walter Crane, *Die Grundlagen der Zeichnung* (Leipzig, 1897)

23 For the lasting legacy of these ideals, see Tanya Harrod, *The Crafts in Britain in the Twentieth Century* (London and New Haven, ct, 1999).

24 Kai Buchholz, ed., *Die Lebensreform: Entwürfe zur Neugestaltung von Leben und Kunst um 1900*, exh. cat., Institut Mathildenhöhe, Darmstadt (2001).

25 Quote from a Gmelin advertisement, in the *Officieller Haupt-Katalog: Illustrirte Prachtausgabe* (1896), p. 72: 'Es finden sich hier Zimmereinrichtungen in sämtlichen Stilarten und kostbarer Ausführung; der Rococo-, Renaissance- (Früh und Spätrenaissance), Régence-, Empirestil ist in kunstgerechter Durchführung ebenso zu finden, wie der Barock-, der Chippendale-, der altnlische und der ganz moderne Stil; Eiche, Nussbaum, Mahagoni, Polkisander, Ebenholz, Bambus u.a. Holzarten sind in den verschiedensten Formen verwandt.'

26 Maria Makela, *The Munich Secession: Art and Artists in Turn of the Century Munich* (New York, 1990).

27 Hans Wichmann, *Deutsche Werkstätten und wk Verband, 1898–1990: Aufbruch zum neuen Wohnen* (Munich, 1992), pp. 16–17.

28 Gabriel P. Weisberg, Edwin Becker and Evelyne Posseme, eds, *Origins of 'L'Art Nouveau': The Bing Empire*, exh. cat., The Van Gogh Museum, Amsterdam (Antwerp, 2004).

29 Werner Schweiger, *Wiener Werkstätte: Design in Vienna, 1903–1932* (London, 1984), and Peter Noever, ed., *Der Preis der Schönheit: 100 Jahre Wiener Werkstätte* (Ostfildern-Ruit, 2003).

30 The literature on the *Gesamtkunstwerk* is extensive. See Debra Shafter, *The Order of Ornament, the Structure of Style: Theoretical Foundations of Modern Art and Architecture* (Cambridge, 2003).

31 Jeremy Aynsley, 'From Applied Art to Graphic Design, 1890–1914', in *Graphic Design in Germany, 1890–1945* (London, 2000), pp. 10–57.

32 Paul Ruben, *Die Reklame: ihre Kunst und Wissenschaft* (Berlin, 1914).

33 Hermann Muthesius in 'Kunst und Volkswirtschaft', in *Dokumente des Fortschrittes* (January 1908), p. 118; quoted in Hans Wichmann, *Deutsche Werkstätten und wk Verband, 1898–1990: Aufbruch zum neuen Wohnen* (Munich, 1992), pp. 15–16: 'Doch zeigten sie (die Dresdener Werkstätten gegenüber den Vereinigten Werkstätten) einen gewissen Fortschritt in volkswirtschaftlicher Beziehung insofern, als sie die Künstler nicht, wie anfänglich in München der Fall gewesen war, zu geschäftlichen Teilhabern des Unternehmens machten, sondern in ein durch Vertrag geregeltes Verhältnis zu der Produktionsstätte setzten, das dem bei literarischen Produktionen üblichen Abkommen zwischen Autor und Verleger entsprach. In beiden Fällen aber – und hierin unterschieden sich die neuen Betriebe grundsätzlich von den alten – standen die Namen der entwerfenden Künstler an der Spitze dessen, was pro-

duziert wurde, gerade so, wie in der Literatur der Name des Autors das Buch bezeichnet und von dem des Verlegers steht.' Translated by Sarah Owens.

34 Walter Benjamin, 'Louis-Philippe; or, The Interior' [1955]; reprinted in 'Paris, Capital of the Nineteenth Century', in *Reflections*, ed. Peter Demetz, trans. Edmund Jephcott (New York, 1979), pp. 154–5.

35 'Friedrich Bruckmann', *Neue Deutsche Biographie* (Berlin, 1985), vol. XII, pp. 648–9.

36 *Deutsche Kunst und Dekoration* (Darmstadt and Stuttgart, 1897–1932) and *Innendekoration* (Darmstadt and Stuttgart, 1890–1944). For commentary on these, see Sigrid Randa, *Alexander Koch: Publizist und Verleger in Darmstadt* (Worms, 1990), and Jeremy Aynsley, 'Graphic Change, Design Change: Magazines for the Domestic Interior, 1890–1930', *Journal of Design History*, XIX/1 (2005), pp. 43–60.

37 Alexander Koch and Hermann Werle, *Das vornehme deutsche Haus: Innenräume, Möbel und Dekorationen* (Darmstadt, Leipzig and Vienna, 1896).

38 Renate Ulmer, *Jugendstil Darmstadt* (Darmstadt, 1997).

39 Behrens issue, *Deutsche Kunst und Dekoration* (Darmstadt, 1902).

40 The portfolios appeared as *Meister der Innen-Kunst, I: Baillie Scott, London, Haus eines Kunstfreudes*, text by Hermann Muthesius (1902); *Meister der Innenkunst, II: Charles Rennie Mackintosh, Haus eines Kunstfreundes*, text by Hermann Muthesius (1902); and *Das Haus eines Kunstfreundes: Ein Entwurf in zwölf Tafeln von Leopold Bauer, Wien*, text by Felix Commichau (1902), all published by Alexander Koch, Darmstadt.

41 Joan Campbell, 'The Founding of the Werkbund', in *The German Werkbund: The Politics of Reform in the Applied Arts* (Princeton, NJ, 1978), pp. 9–32. See also Peter Bruckmann, 'Die Gründung des Deutschen Werkbundes, 6. Oktober 1907', *Die Form*, VII/10 (1932), pp. 297–9.

42 Cheryl Buckley, *Designing Modern Britain* (London, 2007), pp. 49–54 and 78–80.

43 John Heskett, 'Modernism and Archaism in Design in the Third Reich', in *The Nazification of Art: Art, Design, Music, Architecture and Film in the Third Reich*, ed. Brandon Taylor and Wilfried van der Will (Winchester, 1990), pp. 128–43. On standardization in the paper industry and the implications for graphic design and typography, see Robin Kinross, *Modern Typography: An Essay in Critical History* (London, 1992), pp. 90–92. For a full characterization of the Werkbund debate, see Schwartz, *The Werkbund*, pp. 147–50.

44 Deutscher Werkbund, *Die Durchgeistigung der deutschen Arbeit: ein Bericht vom Deutschen Werkbund* (Jena, 1911).

45 Michael Fehr and Gerhard Storck, eds, *Das Schöne und der Alltag: Deutsches Museum für Kunst in Handel und Gewerbe, 1909–1919*, exh. cat., Kaiser Wilhelm Museum, Krefeld (Ghent, 1998).

46 Jörg Meissner, ed., *Strategien der Werbekunnst, 1850–1933*, exh. cat., Deutsches Historisches Museum, Berlin (2004), pp. 174–81.

47 Tilmann Buddensieg, with Henning Rogge, *Industriekultur: Peter Behrens und die AEG, 1907–1914* (Cambridge, MA, 1984), and Gisela Moeller, *Peter Behrens in Düsseldorf: die Jahre 1903–07* (Heidelberg Weinheim, 1991).

48 *Berliner Tageblatt* (29 August 1907); quoted in Eva-Maria Demuth, *Informationen aus der AEG Geschichte*, 1/90 (Frankfurt am Main, 1990): 'Es ist wohl kein Zweifel mehr, dass die Zukunft der Industrie auch auf künstlerischem Gebiet gehört, und dass unsere Zeit zu der Produktionsart, die ihr am gemässesten ist, zur Industrie drängt, solange es sich um Werke der Gebrauchskunst handelt.' Translated by Sarah Owens.

49 Christopher Burke, 'Peter Behrens and the German Letter: Type Design and Architectural Lettering', *Journal of Design History*, V/1 (1992), pp. 19–37.

50 Alfred Ziffer, ed., *Bruno Paul: Deutsche Raumkunst und Architektur zwischen Jugendstil und Moderne* (Munich, 1992).

51 Paul Scheerbart, *The Gray Cloth: A Novel on Glass Architecture*, ed. and trans. John A. Stuart (Cambridge, MA, 2003).

52 Emil Waldmann, *Moderne Schiffsräume des Norddeutschen Lloyd, nach Entwürfen von Bruno Paul, R. A. Schröder und F.A.O. Krüger* (Munich, 1908), p. 3 [special issue of *Dekorativer Kunst*]

53 Ibid., p. 4: 'Durch die Zusammenfügung gemaserter und geflammter Holzflächen, heller und dunkler, glänzender und matter Hölzer, schafft Bruno Paul, fast ganz ohne Ornament, nur mit geometrischer Einfassungslinie oder akzentuierender geometrischer Intarsia "Muster" von nie versagendem Reiz. Wesentlich dabei ist natürlich die Farbe, ja sie ist oft Hauptträger der Stimmung eines ganzen Raumes. Bisher war Bruno Paul in seinen Harmonien zurückhaltend und diskret im Ton, dabei nuancenreich. Jetzt setzt er starke Farben häufiger gegeneinander und wird dadurch volltönender im Ausdruck.' Translated by Sarah Owens.

54 Gustav Stresemann, 'Die Warenhäuser: Ihre Entstehung, Entwicklung und volkswirtschaftliche Bedeutung', in *Zeitschrift für die gesammte Staatswissenschaft* (Berlin, 1900); cited in Klaus Strohmeyer, 'Kathredalen des Konsums: Zur Kulturgeschichte des Warenhauses im 19. und frühen 20. Jahrhundert', in *Strategien der Werbekunnst*, ed. Meissner, pp. 46–57: 'Wenn man heute in einer Familie hört: Wir gehen zu Wertheim, so heisst das nicht in erster Linie, wir brauchen irgend etwas besonders notwendig für unsere Wirtschaft, sondern

man spricht wie von einem Ausflüge, den man etwa
nach irgend einem schönen Orte der Umgebung macht.
Man wählt sich dazu einen Nachmittag, an dem man
möglichst viel Zeit hat, verabredet sich womöglich noch
mit Bekannten. In der Leipziger Strassse angekommen,
bewundert man erst eine ganze Zeit lang die Schau-
fenster, dann ergaht man sich in den Erdgerschoss-
räumen, sieht sich die vershschiedensten Auslagen an,
kauft vielleicht hier und da, lässt sich durch den
Fahrstuhl nach dem ersten Stock befördern und nimmt
womöglich eine Tasse Chocolade nebst dem obligaten
Stück Torte oder Apfelkuchen. Hat man Bekannte
gefunden oder mitgebracht, so beliebt man wohl
plauernd längere Zeit sitzen, zeigt die gegenseitigen
Einkäufe und reizt sich dadurch zu den neuen
Ausgaben. Die Zeit verfliegt mit dem Betrachten der
verschiedensten Rayons, der Toiletten der einkaufenden
Damen, der Unterhaltung und anderem, und wenn man
an der Uhr plötzlich sieht, dass es hüchste Zeit sei
heimzukehren.'

55 Emile Zola, *Au Bonheur des Dames* [1883]; as *The Ladies'
    Paradise*, trans. Brian Nelson (Oxford, 1995).

56 Michael. B. Miller, *The Bon Marché: Bourgeois Culture and
    the Department Store, 1869–1920* (London, 1981); Rosalind
    Williams, *Dream Worlds: Mass-Consumption in Late
    Nineteenth Century France* (Berkeley, CA, and Oxford,
    1982); and Erika D. Rappaport, *Shopping for Pleasure:
    Women in the Making of London's West End* (Princeton,
    NJ, and Chichester, 2000).

57 Paul Göhre, *Das Warenhaus* (Frankfurt am Main, 1907).

58 Ibid., p. 15: 'Wer das Haus Wertheim zum ersten Male
    betritt, empfängt den Eindruck eines erdrückenden
    Gewirres. Menschen fast zu jeder Tageszeit in ununter-
    brochenem Strömen; unabsehbare, immer eine Reihen
    von Verkaufsständen; ein Meer von Warenmassen, aus-
    gebreitet; Treppen, Aufzüge, Etage, sichtbar wie Rippen
    eines Skeletts; Säle, Höfe, Hallen; Gänge, Winkel,
    Kontore; Enge und Weite, Tiefe und Höhe; Farben,
    Glanz, Licht und Lärm: ein ungeheuriches
    Durcheinander, scheinbar ohne Plan und Ordnung.'
    Translated by Sarah Owens.

59 Ibid., p. 35.

60 Ibid., pp. 92–3: 'Ebenso ists übrigens, um das noch zu
    sagen, mit den Schaufensterdekorationen: bei Wertheim
    erlesener künstlerischer Geschmack, bei Tietz elegan-
    teste Effekt. Jandorf-Spittelmarkt aber kann ästhetisch
    angesehen, erst recht nicht mit, weder mit Tietz, noch
    viel weniger mit Wertheim. Bei ihm ist nichts wie Ware,
    Ware, Ware, die mit den kaufenden zusammen die
    engen, kleinen Räume fast zu Ersticken füllt, und zwar
    eine Ware, die ebenso aller Schönheit bar ist wie das
    Haus, in dem sie aufgestapelt zum Verkaufe liegt.'

61 Ibid., p. 142: 'Kein Bratwurst- und Bierdunst, kein

Tabak- ind Zigarrenqualm, kein Durcheinander von
allerhand in Tätigkeit befindlichen lauten
Musikinstrumenten, sondern nur ein gleichmässiges,
verhallendes Rauschen, Reden und Rufen, hier und da
Glockenschläge, Lichterglanz und zarte Düfte von
Parfums, von Obst, von frischem Lack, von Blumen,
Schokoladen, Kaffee, Tee und Seifen. Frohes Bewegen
ringsum, Sauberkeit. Dazu die Jugend der meisten
Verkäuferin und Verkäufer: da eine Lust zu kaufen.
Die Güter der modernen Kultur sind in Reichtum und
Schönheit um uns her.'

62 Ibid., p. 64: 'Hier kostet allein das Musterlager, d.h. die
    schöne Sammlung von etwa 20 Zimmereinrichtungen
    nach den Entwürfen bekannter deutscher
    Kunstgewerbearchitekten, 200,000 Mark, während im
    Laufe des Jahres nicht viel mehr als die gleiche Summe
    umgesetzt wird, nämlich, eine knappe Viertelmillion.'
    The Wertheim special issue was published as *Deutsche
    Kunst und Dekoration*, VI/6 (March 1903).

63 Schwartz, *The Werkbund*, p. 145.

64 Robert Breuer, 'Die Cölner Werkbund-Ausstellung,
    Mai–Okober 1914', *Deutsche Kunst und Dekoration*, XXXIV
    (1914), pp. 416–41: 'Dies Architektur ist ein Kampf,
    durch Kurven einen Raum aus dem Kosmos zu schnei-
    den.'

65 Iain Boyd Whyte, *The Crystal Chair Letters: Architectural
    Fantasies by Bruno Taut and his Circle* (Cambridge, MA,
    1985).

66 Alexander Koch, *Eine Deutsche Ausstellung?* (Darmstadt,
    1910).

67 Ibid.

68 Ibid.

2 Experiment and Tradition in Design, 1917–33

1 Stephen Spender, *World within World* (London, 1951),
   pp. 109–10.

2 Siegfried Kracauer, 'Mädchen im Beruf' [1932]; as
   'Working Women' in *The Weimar Republic Sourcebook*,
   ed. Anton Kaes, Martin Jay and Edward Dimendberg
   (Berkeley, CA, 1994), pp. 216–17.

3 Marsha Meskimmon and Shearer West, eds, *Visions of
   the 'Neue Frau': Women and the Visual Arts in Weimar
   Germany* (Aldershot, 1995).

4 e. c. z., 'Das Heim einer Junggesellin', *die neue linie*
   (October 1929): 'Berlin ist die amerikanischste Stadt
   Deutschlands, sagen die hier zu Besuch weilenden
   Amerikaner. Immer neue Einrichtungen, die das Leben
   geplagten, gehtzten Groszstadtmenschen erleichtern
   und bequemer gestalten, entstehen und bestätigen das
   amerikanische Urteil. Da gibt es nicht nur
   Quickrestaurants, Rolletreppen und Automaten jeder
   Art. Auch das Wohnen wird reformiert, wird

angenehmer und schöner. Architekt Professor Hans Scharoun hat am Kaiserdamm ein Haus gebaut, das es einzelstehenden Menschen, Junggesellen und Junggesellinnen, denen die mobilierten zimmer ein Graus sind, ermöglicht, ein Heim und doch nur ein Zimmer zu besitzen. Aus vielen Einzimmer Wohnungen besteht das HAUS. Wer glaubt, dasz eine solche Einzimmer-Wohnung weder praktisch noch schön sein könne, der sehe sich doch einmal hier abgebildete, von der Innenarchitektin Toni Mayer-Crailsheim eingerichtete reizende Wohnung an.' Translated by Sarah Owens.

5   Patrick Rössler, *Die neue linie, 1929–1943: das Bauhaus am Kiosk* (Bielefeld, 2007).

6   *die neue linie* (September 1929), no. 2: 'die neue linie / Gnädige Frau, / Sie und wir stehen auf einem Platz, von dem aus 3 Wege in die Welt laufen: / Auf dem einen marschieren Männer und Frauen mit Kopf und Perücke und stimmen den Refrain an von der "guten alten Zeit". / Auf dem anderen wandern die Snobs und verkünden mit herabgezogenen Mundwinkeln, dass man in Paris sich neuerdings die Augenwimpern mit Fliegebeinen verlängert und dass Gloria Swanson das Vorbild für jede Lady sein müsse. / Gnädige Frau, sie fühlen es wie wir, dass "die gute alte Zeit" unwiederbringlich vorüber ist, und dass eine Dame ihr Vorbild nicht aus Hollywood bezieht. Sie wissen, dasz es einen dritten Weg gibt, den Weg der wirklichen Dame.' Translated by Sarah Owens.

7   *die neue linie* (September 1929), no. 1. The magazine was published monthly by the publisher Otto Beyer of Leipzig, although its editorial office was given as Berlin sw68.

8   Hans M. Wingler, *The Bauhaus: Weimar Dessau Berlin Chicago* [1962] (Cambridge, MA, and London, 1976), and Magdalena Droste, *Bauhaus, 1919–1933* (Cologne, 1990).

9   Walter Gropius quoted in Wingler, *The Bauhaus*, p. 31.

10 John Willett, 'Revolution and the Arts: Germany, 1918–20', in *The New Sobriety, 1917–1933: Art and Politics in the Weimar Period* (London, 1978), pp. 35–44.

11 Wingler, *The Bauhaus*, pp. 64 – 77.

12 Johannes Itten, *Design and Form: The Basic Course at the Bauhaus* [1963] (London, 1964).

13 Rainer K. Wick, *Teaching at the Bauhaus* (Ostfildern-Ruit, 2000).

14 Droste, *Bauhaus, 1919–1933*, p. 58.

15 Lyonel Feininger in a letter to Julia Feininger of 5 October 1922, in Wingler, *The Bauhaus*, p. 56.

16 Wingler, *The Bauhaus*, pp. 64–8.

17 Gillian Naylor, *The Bauhaus Reassessed: Sources and Design Theory* (London, 1985), pp. 114–17.

18 Hans Engeland and Ulf Meyer, *Bauhaus-Architektur / Bauhaus Architecture* (Munich, London and New York, 2001).

19 Ute Brüning, ed., *Das A und O des Bauhauses*, exh. cat.,
Bauhaus Archiv, Berlin (Leipzig, 1995).

20 Otakar Mácel, 'Avant-garde Design and the Law: Litigation over the Cantilever Chair', *Journal of Design History*, III/2–3 (1990), pp. 125–43.

21 Hans Brockhage and Reinhold Lindner, *Marianne Brandt: 'Hab ich je an Kunst gedacht'* (Chemnitz, 2001).

22 Alain Findeli, 'László Moholy-Nagy and das Projekt der Bauhausbücher', in *Das A und O des Bauhauses*, ed. Bruning, pp. 22–6.

23 Georg Muche, 'Fine Art and Industrial Form' [1926], in *Form and Function: A Source Book for the History of Architecture and Design, 1890–1939*, ed. Charlotte Benton, Tim Benton and Dennis Sharpe (St Albans, 1975), pp. 151–2.

24 Anja Baumhoff, *The Gendered World of the Bauhaus: The Politics of Power at the Weimar Republic's Premier Institute, 1919–1932* (Frankfurt am Main, 2001), and Sigrid Wortmann Weltge, *Women's Work: Textile Art from the Bauhaus* (San Francisco, 1993).

25 Wortmann Weltge, *Women's Work*, p. 102; originally published as 'Die entwicklung der Bauhaus-weberei', *Bauhaus Zeitschrift für Gestaltung*, VII/2 (1931).

26 Hans M. Wingler, *Kunstschulreform, 1900–1933* (Berlin, 1977).

27 Ibid., pp. 246–7, and the Reimannschule's periodical *Farbe und Form* (Berlin, 1927–30).

28 Naylor, *The Bauhaus Re-assessed*, p. 167.

29 Hannes Meyer in 'Die neue Welt', *Das Werk*, XIII/7 (1926), pp. 205–24; reprinted in translation in *The Weimar Republic Sourcebook*, ed. Kaes, Jay and Dimendberg, p. 447.

30 Werner Kleinerüschkamp, *Hannes Meyer, 1889–1954: Architekt, Urbanist, Lehrer* (Berlin, 1989).

31 Christiane Lange, *Ludwig Mies van der Rohe and Lilly Reich: Furniture and Interiors*, exh. cat., Lange House, Krefeld (Ostfildern-Ruit, 2006).

32 Chairman of Dessau city council, Hoffmann, 'What Will Become of the Bauhaus?', *Anhalter Tageszeitung* [Dessau] (10 July 1932); quoted in translation in Wingler, *The Bauhaus*, p. 177.

33 Heinz Hirdina, ed., *Neues Bauen Neues Gestalten: Das neue Frankfurt, eine Zeitschrift zwischen 1926 und 1933* (Dresden, 1991).

34 Winfried Nerdinger, *Bruno Taut, 1880–1938: Architekt zwischen Tradition und Avantgarde* (Stuttgart, 2001), and Wolfgang Ribbe and Wolfgang Schäche, *Die Siemensstadt: Geschichte und Architektur eines Industriestandortes* (Berlin, 1985).

35 Beate Eckstein and Christine Nielsen, *Auf dem Weg zum Neuen Wohnen: Die Werkbundsiedlung, Breslau, 1929 / Towards a New Kind of Living: The Werkbund Housing Estate, Breslau, 1929* (Basel, Boston, MA, and Berlin, 1996).

36 Karin Kirsch, *Die Weissenhofsiedlung: Werkbund-Ausstellung, 'Die Wohnung' – Stuttgart, 1927* (Stuttgart, 1987), and Jürgen Joedicke, *Weissenhofsiedlung Stuttgart* (Stuttgart, 1989).

37 *Das Neue Frankfurt: Monatsschrift für die Fragen der Groszstadtgestaltung* (Frankfurt am Main, 1926–34).

38 Hilde Heynen, 'Modernity and Domesticity: Tensions and Contradictions', in *Negotiating Domesticity: Spatial Productions of Gender in Modern Architecture* (London, 2005).

39 Bruno Taut, *Die neue Wohnung: die Frau als Schöpferin* [1924] (Leipzig, 1926).

40 Frank Gilbreth and Lillian Gilbreth, *Fatigue Study: The Elimination of Humanity's Greatest Unnecessary Waste, etc.* (London, 1916). This was followed by *Applied Motion Study: A Collection of Papers on the Efficient Method to Industrial Preparedness* (New York, 1917).

41 Erna Meyer, *Der neue Haushalt: ein Wegweiser zur wirtschaftlichen Hausführung* [1926] (Stuttgart, 1928).

42 Peter Noever, *Die Frankfurter Küche von Margarete Schütte-Lihotzky* (Berlin, 1992).

43 Nicholas Bullock, 'First the Kitchen – then the Façade', *Journal of Design History*, I/3–4 (1988), pp. 177–92, and Susan R. Henderson, 'A Revolution in the Woman's Sphere: Grete Lihotzky and the Frankfurt Kitchen', in *Architecture and Feminism*, ed. Debra Coleman, Elizabeth Danze and Carol Henderson (New York, 1996).

44 Bruno Taut, *Die neue Wohnung* (Leipzig, 1926).

45 Volker Rattemeyer and Dietrich Helms, *Typographie kann unter Umständen Kunst Sein*, exh. cat., 5 vols, Landesmuseum, Wiesbaden (1990).

46 Jan Tschichold, *The New Typography: A Handbook for Modern Designers* [1928], trans. Ruari McLean, ed. Robin Kinross (Berkeley, CA, 1995).

47 Jan Tschichold, 'The New Typography', in *Circle: An International Survey of Constructive Art*, ed. Leslie J. Martin, Naum Gabo and Ben Nicholson (London, 1937), pp. 249–55.

48 Ute Eskildsen and Jan-Christopher Horak, eds, *Film und Foto der zwanziger Jahre: eine Betrachtung der internationalen Werkbundausstellung Film und Foto, 1929* (Stuttgart, 1979).

49 For further commentary on this, see Jeremy Aynsley, *Graphic Design in Germany, 1890–1945* (London, 2000), pp. 118–77.

50 Paul Schuitema in *Gefesselter Blick*, ed. Heinz Rasch and Bodo Rasch (Stuttgart, 1930).

51 Christopher Burke, *Paul Renner: The Art of Typography* (London, 1998), chapter 4, pp. 77–120.

52 Elsa Taterka, in *Farbe und Form* (February 1927), pp. 88–9.

53 Hubert Riedel, ed., *Lucian Bernhard: Werbung und Design im Aufbruch des 20. Jahrhunderts*, exh. cat., Institut für Ausslandsbeziehungen, Stuttgart (1999).

54 Pat Schleger, *Hans Schleger: A Life of Design* (London, 2001).

55 Adolf Loos, *Ornament and Crime: Selected Essays*, ed. Adolf Opel, trans. Michael Mitchell (Riverside, CA, 1998).

56 Walter Riezler, *Form ohne Ornament* (Stuttgart, 1924). See also Barbara Mundt with Babette Warncke, *Form ohne Ornament?: angewandte Kunst zwischen Zweckform und Objekt*, exh. cat., Kunstgewerbemuseum, Berlin (1999).

57 Charlotte Benton, Tim Benton and Ghislaine Wood, eds, *Art Deco, 1910–1939*, exh. cat., Victoria and Albert Museum, London (2003).

58 Catharina Berents, *Art Deco in Deutschland: Das moderne Ornament* (Berlin, 1998).

59 See the special issue, 'Deutsche Gewerbeschau', in *Dekorative Kunst*, XLVI (1922).

60 Bruno Paul in Guido Marangoni, *An International Exposition of Art in Industry, May 14 to May 26, Macy's* (New York, 1928), p. 35.

61 Berents, *Art Deco in Deutschland*, p. 9.

62 Kenneth Silver, *Esprit de Corps: The Art of the Parisian Avant-Garde and the First World War, 1914–1925* (London, 1989).

63 Ernst Haiger, 'Josef Wackerle, Umrahmung des Durchgangs in das Damenzimmer des Hauses H., Dresden, Zimmereinrichtung', *Dekorative Kunst*, LVI (1927).

64 Ingeborg Becker and Dieter Högermann, *Berliner Porzellan vom Jugendstil zum Funktionalismus, 1889–1939*, exh. cat., Bröhan Museum, Berlin (1987), and Margarete Jarchow, *Berliner Porzellan im 20. Jahrhundert* (Berlin, 1988).

65 Marangoni, *An International Exposition of Art in Industry*, p. 52.

66 Hans Ottomeyer, 'Bruno Paul und die andere Moderne', in *Bruno Paul: Deutsche Raumkunst und Architektur zwischen Jugendstil und Moderne*, ed. Alfred Ziffer (Munich, 1992), p. 108.

67 Walter Riezler, *Das deutsche Kunstgewerbe 1925: Bilder von der deutschen Abteilung der internationalen Kunstgewerbeausstellung in Monza*, vol. IV (Stuttgart, 1926): 'Wer versuchen wollte, etwa absichtlich die Kennzeichen nationaler Eigenart zu betonen und ihnen eine grössere Rolle einzuräumen als ihr von der Seit des künstlerischen Temparaments und der Aufgabe von selber zukommt, kann wohl für einen Augenblick Verwirrung stiften. Ein Erfolg, ein entscheidener Einfluss auf die Entwicklung wird ihm nicht beschieden sein. Auch der mächstigste Diktator wird den neuen nationalen Stil nicht schaffen können.' Translated by Sarah Owens.

68 Paul in Marangoni, *An International Exposition of Art in Industry*, p. 35.

69 Ibid.

3 Politics and Design: Reaction and Consolidation, 1933–45

1 Joan Campbell, *The German Werkbund: The Politics of Reform in the Applied Arts* (Princeton, NJ, 1978), p. 244.

2 Berthold Hinz, *Art in the Third Reich* (Oxford, 1980), and Reinhard Merker, *Die bildenden Künste im Nationalsozialismus: Kulturideologie, Kulturpolitik, Kulturproduktion* (Cologne, 1983).

3 Paul Betts, *The Authority of Everyday Objects: A Cultural History of West German Industrial Design* (Berkeley, Los Angeles and London, 2004), pp. 28–9.

4 Ibid., p. 29.

5 Robin Kinross, in Jan Tschichold, *The New Typography: A Handbook for Modern Designers* (Berkeley, CA, 1995), p. xxxviii.

6 Heinz Loew and Helene Nonné Schmidt, *Joost Schmidt: Lehre und Arbeit am Bauhaus, 1919–1932* (Düsseldorf, 1984).

7 Campbell, *The German Werkbund*, pp. 280–82.

8 Ute Brüning, 'Bauhäusler zwischen Propaganda und Wirtschaftswerbung', in *Bauhaus-moderne im Nationalsozialismus: zwischen Anbiederung und Verfolgung*, ed. Winfried Nerdinger, exh. cat., Bauhaus Archiv, Berlin (Munich, 1993), pp. 24–47. For Bayer's designs, see Jeremy Aynsley, *Graphic Design in Germany, 1890–1945* (London, 2000), pp. 198–207.

9 Hinz, *Art in the Third Reich*, and Merker, *Die bildenden Künste im Nationalsozialismus*, pp. 36–91.

10 Mario-Andreas von Lüttichau, '"Deutsche Kunst" und "Entartete Kunst": die Münchener Ausstellungen, 1937', in Peter-Klaus Schuster, *Die 'Kunststadt' München 1937: Nationalsozialismus und 'Entartete Kunst'* (Munich, 1987), pp. 83–119.

11 Max Nordau, *Degeneration* [1893] (Lincoln, NE, and London, 1993).

12 Campbell, *The German Werkbund*, p. 272.

13 Stephanie Barron, ed., *Exiles and Emigrés: The Flight of European Artists from Hitler*, exh. cat., Los Angeles County Museum (New York, 1997), p. 390.

14 John Heskett, 'Modernism and Archaism in Design in the Third Reich', in *The Nazification of Art: Art, Design, Music, Architecture and Film in the Third Reich*, ed. Brandon Taylor and Wilfried van der Will (Winchester, 1990), pp. 128–43.

15 As an example of this point of view, Heskett referred to Erika Gysling-Billeter, 'Die angewandte Kunst: Sachlichkeit trotz Diktatur', in *Die Dreissiger Jahre: Schauplatz Deutschland*, exh. cat., Haus der Kunst, Munich (1977).

16 Heskett, 'Modernism and Archaism in Design in the Third Reich', p. 118. See also Nerdinger, ed., *Bauhaus-moderne im Nationalsozialismus*, and Betts, *The Authority of Everyday Objects*, pp. 25–9.

17 Jeffrey Herf, *Reactionary Modernism: Technology, Culture and Politics in Weimar and the Third Reich* (Cambridge, 1984).

18 Beate Manske, ed., *Wilhelm Wagenfeld, 1900–1990* (Ostfildern-Ruit, 2000).

19 On Kubus Geschirr, see Beate Manske, 'Die Vorratsbehälter Kubus von Wilhelm Wagenfeld', in *Im Designerpark: Leben in künstlichen Welten*, ed. Kai Buchholz and Klaus Wolbert, exh. cat., Mathildenhöhe Institut, Darmstadt (2004), pp. 812–17.

20 Peter Bain and Paul Shaw, *Blackletter: Type and National Identity* (New York, 1998).

21 Ibid., p. 46. See also Aynsley, *Graphic Design in Germany*, chapter 5.

22 The magazine was re-titled *Die Kunst im Deutschen Reich* between 1939 and 1944.

23 Walter Benjamin, 'The Work of Art in the Age of Mechanical Reproduction' [1935], in *Illuminations*, ed. Hannah Arendt (Glasgow, 1970), pp. 219–54.

24 Ibid., p. 243.

25 Susan Sontag, 'Fascinating Fascism', in *Under the Sign of Saturn* (London, 1983), p. 83. For an extended analysis of the film, see Steve Neale, 'Triumph of the Will: Notes on Documentary and Spectacle', *Screen*, XX/1 (1979), pp. 63–86.

26 Sontag, 'Fascinating Fascism', p. 99.

27 Malcolm Quinn, *The Swastika: Constructing the Symbol* (London and New York, 1997).

28 Steven Heller, *The Swastika: Symbol beyond Redemption?* (New York, 2000), p. 69.

29 Siegfried Kracauer, 'The Mass Ornament', in *The Mass Ornament: Weimar Essays*, ed. and trans. Thomas Y. Levin (Cambridge, MA, 1995), p. 79.

30 Ibid., p. 76.

31 Barbara Miller-Lane, *Architecture and Politics in Germany, 1918–1945* (Cambridge, MA, 1968); Robert Taylor, *The Word in Stone: The Role of Zerstiteture in the National Socialist Ideology* (Berkeley, CA, 1974); Iain Boyd Whyte, in *Art and Power: Europe under the Dictators, 1930–45*, ed. Dawn Ades et al., exh. cat., Hayward Gallery, London (1996) ['Berlin, 1 May 1936', pp. 43–9, and 'National Socialism and Modernism, Architecture', pp. 258–69]; and Paul Jaskot, *The Architecture of Oppression: The SS, Forced Labor and the Nazi Monumental Building Economy* (London, 2000)

32 Hans J. Reichhardt and Wolfgang Schäche, *Von Berlin nach Germania: Über die Zerstörungen der Reichhauptstadt durch Albert Speers Neugestaltungsplanungen* (Berlin,

1985), and Alan Balfour, *Berlin: The Politics of Order, 1737–1989* (New York, 1990).

33 Iain Boyd Whyte, 'Berlin, 1 May 1936', in *Art and Power*, ed. Ades et al., p. 43. See also Gernot Böhme, 'Die Ästhetisierung der Politik: Kommunikationsdesign im Nationalsozialismus', in *Im Designpark*, ed. Buchholz and Wolbert, pp. 162–9.

34 Ulrich Kubisch, *Aller Welts Wagen: die Geschichte eines automobilen Wirtschaftswunders* (Berlin, 1986), and Jürgen Krause, ed., *Die Nützliche Moderne: Graphik- und Produkt-Design in Deutschland, 1935–1955*, exh. cat., Westfälisches Landesmuseum für Kunst und Kulturgeschichte, Münster (2000), pp. 15–29.

35 The poster is reproduced in Aynsley, *Graphic Design in Germany*, p. 187.

36 Kubisch, *Aller Welts Wagen*, pp. 30–31.

37 *Das Haus des Deutschen Handwerks* (Berlin, 1937).

38 Ibid.

39 Campbell, *The German Werkbund*, p. 255.

40 See Ernst Wiechert, *In der Heimat* (Munich, 1938), and F. Matthies-Masuren, *Das Atelier des Fotografen* (Halle, 1937), as examples of this photographic tradition.

41 Hermann Gretsch, *Gestaltendes Handwerk* (Stuttgart, 1940).

42 Campbell, *The German Werkbund*, p. 277. See also Sonja Günther, *Innenräume des 'Dritten Reiches'* (Berlin, 1978), and Günther, *Das Deutsche Heim: Luxusinterieurs und Arbeitermöbel von der Gründerzeit bis zum 'Dritten Reich'* (Giessen, 1984).

43 Lore Kramer, 'Marginialien: Zum Industriedesign im national-sozialistischen Deutschland – Erinnerungen, Spuren, Zitate und Reklektionen', in *Design in Deutschland, 1933–45: Ästhetik und Organisation des Deutschen Werkbundes im 'Dritten Reich'*, ed. Sabine Weissler (Giessen, 1990), pp. 56–71.

44 Wolfgang Schultz, 'Auch an seinem Heim erkennt man den Nationalsozialisten!', *Die Hoheitsträger*, 3 (August 1939), pp. 16–18, German Propaganda Archive. I am grateful to Pat Kirkham for introducing me to this source. http://www.calvin.edu/academic/cas/gpa/interiordecoration.htm (accessed April 2008).

45 Ibid.

46 Irene Guenther, *Nazi Chic? Fashioning Women in the Third Reich* (Oxford and New York, 2004).

47 Patrice Petro, 'Weimar Photojournalism and the Female Reader', in *Joyless Streets: Women and Melodramatic Representation in Weimar Germany* (Princeton, NJ, 1989), pp. 79–139.

48 Detlev Peukert, *Inside Nazi Germany: Conformity, Opposition and Racism in Everyday Life*, trans. Richard Deveson (New Haven, CT, 1987).

49 Guenther, *Nazi Chic?*, p. 266.

50 Guenther, '"Purifying" the German Clothing Industry', in ibid., pp. 143–66.

51 Peter Hahn, 'Bauhaus and Exile: Bauhaus Architects and Designers between the Old and the New', in *Exiles and Emigrés*, ed. Barron, p. 216.

52 Ibid., p. 221.

53 *Bauhaus, 1919–28*, exh. cat., Museum of Modern Art, New York (1938).

54 Alain Findeli, *Le Bauhaus des Chicago: l'oeuvre pedagogique de László Moholy-Nagy* (Quebec and Paris, 1995), and Findeli, 'Moholy-Nagy's Design Pedagogy in Chicago (1937–46)', *Design Issues*, VII/1 (1990), pp. 4–19.

4 Reconstruction and the Tale of Two Germanys, 1945–75

1 Wera Meyer-Waldeck and Hans Schwippert, *Architektur und Wohnform*, LVIII/ 5 (1950), p. 99: 'Wiederaufbau bedeutet nicht nur wieder neu aufzubauen, sondern Gestaltung neuer Lebensform und Lebenswillens.'

2 Maren Eichhorn, Jörn Grabowski and Konrad Vanja, eds, *Die Stunde Null: Über Leben 1945*, exh. cat., Staatliche Museen zu Berlin (2005), and Eckhard Siepmann and Angelika Thiekötter, *Blasse Dinge: Werkbund und Waren, 1945–1949* (Berlin, 1989).

3 Theodor Adorno, *Minima Moralia: Reflections from Damaged Life* [1951], trans. Edmund Jephcott (London, 1978), p. 39.

4 David Childs, *The GDR: Moscow's German Ally* (London, 1988), p. 2.

5 Rob Burns, ed., *German Cultural Studies: An Introduction* (Oxford, 1995), p. 167; Childs, *The GDR*, pp. 59–65; and Robert Kee, 'The Wall', in *Encounter*, ed. Stephen Spender and Melvin J. Lasky, XCVIII (November 1961), pp. 13–19.

6 The plan incorporated the reduction of German heavy industrial production to 50 per cent of its 1938 level through strategic bombing or dismantling of factories. Michael J. Hogan, *The Marshall Plan: America, Britain and the Reconstruction of Western Europe, 1947–1952* (Cambridge, 1987).

7 Gordon A. Craig, 'Professors and Students', in *The Germans* (Harmondsworth, 1982), pp. 170–89.

8 Claude Schnaidt, 'Ulm, 1955–1975', *Archithese* [Niederteufen CH], 15 (1975).

9 For examples of early foreign reviews of Germany's post-war development, see Gerhard Rosenberg, 'Germany: Modern Architecture under and after the Nazis', *Architecture Review*, CXIV/684 (December 1953), pp. 379–87, and J. M. Richards, 'Europe Rebuilt, 1946–1956', *Architectural Review*, CXXI/722 (March 1957), pp. 158–76. By 1954 the Federal Republic had built 542,800 dwellings.

10 Brigitte Hausmann in Dagmar Rinker, *ulmer modelle,*

hochschule für gestaltung ulm, 1953–1968, exh. cat., Ulmer Museum, HfG-Archiv, Ulm (Ostfildern-Ruit, 2005), p.25. As to the question of style, Hausmann continued: 'A preventative to Gelsenkirchen Baroque and kidney tables from Reposal, cone lamps and phonograph cabinets they were not, even if the target group was by no means limited to the potential clientele of Knoll International and Herman Miller, to whom interior design owed its leading position.'

11 Kathrin Spohr, 'Im Wandel der Zeiten', *Design Report*, 5 (2003), pp. 82–3, and Lars Quadejacob, 'Plattform statt Guter Form', *Design Report*, 6 (2003), pp. 80–83.

12 *Werk und Zeit, Monatszeitung des deutschen Werkbundes*, (March 1952–). For commentary on the post-war German Werkbund, see Paul Betts, '"Good Form" and the Critique of Liberalism', in *The Authority of Everyday Objects: A Cultural History of West German Industrial Design* (Berkeley, 2004), pp. 92–108.

13 *Architektur und Wohnform*, LVIII/5 (1950). See also Agatha Buski Wuppermann, *Hans Schwippert, 1899–1973: Von der Werkkunst zum Design* (Munich, 2006), and Olaf Alsendorf, Wolfgang Voigt and Wilfried Wang, eds, *Botschaften: 50 Jahre Auslandbauten der Bundesrepublik Deutschland*, exh. cat., DAM, Bonn (2000).

14 *Architektur und Wohnform*, LVIII/5 (1950).

15 Petra Eisele, 'Florence Knoll: Elegante Bescheidenheit', *Werk und Zeit*, no. 2 (2004), pp. 21–2.

16 Bobbye Tigerman, '"I Am Not a Decorator": Florence Knoll, the Knoll Planning Unit and the Making of the Modern Office', *Journal of Design History*, XX/1 (2007), pp. 61–74, and Arno Votteler and Herbert Eilmann, *125 Jahre Knoll: Vier Generationen Sitzmöbel Design* (Stuttgart, 1985).

17 Jeffrey Head, *Herbert Matter: Modernist Photography and Graphic Design* (Stanford, CA, 2005).

18 This and all subsequent quotes are from Heinz Huber, 'The New Apartment', in *Great German Short Stories*, ed. Stephen Spender, trans. Christopher Middleton (New York, 1960), pp. 251–61.

19 Hans Schwippert, 'Aus dem Programmentwurf' [1955], in *Weltausstellung Brüssel, 1958*, exh. cat., Brussels (Düsseldorf, 1958).

20 Theodor Heuss in ibid., p. 3.

21 *Weltausstellung Brüssel, 1958*. See also Annemarie Jaeggi, ed., *Egon Eiermann, 1904–1970, Architect and Designer: The Continuity of Modernism* (Ostfildern-Ruit, 2004), and Arthur Mehlstäubler, *Egon Eiermann: die Möbel*, exh. cat., Badisches Landesmuseum, Karlsruhe (1999).

22 *Weltausstellung Brüssel, 1958*, p. 5.

23 *Weltausstellung Brüssel, 1958*: 'Hätte man sich doch unserer Länder mit ihrer Heimatkunst erinnert und, zum Teufel!, meinetwegen dem deutschen Bier und Sauerkraut einen Kranz geflochten. Das wäre besser und

richtiger gewesen.' Translated by Sarah Owens.

24 Ibid.: 'Verdammt sei, wer dieses deutsche Raritätenkabinetten ausgeheckt hat'; 'Nichts wirkt hier protzig, nichts 'wirtschaftswunderbar'. Deutschland haut nicht auf die Pauke, sondern spielt in Brüssel Geige.' Translated by Sarah Owens.

25 *Weltausstellung Brüssel, 1958*.

26 *Weltausstellung Brüssel, 1958*.

27 *Weltausstellung Brüssel, 1958*.

28 Childs, *The GDR*, pp. 21–5.

29 Erica Carter, *How German Is She?: Postwar West German Reconstruction and the Consuming Woman* (Ann Arbor, MI, 1997). Billy Wilder's filmic comedy *One, Two, Three* (1961) commented on the situation by taking the theme of a Coca-Cola salesman based in West Berlin, played by James Cagney, with responsibility for distribution in the eastern sector of the city, before and after the building of the Wall.

30 Gert-Joachim Glaessner, 'Selbstinszenierung von Partei und Staat', in *Parteiauftrag: ein neues Deutschland: Bilder, Rituale und Symbole der frühen DDR*, ed. Dieter Vorsteher, exh. cat., Deutsches Historisches Museum, Berlin and Munich (1997), pp. 20–39.

31 Klaus-Peter Merta, 'Uniformierung als Mittel der Politik', in ibid., pp. 175–86. Particular importance lay in the individual responsibility given to the blue kerchief, which after 1973 was changed to a red kerchief for the Thälmann Pioneers.

32 Katja Protte, 'Zum Beispiel – der 1. Mai 1951 in Ost-Berlin Agitation, Staatliche Selbtdarstellung und Utopie', in ibid., pp. 118–41.

33 Michael Kunzel, '"Neues Geld für ein Neues Deutschland": Banknoten und Munzen der SBZ und DDR bis 1964', in ibid., pp. 70–76.

34 Doris Müller, '"Wir bauen die erste sozialistische Strasse Berlins": die Stalinallee in der politischen Propaganda im ersten Jahr des "Nationalen Aufbauprogramms Berlin 1952"', in *Parteiauftrag*, ed. Vorsteher, pp. 369–88.

35 C. Jaquand, 'Hermann Henselmann, architecte de la Stalinallee', *L'Architecture d'aujourdhui*, 275 (1991), and Alan Balfour, *Berlin: The Politics of Order, 1737–1989* (New York, 1990).

36 Childs, *The GDR*, pp. 31–3.

37 Extract from Walter Ulbricht, 'Der IV: Parteitag der Sozialistischen Einheitspartei Deutschlands', *Neue Werbung* (September 1954), p. 1: 'Wir verfügen alle Voraussetzungen, um Industriezeugnisse höchster Qualität zu vorteilhaten Bedingungen nach kapitalistischen Ländern – und vor allem nach den kolonialen und halbkolonialen Ländern – zu liefern und deren Landesprodukte abzunehmen. Die Werktätigen in den Betrieben der Deutschen Demokratischen Republik haben dabei die Aufgabe, durch eine hohe Qualität der

Exporterzeugnisse dazu beizutragen, dass wir Waren unserer Republik Weltruf erlangen und in allen Ländern der Erde Achtung erfahren. Deutschland war von jeher das Land des Aussenhandelbetrieb, wiederaufzunehmen und den Aussenhandel mit den volksdemokratischen Ländern zu vertiefen.' Translated by Sarah Owens.

38 On the impact of the cultural thaw, see Burns, *German Cultural Studies*, pp. 159–64.

39 Deutsche Bauinformation, *Baukatalog Bildende Kunst + Architektur, Teil 1/ Berlin* (Berlin [East], 1969).

40 Rainer Gries and Cordula Günther, '"Jeden Tag ein neues Geschenk": Gedanken zum Geschenkgestus in der DDR', in *Parteiauftrag*, ed. Vorsteher, pp. 241–53.

41 Cordula Günther, '"Präsent 20": Der Stoff, aus dem die Träume sind', in *Wunderwirtschaft: DDR-Konsumkultur in den 60er Jahren*, ed. Ina Merkel and Felix Mühlberg, exh. cat., Neue Gesellschaft für bildende Kunst, Berlin (Cologne, 1996), pp. 144–51.

42 Silke Rothkirch, 'Moderne Menschen kaufen Modern', in ibid., pp. 112–19.

43 Merkel and Mühlberg, eds, *Wunderwirtschaft*, pp. 8–20.

44 Katrin Böske, 'Abwesend anwesend: eine kleine Geschichte des Intershops', in ibid., pp. 214–22.

45 Jochen Fetzer, 'Gut verpackt', in ibid., pp. 104–11.

46 This is shown in the range of articles covered by the magazine *Neue Werbung*, discussed in chapter Five.

47 Eli Rubin, 'The Form of Socialism without Ornament: Consumption, Ideology and the Rise and Fall of Modernist Design in the German Democratic Republic', *Journal of Design History*, XIX/2 (2006), pp. 155–68.

48 Wolfgang Schröder, *Trabant und Wartburg: die Motorrad- und PKW-Produktion der DDR* (Bremen, 1995).

49 For a detailed consideration of the consumption of East German goods, including the Trabant, see Ina Merkel, 'From Stigma to Cult: The Change of Interpretation in the East German Culture of Consumption', a paper given at the conference 'Knowing Consumers: Actors, Images, Identities in Modern History' at the Zentrum für Interdisziplinäre Forschung in Bielefeld, Germany, 26–28 February 2004.

50 Jens Kassner, *Clauss Dietel, Lutz Rudolph: Gestaltung ist Kultur*, exh. cat., Kulturbräuerei, Berlin (2003), and 'Scene: Besuch bei Clauss Dietel', *Design Report*, 11 (2004), pp. 42–47. The Volkseigener Betrieb (People-owned Enterprise), or VEB in abbreviation, was the legal form of industrial company in East Germany that was publicly owned.

51 Christa Wolf, 'Errinerungsbericht', in *Kahlschlag: Das 11. Plenum des ZK der SED 1965. Studien und Dokumente*, ed. Günter Agde (Berlin, 1991), p. 266.

52 Most famously in Christa Wolf, *Der Geteilte Himmel* [1963] (Munich, 2004). This narrates the fate of a young couple whose paths lead to separate lives when the man

stays in the West following a chemistry conference, while the woman remains in the GDR, to contribute to building the new state.

53 Walter Ulbricht, quoted in *Neue Werbung* (July 1961): 'Künstlerische Leistung ist nicht nur ein Mittel, um bei der Erfüllung der Aufgabe zu helfen, sondern ein integrierender Bestandteil des ganzen Planes, der zum Sieg des Sozialismus führt.' Translated by Sarah Owens.

54 Heinz Hirdina, *Gestalten für die Serie in der DDR, 1949–1985* (Dresden, 1988), pp. 10–11.

55 Ibid. See also Siegfried Gronert and Elke Beilfuss, eds, *Horst Michel: Formgestalter in Weimar*, exh. cat., Bauhaus-Universität Weimar (Weimar, 2004).

56 Hans Merz quoted in Hirdina, *Gestalten für die Serie*, in conversation with Hirdina, 22 March 1984. Herz, a student of Stam, went on to become a leading ceramic designer.

57 Hirdina, *Gestalten für die Serie*, p. 39.

58 Walter Heisig, director of the Institut für Angewandte Kunst in 1957: 'Ein Besteck ohne Ornament ist Formalismus'. Quoted in ibid., p. 40.

59 Ibid., p. 39: 'Die Starrheit der früherern Formen wird aufgelockert, die puritanische Schmucklosigkeit überwunden. Das neue erscheinen bewegter, liebenswürdiger und warmer. Das ist nicht zuletzt der Rückerinnerung an die Werte der Heimatkunst zu danken.' Translated by Sarah Owens.

60 Ibid., p. 45.

61 'Kost the Ost' in *Design Report*, 02 (2002).

62 The literature on Ulm Hochschule für Gestaltung is now extensive. Recent works include Herbert Lindinger, *Hochschule für Gestaltung: die Moral der Gegenstände* (Berlin, 1987); Marcela Quijano, ed., *HfG Ulm: Programm wird bau, die Gebäude der Hochschule für Gestaltung Ulm* (Stuttgart, 1998); Rinker, *ulmer modelle*; René Spitz, *HfG Ulm: The View behind the Foreground: The Political History of the Ulm School of Design* (Stuttgart and London, 2002). See also the school's own journal, *Ulm: Zeitschrift der Hochschule für Gestaltung* (Ulm, 1959–68).

63 Gerd Fleischmann, Rudolf Bosshard and Christoph Bignens, *Max Bill: Typographie, Reklame, Buchgestaltung/ Typography, Advertising, Book Design* (Sulgen, 1998).

64 Edgar Reitz, himself a former tutor at Ulm, retrospectively depicted the school in this manner in the second part of *Heimat*, his episodic television drama series, *Die Zweite Heimat*, in 1992.

65 Brigitte Hausmann, 'Experiment 53/68', in Rinker, *ulmer modelle*, pp. 16–33.

66 See *Bauhäusler in Ulm: Grundlehre an der HfG, 1953–1955*, exh. cat., Archiv der Hochschule für Gestaltung (1993).

67 François Burkhardt and Inez Franksen, eds, *Dieter Rams and Design* (Berlin [West], 1981), and 'Besuch bei Dieter Rams', *Design Report*, 10 (2002).

68 Rinker, *ulmer modelle*, p. 50.

69 Brigitte Hausmann, 'Experiment 53/68', in ibid.

70 Rinker, *ulmer modelle*, p. 47.

71 Claude Schnaidt, 'Ulm, 1955–1975', *Archithese* [Niederteufen CH], 15 (1975).

72 Rinke, *ulmer modelle*, pp. 31 and 38.

73 Hans Magnus Enzensberger, 'Das Plebiszit der Verbraucher' [1960], in *Einzelheiten 1: Bewusstseins-Industrie* [1962], quoted in ibid., p. 28.

74 Rinke, *ulmer modelle*, p. 28.

75 Quoted in Hartmut Seeling, *Geschichte der Hochschule für Gestaltung Ulm: ein Beitrag zur Entwicklung ihres Programms und der Arbeiten im Bereich der Visuellen Kommunikation* (Cologne, 1985): 'Die hfg hat die Hoffnung auf eine demokratische Renaissance Westdeutschlands konkretisiert und starb mit ihr.'

5 Reunification: Design in a Global Context, 1975–2005

1 Michael Erlhoff, *Designed in Germany since 1949*, exh. cat., Rat für Formgebung, Frankfurt am Main (Munich, 1990), Preface.

2 Jürgen Habermas, 'Modernity: An Incomplete Project', in Hal Foster, *Postmodern Culture* (London and Sydney, 1985), pp. 3–15. For a more extended discussion of civil society and the public sphere, with specific reference to the Federal Republic of Germany, see Jürgen Habermas, *Towards a Rational Society* [1969] (Cambridge, 1987).

3 Robert Venturi and Denise Scott-Brown, *Complexity and Tradition in Architecture* (New York, 1966), and Robert Venturi, Denise Scott-Brown and Steven Izenour, *Learning from Las Vegas* [1972] (Cambridge, MA, and London, 1996).

4 Helmut Bauer, ed., *Ingo Maurer: Making Light*, exh. cat., Museum Villa Stuck, Munich (Tucson, AZ, 1992); Alexander von Wegesack, ed., *Ingo Maurer: Light; Reaching for the Moon*, exh. cat., Vitra Design Museum, Weil am Rhein (2004), and Ingo Maurer et al., *Provoking Magic: Lighting of Ingo Maurer*, exh. cat., Cooper-Hewitt National Design Museum, New York (2007).

5 Thomas Hauffe, *Fantasie und Härte: das 'Neue Deutsche Design' der achtziger Jahre* (Giessen, 1994), and Gerda Breuer, *Die Erfindung des Modernen Klassikers* (Ostfildern-Ruit, 2001).

6 Siegfried Michail Syniuga, in *Kunst Forum*, LXXXII (1984), p. 102; quoted in Stefan Lengyel and Hermann Sturm, *Design–Schnittpunkt–Essen, 1949–1989: von der Folkwangschule für Gestaltung zur Universität Essen: 40 Jahre Industriedesign in Essen* (Berlin, 1989), p. 85.

7 Kathrin Spohr, 'Im Wandel der Zeiten', *Design Report*, 5 (2003), pp. 82–3, and Lars Quadejacob, 'Plattform statt Guter Form', *Design Report*, 6 (2003), pp. 80–83.

8 Gert Selle, 'Institutionalisierung des Design', in *Geschichte des Design in Deutschland* (Frankfurt and New York, 1997), pp. 269–80.

9 Gwendolyn Ristant, in Erlhoff, *Designed in Germany since 1949*, pp. 101–3.

10 Hans Höger, ed., *Bundespreis Produktdesign, 1996: Katalog der Prämierten Produkte*, exh. cat., Rat für Formgebung, Frankfurt am Main (1996).

11 Ulrike Gauss, *Stankowski 06: Aspects of his Oeuvre* (Ostfildern-Ruit, 2006).

12 Bettina Becker, 'Policy Made in Germany', *Design Report*, 07/08 (2003), pp. 74–7.

13 *Neue Werbung* was published by DEWAG, the state publishing house; see Jörn Schütrumpf, 'Die Werbefirma DEWAG: ein Fragment', in *Parteiauftrag: ein neues Deutschland: Bilder, Rituale und Symbole der frühen DDR*, ed. Dieter Vorsteher, Deutsches Historisches Museum, Berlin and Munich (1997), pp. 451–3.

14 As an example of Rademacher's commentary on the various Party congresses and festivals, see Hellmut Rademacher, 'Gebrauchsgraphik auf der VIII Kunstausstellung der DDR', *Neue Werbung*, XXV/1 (1978).

15 'Plaste und Elaste aus Schkopau', *Neue Werbung*, XXV/1 (1978).

16 Rob Burns, ed., *German Cultural Studies: An Introduction* (Oxford, 1995), p. 320. See also the special issue on *Historikerstreit* in *German History: The Journal of the German History Society*, VI/1 (April 1988).

17 Paolo Portoghesi, *First International Exhibition of Architecture*, exh. cat., The Corderia of the Arsenale. La Biennale di Venezia: Architectural Section (London, 1980), p. 17. See also the essays in the book by Vincent Scully, Charles Jencks and Christian Norberg-Schulz.

18 Charles Jencks, 'Towards Radical Eclecticism', in ibid., p. 33.

19 Officina Alessi, *Tea and Coffee Piazza Alessi: 11 Tea and Coffee Sets* (Brescia, 1983), and Steven Kolsteren, *Tea and Coffee Piazza*, exh. cat., Groninger Museum, Groningen (2002).

20 Josef Paul Kleihues and Hämer Hardt-Walther, *Idee, Prozess, Ergebnis: die Reparatur und Rekonstruktion der Stadt: Internationale Bauausstellung Berlin, 1987*, exh. cat., Martin-Gropius-Bau, Berlin (1984).

21 Volker Fischer, *Ornament und Versprechen. Postmoderne und Memphis im Rückblick*, exh. cat., Museum für Angewandte Kunst, Frankfurt am Main (Stuttgart and London, 2005).

22 Wolfgang Reuter, 'Aspects of Cultural Theory: Design and Power', in *Design–Schnittpunkt–Essen: von der Folkwangschule für Gestaltung zur Universität Essen*, ed. Stefan Lengyel and Hermann Sturm (Berlin, 1989), p. 63.

23 Florian Urban, *Berlin/DDR- neo-historisch: Geschichte aus Fertigteilen* (Berlin, 2007).

24 Friedrich Friedl, *Das Gewöhnliche Design: Dokumentation einer Ausstellung des Fachbereichs Gestaltung der Fachhochschule Darmstadt 1976*, exh. cat., Fachhochschule für Gestaltung. Darmstadt (1979).

25 Wolfgang Welsch, *Unserer postmoderne Moderne* (Heidelberg-Weinheim, 1987).

26 Peter Hahn, *Bauhaus Archiv Museum für Gestaltung Sammlungs-Katalog 1981* (Berlin, 1981). For the period of the GDR, see Greg Castillo, 'The Bauhaus in Cold War Germany', in *Bauhaus Culutre from Weimar to the Cold War*, ed. Kathleen James-Chakraborty (Minneapolis, MN, and London, 2006), pp. 171–93.

27 Vitra Museum: www.vitra.com/philosophy (accessed April 2008).

28 The Dokumentationszentrum Alltagskultur der DDR in Eisenhüttenstadt publishes the journal *Museumsblätter Mitteilungen des Museumverbandes Brandenburg*. For commentary on curatorial initiatives in the former GDR, see Kai-Uwe Scholz, 'Entschwundene Welten', *Design Report*, 06 (1996), pp. 38–42, and Kai-Uwe Scholz, 'Kost the Ost', *Design Report*, 02 (2002), pp. 60–65.

29 Exhibition panel from *Die Deutsche Demokratische Republik, 1949–1990* in the Deutsches Historisches Museum, Berlin, visited on 22 July 2007.

30 Michael Erlhoff suggested in 1990 that 'Made in Germany' could be equated with the Federal Republic of Germany since 1949; see Erlhoff, *Designed in Germany since 1949*, Preface. On the exodus of designers from the former GDR, see Günther Höhne, 'Das neue Deutschland gestaltet sich: nur wo bleiben die Gestalter?', *Form*, 135 (1991), pp. 11–12. For further commentary on the history of the marque 'Made in Germany', see Andrej Kupetz, 'Made in Germany', in *Im Designerpark: Leben in künstlichen Welten*, ed. Kai Buchholz and Klaus Wolbert, exh. cat., Mathildenhöhe Institut, Darmstadt (2004), pp. 130–34.

31 Gertrud Lehnert, *Frauen Machen Mode* (Berlin, 1998).

32 Susanne Anna, Eva Gronbach and Ute Brandes, *Generation Mode*, exh. cat., Düsseldorf Stadtmuseum (Ostfildern-Ruit, 2006).

33 Konstantin Grcic quoted in 'Putting Krups Back in the Mix', *Business Week* (24 May 2006). For commentary, see Klaus Meyer, 'Konstantin Grcic', *Design Report*, 12 (2002), pp. 32–5.

34 Fay Sweet, *MetaDesign: Design from the Word Up* (London, 1999), and Erik Spiekermann and Jan Middendorp, *Made with Fontfont: Type for Independent Minds* (Amsterdam, 2006).

35 Richard Sapper quoted in Kai-Uwe Scholz, 'Was heisst hier "deutsches Design"?', *Design Report*, 6 (1996), p. 9.

36 Michel Chanaud, *5x Berlin, Cyan, Anschlaege, Fons Hickmann m23, ATAK/Georg Barber, Angela Lorenz*, exh. cat., Festival International de l'Affiche et des Arts Graphiques de Chaumont, Paris (2006), and www.anschlaege.de.

37 Ibid. Dawn Ades, et al., *Art and Power: Europe under the Dictators, 1930–45*, exh. cat., Hayward Gallery, London (1996).

Select Bibliography

Adorno, Theodor, *Minima Moralia: Reflections from Damaged Life* [1951], trans. Edmund Jephcott (London, 1978)

—, and Max Horkheimer, *Dialectic of the Enlightenment* [1944], trans. John Cumming (London, 1986)

Agde, Günter, ed., *Kahlschlag: Das 11. Plenum des ZK der SED 1965: Studien und Dokumente* (Berlin, 1991)

Allgemeine Deutsche Biographie (Leipzig, 1891)

Alsendorf, Olaf, Wolfgang Voigt and Wilfried Wang, eds, *Botschaften: 50 Jahre Auslandbauten der Bundesrepublik Deutschland*, exh. cat., DAM, Bonn (2000)

Amtlicher Katalog der internationalen Bauaustellung (Berlin, 1957)

Anderson, Benedict, *Imagined Communities: Reflections on the Origin and Spread of Nationalism* (London, 1983)

Anderson, Perry, *Considerations on Western Marxism* (London, 1976)

Anna, Susanne, Eva Gronbach and Ute Brandes, *Generation Mode*, exh. cat., Düsseldorf Stadtmuseum (Ostfildern-Ruit, 2006)

Arbeitsausschusses der Berliner Gewerbe Ausstellung, *Officieller Haupt-Katalog: Illustrirte Prachtausgabe* (Berlin, 1896)

Asche, Kurt, *Peter Behrens und die Oldenburger Ausstellung, 1905: Entwürfe, Bauten, Gebrauchsgraphik* (Berlin, 1992)

Attfield, Judy, *Wild Things: The Material Culture of Everyday Life* (Oxford and New York, 2000)

Aynsley, Jeremy, *Graphic Design in Germany, 1890–1939* (London, 2000)

Backmeier, Doris, *Josef Hillerbrand: Design in Munchen in der 20er und 30er Jahren* (Munich, 1985)

Bain, Peter, and Paul Shaw, *Blackletter: Type and National Identity* (New York, 1998)

Baker, Malcolm, and Brenda Richardson, eds, *A Grand Design: A History of the Victoria and Albert Museum*, exh. cat., Victoria and Albert Museum / Baltimore Museum of Art (London and New York, 1997)

Balfour, Alan, *Berlin: The Politics of Order, 1737–1989* (New York, 1990)

Barck, Simone, and Siegfried Lokatis, eds, *Fenster zur Welt: eine Geschichte des DDR-Verlages Volk & Welt*, exh. cat., Dokumentationszentrum Alltagskultur, Eisenhüttenstadt (Berlin, 2003)

Barron, Stephanie, ed., *Exiles and Emigrés: The Flight of European Artists from Hitler*, exh. cat., Los Angeles County Museum (New York, 1997)

Bayer, Herbert, Walter Gropius and Ise Gropius, *Bauhaus, 1919–28*, exh. cat., Museum of Modern Art, New York (1938)

Bauer, Helmut, ed., *Ingo Maurer: Making Light*, exh. cat., Museum Villa Stuck, Munich (Tucson, AZ, 1992)

Baumhoff, Anja, *The Gendered World of the Bauhaus: The Politics of Power at the Weimar Republic's Premier Art Institute, 1919–1932* (Frankfurt am Main, 2001)

Bayer, Herbert, *Herbert Bayer: Painter, Designer, Architect* (New York, 1967)

Behnken, Klaus, *Inszenierung der Macht: Ästhetische Faszination im Faschismus*, exh. cat., Neue Gesellschaft für bildende Kunst, Berlin (1987)

Benjamin, Walter, 'The Work of Art in the Age of Mechanical Reproduction' [1935], in *Illuminations*, ed. Hannah Arendt, trans. Harry Zohn (Glasgow, 1970)

—, 'Louis-Philippe; or, The Interior', reprinted in 'Paris: Capital of the Nineteenth Century' [1955], in *Reflections*, ed. Peter Demetz, trans. Edmund Jephcott (New York, 1979)

Benton, Charlotte, Tim Benton and Dennis Sharp, eds, *Form and Function: A Source Book for the History of Architecture and Design, 1890–1939* (St Albans, 1975)

—, — and Ghislaine Wood, *Art Deco, 1910–1939*, exh. cat., Victoria and Albert Museum, London (2003)

Berents, Catherina, *Art Deco in Deutschland: das moderne Ornament* (Berlin, 1998)

Berghahn, Volker, *The Americanisation of West German Industry* (Leamington Spa, 1986)

Bertsch, Georg C., and Ernst Hedler, *SED: Schöne Einheits Design* (Cologne, 1994)

Betts, Paul, 'The Twilight of the Idols', *Journal of Modern History*, LXXII/3 (2000), pp. 731–65

—, *The Authority of Everyday Objects: A Cultural History of West German Industrial Design* (Berkeley, CA, 2004)

Boyd Whyte, Iain, *The Crystal Chair Letters: Architectural Fantasies by Bruno Taut and his Circle* (Cambridge, MA, 1985)

—, *Modernism and the Spirit of the City* (London and New York, 2003)

Breuer, Gerda, ed., *Der Westdeutsche Impuls, 1900–1914: Kunst und Umweltgestaltung im Industriegebiet: von der Künstlerseide zur Industriefotografie: das Museum zwischen Jugendstil und Werkbund*, exh. cat., Kaiser Wilhelm Museum, Krefeld (1984)

—, *Die Erfindung des Modernen Klassikers* (Ostfildern-Ruit, 2001)

—, *Jupp Ernst, 1905–1987: Designer, Grafiker, Pädagoge* (Tübingen, 2007)

—, ed., *Das Gute Leben die deutsche Werkbund nach 1945* (Tübingen, 2007)

Brockhage, Hans, and Reinhold Lindner, *Marianne Brandt: 'Hab ich je an Kunst gedacht'* (Chemnitz, 2001)

Brüning, Ute, ed., *Bauhaus Moderne im Nationalsocialismus: zwischen Anbiederung und Verfolgung* (Munich, 1993)

—, ed., *Das A und O des Bauhauses*, exh. cat., Bauhaus Archiv, Berlin (Leipzig, 1995)

Buchholz, Kai, ed., *Die Lebensreform: Entwürfe zur Neugestaltung von Leben und Kunst um 1900*, exh. cat., Institut Mathildenhöhe, Darmstadt (2001)

—, and Klaus Wolbert, eds, *Im Designerpark: Leben in künstlichen Welten*, exh. cat., Institut Mathildenhöhe, Darmstadt (2004)

Buddensieg, Tilmann, ed., *Berlin, 1900–1933: Architecture and Design / Architektur und Design*, exh. cat., Cooper-Hewitt Museum, The Smithsonian Institution's National Museum of Design (Berlin, 1997)

—, with Henning Rogge, *Industriekultur: Peter Behrens und die AEG, 1907–1914* (Cambridge, MA, 1984)

Bullock, Nick, 'First the Kitchen – then the Façade', *Journal of Design History*, 1/3–4 (1988), pp. 177–92

Burke, Christopher, *Paul Renner: The Art of Typography* (London, 1998)

Burkhardt, François, and Inez Franksen, eds, *Dieter Rams and Design* (Berlin, 1981)

Burkhardt, Lucius, ed., *The Werkbund: History and Ideology, 1907–1933* (New York, 1980)

Burns, Rob, ed., *German Cultural Studies: An Introduction* (Oxford, 1995)

Burschel, Carlo, ed., *Heinrich Löffelhardt: Industrieformen der 1950er und 1960er Jahre aus Porzellan und Glas: die 'Gute Form' als Vorbild für nachhaltiges Design* (Bremen, 2004)

Burton, Anthony, *Vision and Accident: The Story of the Victoria and Albert Museum* (London, 1999)

Butter, Andrea, and Ulrich Hartung, *Ostmoderne Architektur in Berlin, 1945–1965* (Berlin, 2004)

Campbell, Joan, *The German Werkbund: The Politics of Reform in the Applied Arts* (Princeton, NJ, 1978)

Carter, Erica, *How German is She?: Postwar West German Reconstruction and the Consuming Woman* (Ann Arbor, MI, 1997)

Chanaud, Michel, *5x Berlin, Cyan, Anschlaege, Fons Hickmann m23, ATAK/Georg Barber, Angela Lorenz*, exh. cat., Festival International de l'Affiche et des Arts Graphiques de Chaumont, Paris (2006)

Childs, David, *The GDR: Moscow's German Ally* (London, 1988)

Cillessen, Wolfgang, *Das Olympische Dorf* (Gross Glienicke, 1996)

Cohen, Arthur A., *Herbert Bayer: The Complete Work* (Cambridge, MA, 1984)

Coleman, Debra, Elizabeth Danze and Carol Henderson, eds, *Architecture and Feminism* (New York, 1996)

Commichau, Felix, *Das Haus eines Kunst-Freundes: ein Entwurf in zwölf Tafeln* (Darmstadt, 1902)

Craig, Gordon A., *The Germans* (Harmondsworth, 1982)

Demuth, Eva-Maria, *Informationen aus der AEG Geschichte*, 1/90 (Frankfurt am Main, 1990)

Deutsche Bauinformation, *Baukatalog Bildende Kunst + Architektur, Teil 1/ Berlin* (Berlin [East], 1969)

Deutsche Werkbund, *Die Durchgeistigung der deutschen Arbeit: ein Bericht vom Deutschen Werkbund* (Jena, 1912)

Droste, Magdalena, *Bauhaus, 1919–1933* (Cologne, 1990)

Eckstein, Beate, and Christine Nielsen, *Auf dem Weg zum Neuen Wohnen: die Werkbundsiedlung Breslau, 1929 / Towards a New Kind of Living: The Werkbund Housing Estate, Breslau, 1929* (Basel, Boston, MA, and Berlin, 1996)

Engeland, Hans, and Ulf Meyer, *Bauhaus-Architektur / Bauhaus Architecture* (Munich, London and New York, 2001)

Enzensberger, Hans Magnus, *Dreamers of the Absolute: Essays on Ecology, Media and Power* (London, 1988)

Erlhoff, Michael, ed., *Designed in Germany since 1949* (Munich, 1990)

Eskildsen, Ute, and Jan-Christopher Horak, eds, *Film und Foto der zwanziger Jahre: eine Betrachtung der internationalen Werkbundausstellung Film und Foto 1929* (Stuttgart, 1979)

Fehr, Michael, and Gerhard Storck, eds, *Das Schöne und der Alltag: Deutsches Museum für Kunst in Handel und Gewerbe, 1909–1919*, exh. cat., Kaiser Wilhelm Museum, Krefeld (Ghent, 1998)

Findeli, Alain, 'Moholy-Nagy's Design Pedagogy in Chicago, 1937–46', *Design Issues*, VII/1 (Autumn 1990), pp. 4–19 [special issue: 'Educating the Designer']

—, *Le Bauhaus des Chicago: l'oeuvre pedagogique de László Moholy-Nagy* (Sillery, Quebec, and Paris, 1995)

Fischer, Volker, *Die Schwingen des Kranichs: 50 Jahre Lufthansa-Design*, exh. cat., Museum für angewandte Kunst, Frankfurt (Stuttgart, 2005)

—, *Ornament und Versprechen Postmoderne und Memphis im Rückblick*, exh. cat. Museum für angewandte Kunst, Frankfurt am Main (Stuttgart and London, 2005)

Fleischmann, Gerd, Hans Rudolf Bosshard and Christoph Bignens, *Max Bill: typographie, reklame, buchgestaltung / typography, advertising, book design* (Sulgen, 1998)

Form und Zweck, *1960 Jahrbuch*, Institut für Angewandte Kunst, Berlin,

Foster, Hal, ed., *Postmodern Culture* (London and Sydney, 1985)

Franciscono, Marcel, *Walter Gropius and the Creation of the Bauhaus in Weimar: The Ideals and Artistic Theories of its Founding Years* (Urbana, IL, 1971)

Friedl, Friedrich, *Das Gewöhnliche Design: Dokumentation einer Ausstellung des Fachbereichs Gestaltung der Fachhochschule Darmstadt 1976*, exh. cat., Fachhochschule für Gestaltung, Darmstadt (1979)

Friedman, Marilyn, *Selling Good Design: Promoting the Early Modern Interior* (New York, 2003)

Frisby, David, and Mike Featherstone, *Simmel on Culture* (London, Thousand Oaks, CA, and New Delhi, 2006)

Gauss, Ulrike, *Stankowski 06: Aspects of his Oeuvre* (Ostfildern-Ruit, 2006)

Göhre, Paul, *Das Warenhaus* (Frankfurt am Main, 1907)

Graeff, Werner, *Innenräume: Räume und Inneneinrichtungsgegenstände aus der Werkbundausstelllung 'Die Wohnung'* (Stuttgart, 1928)

—, *Es kommt der neue Fotograf!* (Berlin, 1929)

Gretsch, Hermann, *Gestaltendes Handwerk* (Stuttgart, 1940)

Gronert, Siegfried, ed., *Form und Industrie: Wilhelm Braun Feldweg* (Frankfurt am Main, 1998)

—, and Elke Beilfuss, eds, *Horst Michel: Formgestalter in Weimar*, exh. cat., Bauhaus-Universität, Weimar (2004)

Grothe, Jürgen, *Berlin-Mitte um die Jahrhundertwende 103 Fotos aus dem Bildarchiv der Berliner Verkehrs-gesellschaft* (Berlin, 1991)

Gropius, Walter, *Staatliches Bauhaus in Weimar, 1919–1923* (Munich, 1923)

Guenther, Irene, *Nazi Chic? Fashioning Women in the Third Reich* (Oxford and New York, 2004)

Günther, Sonja, *Innenräume des 'Dritten Reiches'* (Berlin, 1978)

—, *Das Deutsche Heim: Luxusinterieurs und Arbeitermöbel von der Gründerzeit bis zum 'Dritten Reich'* (Giessen, 1984)

—, *Lilly Reich, 1885–1947: Innenarchitektin, Designerin, Ausstellungsgestalterin* (Stuttgart, 1988)

—, *Design der Macht: Möbel für Räpräsentanten des 'Dritten Reiches'* (Stuttgart, 1993)

—, *Die fünfziger Jahre: Innenarchitektur und Wohndesign* (Stuttgart, 1994)

Habermas, Jürgen, *Towards a Rational Society* [1969] (Cambridge, 1987)

Hahn, Peter, *Bauhaus Archiv Museum für Gestaltung Sammlungs-Katalog 1981* (Berlin, 1981)

Halter, Regina, ed., *Vom Bauhaus bis Bitterfeld: 41 Jahre DDR Design* (Giessen, 1991)

Harrod, Tanya, *The Crafts in Britain in the Twentieth Century* (London and New Haven, CT, 1999)

Harvey, Charles, and Jon Press, *William Morris: Design and Enterprise in Victorian Britain* (Manchester, 1991)

Harvey, David, *The Condition of Postmodernity: An Enquiry into the Origins Of Cultural Change* (Oxford, 1989)

Hauffe, Thomas, *Fantasie und Härte: das 'Neue Deutsche Design' der achtziger Jahre* (Giessen, 1994)

Head, Jeffrey, *Herbert Matter: Modernist Photography and Graphic Design* (Stanford, CA, 2005)

Heller, Steven, *The Swastika: Symbol beyond Redemption?* (New York, 2000)

Herf, Jeffrey, *Reactionary Modernism: Technology, Culture and Politics in Weimar and the Third Reich* (Cambridge, 1984)

Heskett, John, *Design in Germany, 1870–1919* (London, 1986)

—, 'Modernism and Archaism in Design in the Third Reich', in *The Nazification of Art: Art, Design, Music, Architecture and Film in the Third Reich*, ed. Brandon Taylor and Wilfried van der Will (Winchester, 1990), pp. 128–43

Heynen, Hilde, *Negotiating Domesticity: Spatial Productions of Gender in Modern Architecture* (London, 2005)

Hickethier, Knut, ed., *Mythos Berlin: zur Wahrnahmungsgeschichte einer industriellen Metropole: eine szenische Ausstellung an dem Gelände des Anhalter Bahnhofs, Aesthetik und Kommunikation* (Berlin, 1987)

Hinz, Berthold, *Art in the Third Reich* (Oxford, 1980)

Hirdina, Heinz, *Gestalten für die Serie in der DDR, 1949–1985* (Dresden, 1988)

—, ed., *Neues Bauen Neues Gestalten: das neue Frankfurt, eine Zeitschrift zwischen, 1926 und 1933* (Dresden, 1991)

Hoffmann, Heinrich, *Deutschland in Paris, 1937* (Munich, 1937)

Hoffmann, Julius, *La Décoration interièure allemande et les métiers d'arts à l'exposition de Bruxelles, 1910*, exh. cat., Brussels (Stuttgart and Brussels, 1910)

Hogan, Michael J., *The Marshall Plan: America, Britain and the Reconstruction of Western Europe, 1947–1952* (Cambridge, 1987)

Höger, Hans. ed., *Bundespreis produktdesign, 1996: Katalog der Prämierten Produkte*, exh. cat., Rat für Formgebung, Frankfurt am Main (1996)

Hopf, Susanne, and Natalja Meier, *Plattenbau Privat: 60 Interieurs* (Berlin, 2004)

Itten, Johannes, *Mein Vorkurs am Bauhaus: Gestaltungs und Formenlehre* [1963]; as *Design and Form: The Basic Course at the Bauhaus* (London, 1964)

Jaeggi, Annemarie, ed., *Egon Eiermann, 1904–1970: Architect and Designer: The Continuity of Modernism* (Ostfildern-Ruit, 2004)

Jahrbuch des Deutschen Werkbundes (Jena, 1912–15, and Munich, 1915–20)

James-Chakraborty, Kathleen, ed., *Bauhaus Culture from Weimar to the Cold War* (Minneapolis, MN, and London, 2006)

Jaquand, C., 'Hermann Henselmann: architecte de la Stalinallee', *L'Architecture d'aujourd'hui*, no. 275 (1991), pp. 60–61

Jarchow, Margarete, *Berliner Porzellan im 20. Jahrhundert* (Berlin, 1988)

Jaskot, Paul, *The Architecture of Oppression: The ss, Forced Labor and the Nazi Monumental Building Economy* (London, 2000)

Joachimides, Alexis, *Museumsinszenierungen: zur Geschichte der Institution des Kunstmuseums: die Berliner Museumslandschaft, 1830–1990* (Dresden, 1995)

Joedicke, Jürgen, *Weissenhofsiedlung Stuttgart* (Stuttgart, 1989)

Jones, Owen, *The Grammar of Ornament* (London, 1856)

Julier, Guy, *The Culture of Design* (London, 2000)

Kaes, Anton, Martin Jay and Edward Dimendberg, eds, *The Weimar Republic Sourcebook* (Berkeley, CA, 1994)

Kahle, Katharine Morrison, *Modern French Decoration* (New York and London, 1930)

Kant, Immanuel, *The Critique of Judgement* [1790], ed. and trans. Meredith James Creed (Oxford, 1980)

Kaplan, Wendy, ed., *Designing Modernity: The Arts of Reform and Persuasion, 1885–1945*, exh. cat.,The Wolfsonian, Miami Beach (New York, 1995)

Kassner, Jens, *Clauss Dietel, Lutz Rudolph: Gestaltung ist Kultur*, exh. cat., Kulturbräuerei, Berlin (2003)

Kermer, Wolfgang, *Willi Baumeister: Typographie und Reklamegestaltung* (Ostfildern-Ruit, 1989)

—, *Willi Baumeister und die Werkbund: Ausstellung 'Die Wohnung', 1927*, exh. cat., Staatliche Akademie der Bildenden Künste, Stuttgart (2003)

Kinross, Robin, *Modern Typography: An Essay in Critical History* (London, 1992)

Kirsch, Karin, *Die Weissenhofsiedlung: Werkbund-Ausstellung, 'Die Wohnung' – Stuttgart 1927* (Stuttgart, 1987)

Kleihues, Josef Paul, and Hämer Hardt-Waltherr, *Idee, Prozess, Ergebnis: die Reparatur und Rekonstruktion der Stadt: Internationale Bauausstellung Berlin 1987*, exh. cat., Martin-Gropius-Bau, Berlin (1984)

Kleinerüschkamp, Werner, *Hannes Meyer, 1889–1954: Architekt, Urbanist, Lehrer* (Berlin, 1989)

Koch, Alexander, and Hermann Werle, *Das vornehme deutsche Haus: Kunstgewerblicher Verlag Alexander Koch* (Darmstadt, Leipzig and Vienna, 1888)

Koch, Hofrat Alexander, *Eine Deutsche Ausstellung?* (Darmstadt, 1910)

Koehler, Carola, *Unterwegs zwischen Gründerzeit und Bauhaus: Wohnverhältnisse in Berlin in Romanen der Neuen Sachlichkeit* (Münster, 2003)

Konsum: Konsumgenossenschaften in der DDR, exh. cat., Fürst Puckler Museum, Cottbus (2007)

Krampen, Martin, *Otl Aicher: 328 Plakate für die Ulmer Volkshochschule* (Berlin, 2000)

Krause, Jürgen, ed., *Die nützliche Moderne: Graphik- und Produkt-Design in Deutschland, 1935–1955*, exh. cat., Westfälisches Landesmuseum für Kunst und Kulturgeschichte, Münster (2000)

Kubisch, Ulrich, *Aller Welts Wagen: die Geschichte eines automobilen Wirtschaftswunders* (Berlin, 1986)

Kühnel, Anita, ed., *Verführungen Plakate aus Österreich und Deutschland von 1914 bis 1945*, exh. cat., Kunstbibliothek, Berlin, Museum für Kunst und Gewerbe, Hamburg, and Österreichische Nationalbibliothek, Vienna (Berlin, 1999)

Lampugnani, Vittorio Magnano, and Michael Mönninger eds, *Berlin Morgen: Ideen für das Herz einer Groszstadt*, exh. cat., Deutsches Architektur Museum, Frankfurt am Main (Stuttgart, 1991)

Lange, Christiane, *Ludwig Mies van der Rohe and Lilly Reich: Furniture and Interiors*, exh. cat., Lange House, Krefeld (Ostfildern-Ruit, 2006)

Lehnert, Gertrud, *Frauen Machen Mode* (Berlin, 1998)

Lengyel, Stefan, and Hermann Sturm, eds, *Design–Schnittpunkt–Essen, 1949–1989: von der Folkwangschule für Gestaltung zur Universität Essen: 40 Jahre Industriedesign in Essen* (Berlin, 1989)

Lessing, Julius, *Führer durch die Ausstellung älterer kunstgewerblicher Gegenstände* exh. cat., Berlin Kunstgewerbemuseum (1872)

—, *Die Berliner Gewerbeausstellung* (Berlin, 1896)

Levin, Thomas Y., ed. and trans., *Siegfried Kracauer: The Mass Ornament* (Cambridge, MA, 1995)

Lindinger, Herbert, *Hochschule für Gestaltung: die Moral der Gegenstände* (Berlin, 1987)

Loehlin, Jennifer, *From Rugs to Riches: Housework, Consumption and Modernity in Germany* (Oxford, 1999)

Loew, Heinz, and Helene Nonne Schmidt, *Joost Schmidt: Lehre und Arbeit am Bauhaus, 1919–1932* (Düsseldorf, 1984)

Lohse, Richard P., *Neue Ausstellungsgestaltung: 75 Beispiele neuer Ausstellungsform* (Erlenbach-Zürich, 1953)

Lotringer, Sylvere, 'The German Issue', *Semiotext(e)*, IV/2 (1982)

Makela, Maria, *The Munich Secession: Art and Artists in Turn of the Century Munich* (New York, 1990)

Malke, Lutz, ed., *Europäische Moderne: Buch und Graphik aus Berliner Kunstverlagen, 1890–1933*, exh. cat., Kunstbibliothek, Berlin (1989)

Manske, Beate, ed., *Wilhelm Wagenfeld, 1900–1990* (Ostfildern-Ruit, 2000)

Martin, Leslie J., Naum Gabo and Ben Nicholson, eds, *Circle: An International Survey of Constructive Art* (London, 1937)

Matthies-Masuren, F., *Das Atelier des Fotografen* (Halle, 1937)

Mehlstäubler, Arthur, *Egon Eiermann: die Möbel*, exh. cat., Badisches Landesmuseum, Karlsruhe (1999)

Meissner, Jörg, ed., *Strategien der Werbekunst, 1850–1933*, exh. cat., Deutsches Historisches Museum, Berlin (2004)

Mendell, Pierre, and Carlos Oberer, *Design ist Kunst die sich nützlich macht*, exh. cat., Die Neue Sammlung, Munich (1984)

Merkel, Ina, *Utopie und Bedürfnis: die Geschichte der Konsumkultur in der DDR* (Cologne, 1999)

—, and Felix Mühlberg, eds, *Wunderwirtschaft: DDR-Konsumkultur in den 60er Jahren*, exh. cat., Neue Gesellschaft für bildende Kunst, Berlin (Cologne, 1996)

Merker, Reinhard, *Die bildenden Künste im Nationalsozialismus: Kulturideologie, Kulturpolitik, Kulturproduktion* (Cologne, 1983)

Meskimmon, Marsha, and Shearer West, eds, *Visions of the 'Neue Frau': Women and the Visual Arts in Weimar Germany* (Aldershot, 1995)

Meyer, Erna, *Der neue Haushalt: ein Wegweiser zur wirtschaftlichen Hausführung* (Stuttgart, 1928)

Miller, Michael. B., *The Bon Marché: Bourgeois Culture and the Department Store, 1869–1920* (London, 1981)

Miller-Lane, Barbara, *Architecture and Politics in Germany, 1918–1945* (Cambridge, MA, 1968)

Moeller, Gisela, *Peter Behrens in Düsseldorf: die Jahre 1903–07* (Heidelberg-Weinheim, 1991)

Moholy-Nagy, László, *Painting Photography Film* [1925], trans. Janet Seligman (London, 1969)

Morris, William, *Die Kunst und die Schönheit*, trans. M. Schwabe (Leipzig, 1901)

—, *Kunsthoffnungen und Kunstsorgen* (Leipzig, 1901) [contains five separately bound essays: *Die niederen Künste, Die Kunst des Volkes, Die Schönheit des Lebens, Wie wir aus dem Bestehenden das Beste machen können, Die Aussichten der Architekten in der Civilisation*]

Mundt, Barbara, ed., *Interieur und Design in Deutschland, 1945–1960*, exh. cat., Kunstgewerbemuseum, Berlin (1993)

Mundt, Barbara, with Babette Warncke, *Form ohne Ornament? angewandte Kunst zwischen Zweckform und Objekt*, exh. cat., Kunstgewerbemuseum, Berlin (Berlin, 1999)

Muthesius, Hermann, *The English House* [1904–5], ed. Dennis Sharp, trans. Janet Seligman (London, 1987)

Naylor, Gillian, *The Bauhaus Reassessed: Sources And Design Theory* (London, 1985)

Neale, Steve, 'Triumph of the Will: Notes on Documentary and Spectacle', *Screen*, XX/1 (1979), pp. 63–86

Nerdinger, Winfried, ed., *Bauhaus-moderne im Nationalsozialismus: zwischen Anbiederung und Verfolgung*, exh. cat., Bauhaus Archiv, Berlin (Munich, 1993)

—, *Bruno Taut, 1880–1938: Architekt zwischen Tradition und Avantgarde* (Stuttgart, 2001)

—, ed., *100 Jahre Deutscher Werkbund, 1907/2007*, exh. cat., Architektur Museum der Technischen Universität, Munich (2007)

Neue Deutsche Biographie (Berlin, 1985)

Nicolaus, Herbert, and Alexander Obeth, *Die Stalinallee: Geschichte einer deutschen Strasse* (Berlin, 1997)

Noever, Peter, *Die Frankfurter Küche von Margarete Schütte-Lihotsky* (Berlin, 1992)

—, ed., *Der Preis der Schönheit: 100 Jahre Wiener Werkstätte* (Ostfildern-Ruit, 2003)

Nolan, Mary, *Visions of Modernity: American Business and the Modernisation of Germany* (Oxford, 1994)

Nordau, Max, *Degeneration*, ed. George L. Mosse (Lincoln, NE, and London, 1993)

Oestereich, Christopher, *'Gute Form' im Wiederaufbau: Geschichte der Produktgestaltung in Westdeutschland nach 1945* (Berlin, 2000)

Otto, Christian F., and Richard Pommer, *Weissenhof 1927 and the Modern Movement in Architecture* (Chicago and London, 1991)

Overy, Paul, 'Visions of the Future and the Immediate Past: The Werkbund Exhibition, Paris 1930', *Journal of Design History*, XVII/4 (2004), pp. 337–57

—, *Light, Air and Openness: Modern Architecture between the Wars* (London, 2007)

Paret, Peter, *The Berlin Secession: Modernism and its Enemies in Imperial Germany* (Cambridge, MA, 1980)

Peukert, Detlev, *Inside Nazi Germany: Conformity, Opposition and Racism in Everyday Life*, trans. Richard Deveson (New Haven, CT, 1987)

Petro, Patrice, *Joyless Streets: Women and Melodramatic Representation in Weimar Germany* (Princeton, NJ, 1989)

Pevsner, Nikolaus, *Pioneers of Modern Design from William Morris to Gropius* (Harmondsworth, 1964)

Portoghesi, Paolo, ed., *First International Exhibition of Architecture*, exh. cat., The Corderia of the Arsenale. La Biennale di Venezia: Architectural Section (London, 1980)

Posener, Julius, *Anfänge des Funktionalismus von Arts and Crafts zum Deutschen Werkbund* (Berlin, 1964)

Quijano, Marcela, ed., *HfG Ulm: Programm wird Bau, die Gebäude der Hochschule für Gestaltung Ulm* (Stuttgart, 1998)

Quinn, Malcolm, *The Swastika: Constructing the Symbol* (London and New York, 1997)

Rademacher, Hellmut, and René Grohnert, *Kunst! Kommerz! Visionen! Deutsche Plakate, 1888–1933*, exh. cat., Deutsches Historisches Museum, Berlin (1992)

Randa, Sigrid, *Alexander Koch: Publizist und Verleger in Darmstadt* (Worms, 1990)

Rappaport, Erika. D., *Shopping for Pleasure: Women in the Making of London's West End* (Princeton, NJ, and Chichester, 2000)

Rasch, Heinz, and Bodo Rasch, eds, *Gefesselter Blick* (Stuttgart, 1930)

Rattemeyer, Volker, and Dietrich Helms, *Typographie kann unter Umständen Kunst Sein*, exh. cat., 5 vols, Landesmuseum, Wiesbaden (1990)

Reichhardt, Hans J., and Wolfgang Schäche, *Von Berlin nach Germania: Über die Zerstörungen der Reichhauptstadt durch Albert Speers Neugestaltungsplanungen* (Berlin, 1985)

Ribbe, Wolfgang, and Wolfgang Schäche, *Die Siemensstadt: Geschichte und Architektur eines Industriestandortes* (Berlin, 1985)

Richards, J. M., 'Europe Rebuilt, 1946–1956', *Architectural Review*, CXXI/722 (1957), pp. 158–76

Riedel, Hubert, ed., *Lucian Bernhard: Werbung und Design im*

Aufbruch des 20. Jahrhunderts, exh. cat., Institut für Ausslandsbeziehungen, Stuttgart (1999)

Riley, Terence, and Barry Bergdoll, eds, *Mies in Berlin*, exh. cat., Museum of Modern Art, New York (2001)

Rinker, Dagmar, *ulmer modelle, hochschule für gestaltung ulm, 1953–1968*, exh. cat., Ulmer Museum, HFG-Archiv, Ulm (Ostfildern-Ruit, 2005)

Rittaway, Mark, ed., *Globalization and Europe* (Milton Keynes, 2003)

Rössler, Patrick, *Die Neue Linie, 1929–1943: das Bauhaus am Kiosk* (Bielefeld, 2007)

Roth, Fedor, *Hermann Muthesius und die Idee der Harmonischen Kultur* (Berlin, 2001)

Rowe, Dorothy, *Representing Berlin: Sexuality and the City in Imperial and Weimar Germany* (Aldershot, 2003)

Rubin, Eli, 'The Form of Socialism without Ornament: Consumption, Ideology and the Rise and Fall of Modernist Design in the German Democratic Republic', *Journal of Design History*, XIX/2 (2006) pp. 155–68

Sachsse, Rolff, *Bild und Bau: zur Nutzung technischer Medien beim Entwerfen von Architektur* (Brunswick and Wiesbaden, 1997)

Scheerbart, Paul, *The Gray Cloth: A Novel on Glass Architecture*, ed. and trans. John A. Stuart (Cambridge, MA, 2003)

Schleger, Pat, *Hans Schleger: A Life of Design* (London, 2001)

Schnaidt, Claude, 'Ulm, 1955–1975', *Archithese*, 15 [Niederteufen CH] (1975)

Schneck, Adolf, *Die Billige Wohnung*, exh. cat., Deutsche Werkstätten, Dresden Hellerau (Dresden, 1928)

Schröder, Wolfgang, *Trabant und Wartburg: die Motorrad- und PKW-Produktion der DDR* (Bremen, 1995)

Schultz, Wolfgang, 'Auch an seinem Heim erkennt man den Nationalsozialisten!', *Die Hoheitsträger*, 3 (August 1939), pp. 16–18: German Propaganda Archive http://www.calvin.edu/academic/cas/gpa/interiordeco ration.htm (accessed April 2008)

Schuster, Peter-Klaus, *Die 'Kunststadt' München 1937: Nationalsozialismus und 'Entartete Kunst'* (Munich, 1987)

Schwabe, Hermann, *Die Organisation von Kunstgewerbeschulen in Verbindung mit dem deutschen Gewerbemuseum in Berlin* (Berlin, 1869)

—, *Kunstindustrie Bestrebungen in Deutschland in Verbindung mit dem deutschen Gewerbe Museum in Berlin* (Leipzig, 1871)

Schwartz, Frederic J., *The Werkbund: Design Theory and Mass Culture before the First World War* (New Haven, CT, and London, 1996)

Schwarzer, Mitchell, 'The Design Prototype as Artistic Boundary: The Debate on History and Industry in Central European Applied Arts Museums, 1860–1900', *Design Issues*, IX/1 (1992) pp. 30–44

—, *German Architectural Theory and the Search for Modern Identity* (Cambridge, 1995)

Schweiger, Werner, *Wiener Werkstätte: Design in Vienna, 1903–1932* (London, 1984)

Seeger, Mia, *Gute Möbel Schöne Räume* (Stuttgart, 1953)

—, and Stephan Hirzel, *Deutsche Warenkunde: eine Bildkartei des Deutschenwerkbundes* (Stuttgart, 1956–61)

Seeling, Hartmut, *Geschichte der Hochschule für Gestaltung Ulm: ein Beitrag zur Entwicklung ihres Programms und der Arbeiten im Bereich der Visuellen Kommunikation* (Cologne, 1985)

Selle, Gert, *Geschichte des Designs in Deutschland* [1978] (Frankfurt am Main and New York, 1997)

Semper, Gottfried, *Der Stil in den technischen und tektonischen Künsten, oder, Praktische Aesthetik: ein Handbuch für Techniker, Künstler und Kunstfreunde* (Frankfurt am Main, 1860)

Shafter, Debra, *The Order of Ornament, the Structure of Style: Theoretical Foundations of Modern Art and Architecture* (Cambridge, 2003)

Siepmann, Eckhard, and Angelika Thiekötter, *Blasse Dinge: Werkbund und Waren, 1940–1949* (Berlin, 1989)

Silver, Kenneth, *Esprit de Corps: The Art of the Parisian Avant-Garde and the First World War, 1914–1925* (London, 1989)

Simmel, Georg, 'Das Problem des Stiles', *Deutsche Kunst und Dekoration*, XI/7 (1908)

Sontag, Susan, *Under the Sign of Saturn* (London, 1983)

Spender, Stephen, *World within World* (London, 1951)

—, ed., *Great German Short Stories* (New York, 1960)

Spiekermann, Erik, and Jan Middendorp, *Made with Fontfont: Type for Independent Minds* (Amsterdam, 2006)

Spitz, René, *HfG Ulm: The View behind the Foreground: The Political History of the Ulm School of Design* (Stuttgart and London, 2002)

Stalla, Robert, and Florian Hufnagl, *Blickpunkt 1926: die Anfänge der neuen Sammlung München: Internationale Plakate*, exh. cat., Die Neue Sammlung, Staatliches Museum für angewandte Kunst, Munich (Munich and Berlin, 2002)

Stern, J. P., *The Politics of Cultural Despair: A Study in the Rise of Germanic Ideology* (New York, 1965)

Sweet, Fay, *MetaDesign: Design from the Word Up* (London, 1999)

Taterka, Elsa, *Farbe und Form*, XII/ 2 (1927), pp. 88–9

Taut, Bruno, *Die neue Wohnung: die Frau als Schöpferin*, 4th edn (Leipzig, 1926)

—, *Ein Wohnhaus* (Stuttgart, 1927)

—, *Modern Architecture* (London, 1929)

Taylor, Brandon, and Wilfried van der Will, eds, *The Nazification of Art: Art, Design, Music, Architecture and Film in the Third Reich* (Winchester, 1990)

Thöner, Wolfgang, *Das Bauhaus Wohnt: Leben und Arbeiten in der Meister Haus Siedlung Dessau* (Dessau and Leipzig, 2002)

Tigerman, Bobbye, '"I Am Not a Decorator": Florence Knoll, the Knoll Planning Unit and the Making of the Modern Office', *Journal of Design History*, XX/1 (2007), pp. 61–74

Tschichold, Jan, *The New Typography: A Handbook for Modern Designers*, trans. Ruari McLean, ed. Robin Kinross

(Berkeley, CA, 1995)

Ulmer, Renate, *Jugendstil Darmstadt* (Darmstadt, 1997)

Urban, Florian, *Berlin/DDR – neo-historisch: Geschichte aus Fertigteilen* (Berlin, 2007)

Venturi, Robert, and Denise Scott-Brown, *Complexity and Tradition in Architecture* (New York, 1966)

—, — and Steven Izenour, *Learning from Las Vegas* [1972] (Cambridge, MA, and London, 1996)

Vorsteher, Dieter, ed., *Parteiauftrag: ein neues Deutschland: Bilder, Rituale und Symbole der frühen DDR*, exh. cat., Deutsches Historisches Museum, Berlin (Munich and Berlin, 1997)

Votteler, Arno, and Herbert Eilmann, *125 Jahre Knoll: vier Generationen Sitzmöbel Design* (Stuttgart, 1985)

Waldmann, Emil, *Moderne Schiffsräume des Norddeutschen Lloyd: nach Entwürfen von Bruno Paul, R. A. Schröder und F.A.O. Krüger* (Munich, 1908) [special issue of *Dekorativer Kunst*]

Ward, Janet, *Weimar Surfaces: Urban Visual Culture in 1920s Germany* (Berkeley, Los Angeles and London, 2001)

Wegesack, Alexander von, ed., *Ingo Maurer: Light; Reaching for the Moon*, exh. cat., Vitra Design Museum (Weil am Rhein, 2004)

Weisberg, Gabriel P., Edwin Becker and Evelyne Posseme, eds, *Origins of L'Art Nouveau: The Bing Empire*, exh. cat., Van Gogh Museum, Amsterdam (Antwerp, 2004)

Weissler, Sabine, ed., *Design in Deutschland, 1933–45: Ästhetik und Organisation des Deutschen Werkbundes im 'Dritten Reich'* (Giessen, 1990)

Welsch, Wolfgang, *Unserer postmoderne Moderne* (Heidelberg-Weinheim, 1987)

Westphal, Uwe, *Werbung im Dritten Reich* (Berlin, 1989)

Wichmann, Hans, *Die Realisation eines neuen Museumtyps: die Neue Sammlung: Bilanz, 1980/90*, with essays by Florian Hufnagl and Corinna Rösner (Basel, 1990)

—, *Deutsche Werkstätten und WK Verband, 1898–1990: Aufbruch zum neuen Wohnen* (Munich, 1992)

Wick, Rainer K., *Teaching at the Bauhaus* (Ostfildern-Ruit, 2000)

Wiechert, Ernst, *In der Heimat: Aufnahmen von Walter Gerull-Kardas* (Munich, 1938)

Wie Wohnen, Bautechnik, Möbel, Hausrat, Ausstellungskatalog (Stuttgart and Karlsruhe, 1949–50)

Wilk, Christopher, ed., *Modernism: Designing a New World, 1914–1939*, exh. cat., Victoria and Albert Museum, London (2006)

Willett, John, *The New Sobriety, 1917–1933: Art and Politics in the Weimar Period* (London, 1978)

Williams, Rosalind, *Dream Worlds: Mass-consumption in Late Nineteenth-century France* (Berkeley, CA, and Oxford, 1982)

Wingler, Hans M., *The Bauhaus: Weimar Dessau Berlin Chicago* [1962] (Cambridge, MA, and London, 1976)

—, *Kunstschulreform, 1900–1933* (Berlin, 1977)

Wortmann Weltge, Sigrid, *Women's Work: Textile Art from the*

Bauhaus (San Francisco, 1993)

Wuppermann, Agatha Buski, *Hans Schwippert, 1899–1973: Von der Werkkunst zum Design* (Munich, 2006)

Ziffer, Alfred, ed., *Bruno Paul: Deutsche Raumkunst und Architektur zwischen Jugendstil und Moderne* (Munich, 1992)

Zola, Emile, *The Ladies' Paradise*, trans. Brian Nelson (Oxford, 1995)

Principal Journals Consulted

Architektur und Wohnform
Bau und Wohnen
Dekorative Kunst
Design Report
Deutsche Kunst und Dekoration
Farbe und Form
Die Form: Zeitschrift für Gestaltende Arbeit
Form: Internationale Revue
Gebrauchsgraphik
Innendekoration
Kultur im Heim
Die Kunst im Deutschen Reich
Die Kunst im Dritten Reich
Das Neue Frankfurt
die neue linie
Neue Werbung
Ulm

Acknowledgements

My immediate context while working on this book has been the postgraduate programme in History of Design, run jointly by the Royal College of Art and the Victoria and Albert Museum. I have learnt a great deal over the years from this experience and I would like to think that the following pages may at least start to address some of the fascinating and challenging questions posed by those involved in this most stimulating academic environment. I thank all my colleagues, staff and students alike, on the RCA/V&A History of Design programme. Although far too numerous to name in full, I should particularly mention Glenn Adamson, Juliet Ash, David Crowley, Christine Guth and Viviana Narotzky for their sustained encouragement and interest in the project. I am also grateful to Barbara Berry and Ana Pereira who offered their generous assistance and support during the writing of the book.

The Research Committee of the Royal College of Art and the British Academy Small Research Grant award offered invaluable financial assistance towards the research. I thank Frederic Schwartz and Penny Sparke for acting as my referees. Sarah Owens contributed a great deal to this project, both in translating texts from the original German and her valiant picture research. Similarly, Elizabeth Bisley and Kimberley Chandler offered invaluable help in locating images. I also thank Thomas Wilson for his excellent photography.

I would like to thank staff at the various libraries consulted, and especially the Royal College of Art, the National Art Library in London and the Kunstbibliothek, Berlin.

I have presented papers related to this book in recent years and I would like to thank Christopher Wilk of the V&A Museum; Marianne Lamonaca of The Wolfsonian Florida International University; Wendy Kaplan of Los Angeles County Museum of Art; Pat Kirkham of Bard Graduate Center, New York; and Cheryce Kramer at the Deutsches Museum, Munich, for their generous invitations and the opportunities these gave to receive responses to the work.

At Reaktion, Vivian Constantinopoulos offered her constant support and incisive judgement on the project. I extend my gratitude to her, as well as to Harry Gilonis, Simon McFadden and Martha Jay.

Finally, I express my thanks and love to Sarah, Agnes and Hugh.

Photo Acknowledgements

The author and publishers wish to express their thanks to the following sources of illustrative material and/or permission to reproduce it. Some locations of artworks not mentioned in captions are also given below.

Photos akg-images: pp. 12, 42; ALESSI: p. 204; anschlaege.de: pp. 220, 221; photo author: p. 223; photo Lotte Barleben: p. 120; photo Erich Bauer: p. 138; Bauhaus Archiv, Berlin: pp. 68, 84, 86; Bildarchiv Preussischer Kulturbesitz, Berlin: p. 27; © Braun: p. 182; photo Boris Breuer: p. 216; Bröhan-Museum, Berlin: p. 108 (photo Martin Adam); © DACS 2008: pp. 24, 44, 48, 53, 54, 55, 56, 63, 64, 81, 86, 101, 108, 120, 168 (top), 190, 191, 199; Deutsches Historisches Museum, Berlin: pp. 150, 163, 212; Clauss Dietel: p. 174; Jochen Fiedler: p. 201; Eva Gronbach: p. 216; Gunta Stözl estate: p. 86; Günther-Wagner Pelikan-Werke: p. 148; photo Bernd Heyden: p. 178; HfG-Archiv Ulm: pp. 179, 180; by kind permission, Ingo Maurer GmbH: p. 186; photo Peter Inselmann: p. 211; Konstantin Grcic Industrial Design: p. 217; Reinhard Kranz: p. 198; photo Christel Lehmann: p. 175; Landesarchiv Berlin: p. 15; MetaDesign: p. 219; photo Moegle: p. 136; photo Lucia Moholy: p. 84; by permission of Hattula Moholy-Nagy: p. 142; © Hattula Moholy-Nagy/DACS 2008: p. 74; Museum der Dinge, Werkbund-Archiv, Berlin: p. 146; Ott+Stein: p. 209; photo Werner Peters: p. 125; photo Georg Pollich: p. 159; photo Andreas Praefcke: p. 52; photo Arne Psille: p. 212; Rat für Formgebung/German Design Council: p. 194; Dirk Scheper: p. 82; Senate Department of Urban Development Berlin: pp. 8, 9; Siemens press photo: p. 195; photo Wolfgang Siol: p. 179; photo Sipa Press/Rex Features: p. 215; © Stankowski Stiftung: p. 196; Stiftung Weimarer Klassik und Kunstsammlungen: p. 79; photo Wolf Strache: p. 119; photo ullstein bild – Haeckel Archiv: p. 30; Universität und Landesbibliothek Darmstadt: p. 48 (left); photo Tom Vack: p. 186; Vitra Design Museum, Weil am Rhein: p. 211; courtesy Vitsœ: p. 182; Albrecht von Bodecker: p. 207; photo Wanda von Deschitz-Kunowski: p. 68; Helmut Wengler and Axel Bertram: p. 199; photo Iain Boyd Whyte: p. 208; WMF: p. 206; photo Hans Wotin: p. 198.

Index